News Verdicts, the Debates, and Presidential Campaigns

News Verdicts, the Debates, and Presidential Campaigns

JAMES B. LEMERT
WILLIAM R. ELLIOTT
JAMES M. BERNSTEIN
WILLIAM L. ROSENBERG
KARL J. NESTVOLD

PRAEGER

New York
Westport, Connecticut
London

Library of Congress Cataloging-in-Publication Data

News verdicts, the debates, and presidential campaigns / James B.
  Lemert . . . [et al.].
      p.   cm.
    Includes bibliographical references and index.
    ISBN 0-275-93758-5 (alk. paper)
    1. Presidents—United States—Election—1988.   2. Campaign
  debates—United States.   3. Press and politics—United States.
  4. Press—United States—Influence.   I. Lemert, James B., 1935–
  JK5261988k
  324.973'0927—dc20   91-8749

British Library Cataloguing in Publication Data is available.

Library of Congress Catalog Card Number: 91-8749
ISBN: 0-275-93758-5

First published in 1991

Praeger Publishers, One Madison Avenue, New York, NY 10010
An imprint of Greenwood Publishing Group, Inc.

Printed in the United States of America

The paper used in this book complies with the
Permanent Paper Standard issued by the National
Information Standards Organization (Z39.48-1984).
10 9 8 7 6 5 4 3 2 1

CONTENTS

ILLUSTRATIONS

TABLES

FIGURES

PREFACE

Actual research—as distinguished from the gleam in a researcher's eye—sometimes begins in unexpected ways. Jim Lemert thought he was just having a get-reacquainted coffee break with former student Frank Allen, visiting the School of Journalism from his post in Philadelphia as bureau chief for *The Wall Street Journal*. When asked what research he had been doing lately, Lemert proceeded to describe more than a year of frustrated attempts to interest the big media foundations in funding a study that would separate the impact of news verdicts about debates from the impact of the presidential debates themselves.

(Warning: Never ask scholars what they've been doing lately; they're liable to tell you!)

In any case, after Lemert had concluded—in a weary and exasperated voice—by saying that the study would be the definitive test and could be done "dirt cheap," guess what happened! Frank Allen asked, in a quiet voice, how much it would cost to do the study the way it should be done. Lemert, still not realizing what was happening, blurted out, "Oh, about $5,000 or so." Suddenly, Lemert's antennae went up as Allen replied, "Hmmm. Let me think about that."

Well, he did. He and his family wrote a check to the School of Journalism for that amount, given in memory of Frank's late father, J. M. Allen, Jr., and that is how we got started. Other support for this project followed. The most important, in terms of obtaining our data, was a cash grant of $1,500 from Frank and Margaret Allen to allow us to collect survey data for the vice-presidential debate. As you will see, we would have lived to regret our original decision not to study the Quayle-Bentsen debate.

Because we were spending all the grant money for survey interviewing and videotaped newscasts, we knew that we had sacrificed ease of data entry and data analysis to the imperative of obtaining the richest data sets we could get. We knew we had an arduous task ahead of us, lacking even assistance in entering our data into our mainframe computers.

Fortunately, after the two Allen grants, others began to come forward with offers of help. Oregon Journalism Dean Arnold Ismach funded a graduate research assistant for the 1988–89 academic year. Mervyn Brockett, that graduate assistant, rendered invaluable assistance with interviewing, some data entry, and reconciling the vice-presidential data sets from Drexel University, Southern Illinois University at Carbondale, and the University of Oregon. (We were plagued by the problem of reconciliation throughout the study. A good part of the problem resulted from incompatibilities between our respective computers, especially between the Oregon computer, a VAX 8800, and the IBM computers at the other two campuses. Incompatibility problems have continued to weaken the analyses that can be performed at Drexel.)

In any case, a surprise $3,000 two-for-one matching fund grant from the Dow Jones Fund (for Frank and Margaret Allen's grant) helped us obtain 1976, 1980, and 1984 videotapes from the Vanderbilt Television News Archive, substantially enhancing our ability to place what was happening in 1988 into a comparative perspective. The Dow Jones Fund grant also helped us to pay for coding help and to reimburse our academic programs for some of the nitty-gritty costs of supporting our work.

During the summer of 1989, Lemert used a stipend grant of $3,000 from the Donald McGannon Communication Research Center at Fordham University to free him to write one chapter and to complete data entry and data reconciliation at Oregon. Meanwhile, Elliott received a research fellowship for the same summer from the Graduate School at Southern Illinois University at Carbondale in order to help him with similar activities. Elliott would also like to thank Dr. George A. Ngwa, then a doctoral candidate in Journalism at SIUC, for his assistance in the early stages of the project and for his handling of most of the coding of SIUC's open-ended survey questions.

Graduate student Mike Krippendorf helped Rosenberg with data entry and the survey effort at Drexel's Survey Research Center.

All of us would like to thank our respective schools and centers for the many direct and indirect ways in which this project was encouraged and supported. (Actually, Bernstein, who started out at Oregon and wound up at Indiana, wants to thank two of our academic units). We would like to thank the computing centers of Drexel University, Southern Illinois

University at Carbondale, and the University of Oregon for their allocation of computing time and their occasional programming consultation.

Last, but by no means least, each of us would like to thank our families for their forbearance and support. While this book could have been done only through lots of "sweat equity" on our parts, it was both a labor of love and one that love permitted.

As for the division of responsibilities, one of us handled the analysis and writing of each chapter. Thus, this is not an edited collection of chapters, in the sense that the analytical approach and the writing of each chapter was determined by an overall editor. Although we tried to circulate each chapter for comments from the others, in the last analysis each chapter represents the views and writing style of its author(s).

While each of us handled the analysis and writing of individual chapters, we did share significantly in the collection of the data used in the analyses. Professors William L. Rosenberg (Philadelphia), William R. Elliott (Carbondale), and James B. Lemert and James M. Bernstein (Eugene-Springfield) organized and supervised the telephone interviewing at each site. Each of them also contributed questions to the questionnaires. Videotaping and collection of 1988 newscast content was done by Professors Lemert and Karl J. Nestvold. Bernstein and Lemert arranged for the collection of past videotapes from the Vanderbilt Television News Archive. Transcripts of 1988 network newscasts were done by Nestvold and Lemert. Coding of network newscasts was done by Bernstein and Nestvold, with Lemert resolving disagreements on units. Coding of the post-debate news specials was done by Lemert and Nestvold.

James B. Lemert bears primary responsibility for Chapters 1, 5, 7, and 10. In addition, he coordinated and edited Chapter 12, while writing portions of it as well.

William R. Elliott bears primary responsibility for Chapters 2, 6, and 8 and wrote segments of 12. He also had the responsibility of integrating all of the copy into a single word processing system.

James M. Bernstein bears primary responsibility for Chapters 3 and 11 and contributed portions of Chapters 2, 5, and 12.

William L. Rosenberg bears primary responsibility for Chapter 9 and wrote portions of Chapter 12 as well.

Karl J. Nestvold bears primary responsibility for Chapter 4.

News Verdicts,
the Debates, and
Presidential Campaigns

1

INTRODUCTION

When considering the 1988 presidential campaign, it is hard not to use the old cliche, "The word *ugly* was given a whole new meaning," as:

- The names of campaign wizard Roger Ailes and rapist-murderer Willie Horton became household words to many Americans.
- Observers characterized the Michael Dukakis campaign as amateurish, disorganized, and inept.
- The polls showed many Americans wishing they had somebody else they could vote for on election day.
- A respected, nonpartisan scholar of political ads accused the George Bush campaign of "blatantly" lying in its television ads (Jamieson 1988).
- Voter turnout in the election plunged to a low not seen in more than 60 years.
- Even the eventual winner of the election tried to distance himself from what his own campaign had done.
- The average campaign news sound bite—direct television footage of what the candidate and others actually said—apparently fell from an already low 12 seconds in 1984 to 9 seconds in the 1988 campaign, perhaps further isolating the audience from candidates (Payne, Golden, Marlier, and Ratzen 1989; also see Smith 1989 and Deaver 1988).

With so many other things in this campaign apparently going so wrong, why on earth have we chosen to focus on the 1988 general election presidential debates and news media coverage of them? In other words, why should *anyone* be interested in the results of this study? There are several reasons, we think.

1. Debates (many question, with reason, whether they might better be termed "joint appearances," but we will generally use the less ponderous term "debate") between presidential candidates are showing signs of becoming institutionalized in modern campaigns. At least one fall debate has been held in every presidential election since 1976. If the debates are becoming a political institution in our society, that means voters expect them to be held—and candidates expect that they must participate in them, whether they want to or not.

Therefore, it is very important that we do the best we can to examine and, if necessary, improve them *now*. Why? Because generally, the longer an institution exists, the harder it becomes to make changes in it. Furthermore, because the presidential debates occur only during four-year election cycles, we do not have the luxury of letting a few more of them occur before making any needed changes.

2. Modern, mass-communicated presidential campaign debates began with the Kennedy-Nixon debates in 1960. Since that time, there have been only three different sponsors of the fall debates: network news organizations (1960), the League of Women Voters (1976, 1980, and 1984), and the Commission on Presidential Debates (1988). While the nonpartisan League itself has not been totally immune from criticism of its handling of the debates (see Kraus 1988), it is fair to say that the Commission took over running the 1988 debates because it had the political clout to do so, not because there was any popular demand for it to replace the League. (The Commission was created by the two major political parties, and the rationale for its replacing the League seemed to be that only it could guarantee that the candidates would appear.)

Within days after the Commission had made the gesture of offering the League at least nominal sponsorship of the last 1988 debate, the League angrily rejected the offer, claiming it had discovered that the candidates and their campaign organizations had such control of the format and ground rules that the debate would be a "charade," not a genuine confrontation that would help inform the electorate. In effect, the League was saying, the Commission was merely a remote-control device fronting for, and protecting, the candidates.

Our study will examine popular and news media support for the debates in the context of the 1988 campaign, how much voters thought they could rely on them to make up their minds, and numerous other questions with a bearing on debate sponsorship and format.

3. Judging by the media noise and uproar, 1988 will be remembered as the year of Roger Ailes and the negative "attack ad"—*not* the year of the "great debates." Yet, given the many complaints about the "packaging" of the 1988 candidates and the heavy-handed intrusion of television news

between candidates and voters, the debates stand almost alone now as the best chance for the voters *directly* to observe candidates' behavior, learn something about their policy views, and judge their relative abilities. Diminished as the debates may have been by the events of campaign '88, they remained virtually the only chance for voters to observe the candidates "live" and unedited. (No claim is made here, however, that the debate performances are *unrehearsed*.)

4. The fall debates continue to provide the single greatest television audience shares for any campaign communication in the entire presidential election cycle. According to Nielsen Media Research (1988), the September 25 debate garnered just under half of all U.S. television households. Even this is an underestimate, because it counts only those households viewing the debate on CBS, ABC, or NBC. Other networks, including public broadcasting and CNN (Cable News Network), also carried the debate, not to mention radio.

5. The threat/opportunity provided by the debates in 1988 had profound effects upon the campaign strategies of both sides. For example, the 1988 presidential campaign may have been the first in which a candidate who had agreed to debate so obviously feared their potential risk to his campaign that he and his advisers seemed less interested in winning debates than in *diminishing* their significance. The George Bush campaign did this in at least two fairly obvious ways: (1) by insisting that the final debate be held almost four weeks before election day, thus allowing Bush time to regain the offensive in case he lost the final debate, and (2) by discussing the debates as if they were just another campaign event and a distraction from the "real" campaign, at that (e.g., see Bush campaign manager James Baker's interview with ABC just before the final debate.[1]) One of the campaign's many ironies was that it was actually George Bush—with some aid from a question to Michael Dukakis from CNN's Bernard Shaw—who seemed to apply the *coup de grace* to his opponent in their final debate on October 13.

Ironically, it was Michael Dukakis, the candidate who seemed to have bet more marbles on the debates, who was to spend the nearly four weeks between October 14 and November 8 trying to make up for the political damage done in that October 13 debate. Having been badly outmaneuvered in the battle of negative political ads and having few other resources left after that final debate, Michael Dukakis and Lloyd Bentsen found themselves reduced to offering to be interviewed by just about any national television journalist willing to have them as guests.

6. In the last three presidential election cycles, we have seen an explosion in the number of pre-primary and primary debates, starting with the Republicans in 1980 and Democrats in 1984. Before the end of 1987, the 1988 campaign had begun with debates staged by PBS's William Buckley and NBC's Tom Brokaw as the early-season horizon for the start

of debates was pushed further and further back. Indeed, had both the League of Women Voters and the Commission on Presidential Debates each succeeded in holding its proposed four fall debates, even the fall debate "season" would have seen an astonishing new record of eight debates.

Meanwhile, the amount of research being done on this vastly expanded number of presidential debates seems to have shriveled. What this means is that we do not really know very much even about the 1980 and 1984 debates—but that absence of knowledge hardly justifies not learning about them in 1988!

WHAT THIS BOOK IS ABOUT

We believe that this book reports the largest in-depth study ever done of presidential and vice-presidential debates. The study combines more than 2,000 survey interviews done at three locations (Philadelphia, Pa., Carbondale, Ill., and Eugene-Springfield, Ore.) with simultaneous collection and content analysis of campaign news coverage. The survey data were collected using a potentially powerful time-series design which, when combined with the collection of network news coverage of the debates, allowed us to draw a much more sensitive picture of debate and post-debate news effects than usually can be obtained from surveys of audience members.

Perhaps the single most important focus of our study is this question: *Do news media verdicts about candidates' debate performance have an influence, independent of the debates themselves, on (1) who is perceived to have won a given debate and (2) political attitudes and voting preferences?* It was this focus that led to a research design that gives us a chance to separate the effects of a debate from the effects of performance verdicts in the news after the debate. What we did was to draw and interview comparable but separate samples of people (1) each day (from 1 to 3) before a given debate; (2) the night of the debate, starting immediately after it had ended; and (3) each of several days after the debate.

The people interviewed immediately afterward were presumably reacting to the debate itself—without the intervention of news verdicts—while the people interviewed later obviously could have been exposed to those verdicts. (Chapter 2 provides a detailed discussion of this "short time series" design and its great advantages, when combined with simultaneous collection of news content, over previous efforts to examine a news verdict effect.) If news verdicts about candidates' debate performance do turn out to have an impact independent of the debates themselves, then it seems that the original debates have been *diminished* in another important way: by the interpretations placed on them in the news media.

Given the richness of this set of survey and content data, we are able to examine a number of other important questions about both the debates and the larger campaign. Here are a few examples:

- Were journalists quicker and more willing to reach debate performance verdicts in 1988 than in previous years, when the presidential debates were a newer, "fresher" phenomenon?
- Some authors have argued that the existence of the debates lends legitimacy to the American presidential election system. Perhaps that is so, but what happens if news coverage of the debates in recent years tends to undermine *their* legitimacy? If the debates lose their legitimacy, what ultimately may happen, then, to that of the American electoral system?
- Did negative "attack" ads receive more continuing news coverage than the debates themselves? Did news coverage of these ads extend their "reach" to the audience? Did audiences think the Dukakis campaign ran as many negative ads as the Bush campaign?
- When the League of Women Voters rejected the Commission's sponsorship offer, how much of a network news story was it? Is there any evidence that the networks sided with either of the rivals?
- Do our study's results suggest a need for any changes in debate format or sponsorship?

The first two chapters of this book set the scene for this multi-faceted study. Chapters 3, 4, and 5 present results concerning media content and, in so doing, also set the scene for the survey analyses to come in Chapters 6, 7, 8, and 9 by describing the media environment that surrounded our survey respondents. Chapters 10 and 11 place the debates in the larger context of the campaign, and Chapter 12 examines the policy implications of all our findings for the parties, the debates, and the news media.

We turn now to a review of the evidence—such as it is—of a debate verdict effect.

THE VERDICT EFFECT: POLITICAL MYTH OR NOT?

We have already indicated that surprisingly little research of any kind has been done on presidential debates since the 1976 Ford-Carter debates, which were the first to have been held since the now legendary and myth-surrounded Kennedy-Nixon debates of 1960. The startlingly few studies done about the 1980 and 1984 debates have often failed to follow up well on ideas generated by previous debate studies and have also tended to be superficial, partly because funding sources seemed no longer interested in providing the support needed to do better research. These circumstances leave lots of uncertainties about whether there *is* a news verdict effect, let alone how it might work. In the remainder of this chapter, we will do a careful review of the existing evidence on the effects of post-debate verdicts. Before we do that, however, let us recap briefly some related findings from other areas of debate research.

In general—though perhaps not always (e.g., Just et al. 1990)—researchers agree that people do learn policy-related and candidate-related information from debates (e.g., Katz and Feldman 1962; Sears and Chaffee 1979). They also learn a considerable amount of campaign-related information, especially if they see debates held among contenders for the nomination during the primaries (Lemert, Elliott, Nestvold, and Rarick 1983). In addition, watching a debate generally has stimulated interest, which in turn can lead to both further learning and motivation to participate in the election (see especially Katz and Feldman 1962; Sears and Chaffee 1979; Lemert, Elliott, Nestvold, and Rarick 1983).

For the most part, however, the fall debates do not seem to have changed many minds about whom to vote for. Instead they seem more likely to reinforce most viewers' existing attitudes toward the candidates, though many important scholars (e.g., Katz and Feldman 1962; Comstock, Chaffee, Katzman, McCombs, and Roberts 1978; Hershey 1989) seem to have mistakenly drawn the conclusion from this finding that the debates *therefore* did not change the election outcome (see Lemert 1981a and 1981b).

Perhaps the single most "solid" finding from debate studies is this one: *The best predictor of who people thought "won" a debate is who they preferred prior to the debate.* So the effects of news verdicts—if there are any—will very likely be to *modify* this very powerful "wishful thinking" phenomenon. In other words, a news verdict effect might *weaken or diminish* wishful thinking when the verdict runs against the preferences of the voter. On the other hand, when a news verdict supports a voter's own predisposition to see her/his candidate as winning, the verdict effect would *strengthen or enhance* that person's wishful thinking.

A Verdict Effect: Just Political "Horse Sense"?

The idea that news verdicts tell voters who has just "won" a presidential debate is now so widespread that it is deeply entrenched in the news itself. During the 1988 campaign, journalists' references to this idea could even be heard on the post-debate analysis programs, themselves a very likely first source of the media verdicts.[2]

Nor was it coincidental that the 1988 campaign staffs summoned forth their "spin doctors" to try to control how the news media interpreted their candidate's debate performance, often trying as well to establish pre-debate expectations that would encourage journalists to utter "better than expected"performance verdicts about their candidate. Thus, George Bush and his aides, before the September 25 debate, tried to stress

Michael Dukakis' extensive television and debate experience, in an effort to raise journalists' expectations of Dukakis and lower them for Bush. And, of course, the Bush campaign tried to lower expectations of Dan Quayle by leaking word about the campaign's assignment to him of hand-picked "mentors" and by stressing Lloyd Bentsen's formidable experience and skills.

Indeed, political insiders have believed in the verdict effect at least since 1976's "Eastern Europe" gaffe by President Ford in his second debate with challenger Jimmy Carter:

After both the first and the second debates, we believed the press commentary served to magnify the actual outcome [of the debate] and to shape voter sentiment even though the voters had seen the event themselves. (Charles E. Walker, co-chairman of the 1976 Debates Steering Committee—1979, 134)

. . . The fact of the matter is that the media do have a big role in interpreting the results [of debates]. Even though people watched the second debate themselves . . . the media played a big role in how people responded to the debate two days after the event. . . . (Ford Campaign Manager Richard B. Cheney—1979, 134–135)

In 1980 political insiders were convinced that the seemingly constant television replays of Ronald Reagan's relaxed "There you go again!" put-down of a tense-looking Jimmy Carter had successfully reassured the many voters who dearly wanted Reagan to be a safe haven for their anti-Carter votes.

And in 1984, according to former *Washington Post* polling analyst Barry Sussman (1988), Reagan was hurt much more by media verdicts about his first debate with Walter Mondale than by the debate itself. Similarly, according to Sussman, media verdicts about Reagan's second debate—especially the emphasis on his seemingly off-hand comment about not holding Mondale's "youth" and "inexperience" against him—helped Reagan much more than did his actual debate performance. Sussman backed up his assertion with poll data.

Indirect Support for a Verdict Effect

A debate verdict effect, then, seems firmly ensconced in conventional wisdom. The verdict effect also seems to make a lot of sense, based on our general knowledge about the levels of attention and cognitive effort that people generally seem willing to devote to politics (e.g., see Lemert 1981a, 104–110, and Graber 1988). Consider the following, for example:

• Many voters' interest in and attention to politics is at best skimpy, thus rendering them seemingly susceptible to "quick and easy" fill-ins on how a debate went.

- Having the set tuned to a debate is no guarantee that people will actually be watching and listening closely enough to catch a pivotal moment themselves.
- With the possible exception of the Kennedy-Nixon debates (Katz and Feldman 1962, 190–191), ratings have always been highest for the first debate, falling off some after that, regardless of who is debating. In 1988 as well, ratings fell after the first 1988 debate (Nielsen Media Research 1988). What lower exposure to the later debates implies, of course, is that an even larger number of potential voters may be dependent on media verdicts after the later debates.
- The same reasoning applies to a major historical decline in audience share for the debates. One estimate is that 72.5% of American homes saw the first Ford-Carter debate (1976), compared with 71.2% for the Reagan-Carter debate in 1980, 59.1% for the first Reagan-Mondale debate in 1984, and 49.3% for the first Bush-Dukakis meeting in 1988 (Nielsen Media Research 1988). The fewer people who watch, the more important and influential post-debate verdicts may be, at least *as long as the debates are thought to be relevant and important.*
- Many voters lack sufficient background knowledge to recognize mistakes such as Ford's "Eastern Europe" gaffe, even when they hear and see what will later be termed a mistake.[3]

In view of these points, it should be no wonder at all that post-debate "verdicts" in the news could affect audience reactions as much as, or even more than, the debate itself.

Other Arguments for a Verdict Effect

Debate Format. We think the format of presidential debates also could plausibly be responsible for the occurrence of a verdict effect. The following seems to be almost a prototypical scenario for a debate that will be followed by a verdict effect:

Candidate Y makes a misstatement or seems slightly confused at some point in his debate with Candidate Z. Because of constraints imposed on the journalist panel and on Y's opponent by the debate format itself, Candidate Y's faltering is not made as glaringly apparent as it might have been if direct questioning of Y by Z had been allowed or if the panel were allowed adequate room for follow-up questioning. In the absence of very clear and dramatic evidence *within the debate itself*, many voters therefore will miss the cues that Y has gotten himself in trouble. But in the debate aftermath, the news media quickly dramatize Y's shaky performance, even if the panel of journalists was prevented from doing so in the debate itself.

Ironically, then, the efforts by campaigns to make the debates' format "safe" for their candidates may also put the campaigns in even greater jeopardy from post-debate news verdicts.

Clues from Cognitive Psychology. Support for a verdict effect can be derived from many lines of research and theory in cognitive social psychology. We highlight here only one of them, the "Elaboration Likelihood Model" of Petty and Cacioppo (1981), which is rather consistent with our earlier argument about the ambiguity-creating effects of existing debate formats. According to Petty and Cacioppo (1981, 255–269), there are two primary routes to attitude change, a *central* route and a *peripheral* one. The central route will be taken when the issues being argued about are important and comprehensible to the individual. For any message to change the existing attitude will be very hard, Petty and Cacioppo argue, but *if* the individual changes, the change will probably be a long-lasting one, since the person will have been motivated to do a lot of message-analytical work before making the change. In contrast, the peripheral route involves changes based on "peripheral" cues—that is, cues that have little or nothing to do with the quality of arguments in the message. In contrast to central-route change, change produced through the peripheral route generally will not last very long, since it is tied to more-or-less irrelevant cues. Examples of such peripheral cues might include high communication source credibility, or what seems to be "in" or popular—and (we think) media verdicts about debate performance.

Recall now our earlier arguments about ambiguities created by candidates' wish to control the debate format, about some voters' inability to understand complex policy arguments, and about decreased attention to the debates. Under these conditions, viewers must search for peripheral cues. Post-debate network commentary obviously can produce verdicts that serve as peripheral cues for interpreting the debate and the campaign. This verdict, especially for the uninterested and relatively uninformed voter, would result in at least a temporary shift in attitude in the direction of the verdict. Whether or not this temporary shift results in a more enduring change, and eventually in a changed vote, depends on the types of persuasive messages received after the debate verdict.

Direct Evidence of a Verdict Effect

In any event, a very plausible case can be deduced for a news verdict effect as a serious threat/opportunity to a campaign. But what is the *direct* evidence that news verdict effects actually occur? Plenty of anecdotal evidence for a verdict effect exists from polls done in 1976, 1980, and 1984. The prototypical pattern looks something like this:

Immediately after the debate between our faltering Y and steady Z, voters' perceptions of who won split almost exactly the way the polls were split on voter preferences just before the debate. In the post-debate "instant analysis," one television journalist (by no means all) opines that Y seemed shaky. Later, after all the journalists have had a chance to go off the air and talk to each other privately, a stronger, bolder media consensus emerges on the next morning's news shows and all day thereafter. Polls done the day after the debate show an increasing tilt toward Z as the winner as the day goes along.

The evening news shows emphasize the poll results, and the correspondents covering Y and Z press each campaign for its reactions and/or rationalizations. Eventually something is pulled out from Y's staff that seems to confirm that Y lost. The tilt toward Z as debate winner in media polls grows even stronger over the next few days. Morale in Z's campaign goes sky-high. Z's crowds grow bigger and more enthusiastic, and Z's campaign staff finds that more potential "fat cat" donors are returning their phone calls.

So logical deduction, the polls, and campaign experiences all seem to fit the above scenario. In addition, research reviews since the 1976 debates consistently single out the post-debate verdict effect (see, e.g., Sears and Chaffee 1978; Chaffee and Dennis 1978; Kraus 1988). Somewhat surprisingly, though, careful evidence is slim that directly connects verdicts in the news to verdicts in the minds of voters.

A Verdict Effect in 1976? Perhaps the strongest evidence for the impact of a news verdict comes from the 1976 Ford-Carter debates, but even here there are problems with research design and/or peculiarities of samples. One of two strongly supportive studies is by Steeper (1978), who reported that a Seattle group did not react at all to Ford's "Eastern Europe" gaffe while it was happening. Yet, the next day, perceptions that Ford had not done well in the second debate increased as the day went on and as the evening news emphasized and re-emphasized the error. It appeared that, as more chances to repeat and reinforce the verdict occurred over time in the news, diffusion of the verdict among audience members proceeded. However, the Steeper study results are somewhat limited by the small and perhaps unrepresentative sample of those reacting to the debate while it was broadcast and by its failure explicitly to connect audience perceptions to either media content or diffusion of that content.

Very similar results were reported briefly by Patterson (1980, 123–5). More than half of those interviewed *within* 12 hours of the second Carter-Ford debate thought that Ford had won the debate, yet another sample interviewed later than 12 hours afterward showed an almost mirror-image reversal to Carter as the winner. Unfortunately, Patterson's sketchy report provided no indication of the sample sizes or locations.

Lang and Lang (1978) also reported an apparent verdict effect—this time after the *first* Ford-Carter confrontation. Over time, their undergraduate respondents were increasingly likely to pick Ford as the winner. Unfortunately, numerous differences in the testing conditions between the separate groups interviewed immediately after, and days after, the debate made it fairly easy for skeptics to discount the media verdict (that Ford won) as the cause of the difference between the two groups.

Despite finding apparent support for a verdict effect upon performance perceptions, Hagner and Rieselbach (1978) reported that perceptions of Ford's performance in the second debate were not at all related to changes in voting preferences, though perceptions of Carter's performance might have been.

Using CBS/*New York Times* panel survey data from before and after the first Ford-Carter debate in 1976, Geer (1988) concluded that audience perceptions of who won the debate *did* predict changes in preferences for the candidates, even after the influence of audience predispositions had been controlled. Unfortunately, no results were reported for the infamous gaffe debate. Further, Geer's analysis merely folded together the debate itself with any news verdicts. As a result, it was not possible to separate the debate effect from the verdict effect.

Verdicts in 1980? In view of the increasing clamor about news verdicts in the 1976 campaign, it is remarkable how little academic research was done on the 1980 Reagan-Carter debate, let alone the Reagan-Anderson one. Probably contributing to this lack of attention were (1) a decline in interest on the part of the major private foundations, a decline that continued into the 1984 and 1988 elections as well, and (2) the relatively unique character of the 1980 debates themselves. In 1980 President Carter refused to debate with anybody except Reagan, so researchers, the networks, and voters all were destined to wait until the very last minute before it was clear whether there would be any debates, who would debate—and when (see Kraus 1988). Apparently it was easier to put together the debate on extremely short notice than to put together a research effort!

Sigelman and Sigelman's study (1984) of "winner" perceptions is probably the most widely read study of the 1980 Carter-Reagan debate, but since they were not gathering their own data, they seemed compelled to live with the limitations of the survey data provided them through the Inter-university Consortium for Political and Social Research. Their principal finding was the almost universal one in studies of "winner" perceptions: The single best predictor of who a respondent thinks won is who the respondent wanted to win. In other words, when one allows selective perception of winners to occur, it will occur. Selective perception as the dominant effect by no means precludes a news verdict effect as the next-most-important influence upon winner perceptions, however. Unfortunately, the Sigelmans' focus seemed restricted to testing for the selective perception phenomenon, possibly because of limitations in the CBS/*New York Times* data set with which they were working.

Bothwell and Brigham (1983) divided college students into two groups. The first viewed the Reagan-Carter debate in a classroom and filled out questionnaires before and after the debate (the "lab" group). The second (the "field" group) filled out a questionnaire on Monday before the debate but was neither told to watch the debate nor warned that they would have to fill out a second questionnaire in their Wednesday class. Both "lab" students and those "field" students who watched the Reagan-Carter debate demonstrated selective perceptions of who won—in the usual direction. That is, who they preferred before the debate was also likely to be the candidate they thought won. While it would have been possible to look at post-debate verdict effects among "field" group members, the researchers apparently did not do so.

Davis (1982) once again found the familiar selective perception phenomenon but reported additionally that perceptions of whether Reagan won also seemed to feed back and lead to changes in the intent to vote for Reagan. Once again, however, the study failed to differentiate between the debate itself and media verdicts about the debate. As a predictor of intent to vote for Reagan, the perception (say, that Reagan won) could have been produced by the debate, by a news verdict, or by both. Another weakness of this study was that Davis' respondents were undergraduate volunteers whose participation in pre-test measurements could easily have sensitized them to debate and post-debate stimuli. The lack of a control group makes it almost impossible to tell whether sensitization occurred—and, if it did, with what effect.

Verdicts in 1984? Geer (1988) also used CBS/*New York Times* panel survey data to look at changes in candidate preferences in 1984, using the same regression analyses he used for the 1976 data. Once again, he reported that perceived candidate performance in each of the two Reagan-Mondale debates exerted an important secondary influence on preferences, even after controlling for initial predispositions: "The effect of [pre-existing] partisanship is severely weakened if the respondent thought the other party's candidate emerged victorious (Geer 1988, 494)." Once again, however, the perceived performance measure in this study confounds verdicts after the debate with the debate itself.

Another study of the 1984 debates did, however, try to separate post-debate verdicts from the debate itself. Using a survey panel from the metropolitan Cleveland area that could not have exceeded 139 respondents and might have been considerably smaller for the key analyses, Rouner and Perloff (1988) concluded that predispositions—not a media verdict—essentially explained all the variance in perceptions of who won the first Mondale-Reagan debate. Their attempt to create a post-debate media verdict as a rival to predispositions took the form of self-reported amount of attention paid to debate analysis in the media. There was no independent attempt, apparently, to identify the content or direction of this analysis or to distinguish between those interviewed October 10 vs. 11 vs. 12 vs. 13 vs. 14. Unfortunately, they also did not start interviewing after the October 8 debate until October 10, and they combined all their interviews into one data set without taking the date of the interview into account. Had Rouner and Perloff obtained perceptions from a sample interviewed immediately after the October 8 debate, they might have been in a a better position to have a more potent news verdict variable, since a group interviewed immediately after the debate probably had not yet been exposed to post-debate verdicts.

In one of the few survey research studies to be done so far of reactions to a vice-presidential debate, Rosenberg and Elliott (1987) reported that exposure to the 1984 Bush-Ferraro debate reinforced loyalties to Ferraro among women Democrats. However, media verdicts were not part of their study design.

Perhaps reflecting the general belief that post-debate news verdicts *do* have important effects, Wall, Golden, and James (1988) deliberately designed a series of debate studies that made it impossible to capture the impact of post-debate verdicts. This study design was to have considerable influence on at least one study of the 1988 debates, as well. Wall et al. asked communications and political science students to watch the three 1984 debates, requesting them to fill out questionnaires immediately after each debate. This procedure "was designed to limit the influence of outside forces—especially those emanating from television news commentators . . ." (Wall et al. 1988, 542).

Even if we take the Wall, Golden, and James study on its own terms, several other design difficulties make their findings in many ways rather inconclusive. They did, however, report that winner perception was second only to pre-debate preference in predicting the students' voting preference after the debate. Interestingly, female students were much more likely than males to say that Geraldine Ferraro won her debate with George Bush.

In an interesting test of individual differences in selective perceptions and behavior, Fazio and Williams (1986) found that how *quickly* people could express their attitudes toward Mondale and Reagan (in August) predicted how *biased* people were in their late-October perceptions of who won the Bush-Ferraro debate. The more quickly people could express their attitudes in August, the greater the impact of their preferences on their "winner" perceptions. These researchers asked respondents about who won the first Mondale-Reagan debate as well, but the speed of attitude response ("accessibility," in their terms) did not work as well concerning that early-October first presidential debate. The authors suggested an explanation that sounds very much like our news verdict hypothesis:

Whereas the media seemed to have viewed Mondale as the clear victor in the presidential debate, the vice-presidential debate was viewed much more evenly. . . . If . . . the outcome of the [first] presidential debate was less ambiguous than the vice-presidential debate, then it is not surprising that attitudinal accessibility appeared to exert a larger role with respect to [winner perceptions for] the vice-presidential debate than the presidential debate (Fazio and Williams 1986, 509).

In other words, the more ambiguity in the verdict, the more room for wishful thinking/selective perception to occur. Given this interpretation on the part of Fazio and Williams, it is unfortunate that they did not ask their respondents whether they had heard verdicts about each of the debates.

Verdicts in 1988? Explaining their decision in virtually the same words as did Wall et al., Payne, Golden, Marlier, and Ratzan (1989) also tried to prevent "contamination" of their results by post-debate news verdicts. It should be no surprise, therefore, to find that prior preferences were a powerful and consistent predictor of winner perceptions in each of the three debates.

In their small study of the 1988 campaign, McLeod, Pan, Sun, and Hein (1989) apparently lumped exposure/attention to all three debates together and did not have separate measures of exposure and attention to post-debate verdicts, even though inevitably at least some of their respondents would have seen or heard such verdicts. In addition, their analysis focused on variables other than winner perceptions and, for the most part, voting preferences. However, exposure and attention to one or more of the debates predicted gains in knowledge about the candidates, even after controls for a number of other variables.

In contrast to the Payne and McLeod studies, a series of three reports from the University of Florida did focus on post-debate verdicts. These reports all were based on a single study, however, and yet—collectively at least—did not come up with a very clear message about what was found. The design was simple: A total of 75 mass communications students watched the Quayle-Bentsen debate together, "live," then were split into two groups. One of the groups watched the first eight minutes of PBS's post-debate commentary by David Gergen and Mark Shields, then filled out their questionnaires. Meanwhile, the other group filled out the questionnaires without seeing any post-debate analysis.

The first of these three papers, by Ferguson, Hollander and Melwani (1989), reported that exposure to the Gergen-Shields analysis dampened or diminished reactions to the debate itself. While it was true that exposure to the analysis led students to say that Quayle's performance was more scripted and rehearsed, in general ratings favoring the Dukakis-Bentsen ticket were smaller than when subjects were not exposed to the analysis. You will recall that we said that a verdict effect might *diminish* wishful thinking reactions to a debate when the viewers favored one candidate but the verdict went against their man.

On the face of it, the Ferguson et al. report would be consistent with our verdict hypothesis only if, for some reason, there were more Bush-

Quayle supporters in the "analysis" group than the "debate-only" group. We cannot tell, even though there were many breakdowns by subgroups in this and the two later papers, because the numbers of cases of Bush-Quayle supporters were not provided for each ("analysis" and "debate-only") group.

Two more papers based on the Florida data were released several months after the first one. Each concentrated on differences in how people reacted to the Gergen-Shields analysis of the Quayle-Bentsen debate. One of these reports, by Horvath-Niemeyer and Ferguson (1989), looked at a new dependent variable that had not been examined in the original report: reports by the students of thoughts coming to mind about the debaters while watching the debate (plus analysis, for the "analysis" group). In this report, partisan predispositions strongly interacted with exposure to the analysis to *intensify*, not dampen, reactions to the two debaters. In general, Bush-Quayle supporters seemed more defensive of Quayle when they saw the analysis, and Dukakis-Bentsen supporters piled up more derisive thoughts about Quayle when they saw the Gergen-Shields analysis.

These results seem consistent with our verdict hypothesis, and perhaps inconsistent with the earlier report about a dampening effect. However, we should point out a design problem here: The "analysis" group had eight more minutes of television to watch (and have thoughts about) than did the "debate-only" group. Just to complicate matters further, the final report on the Florida study tends to use the same dependent variables as the original Ferguson report—and to support the original findings.

Engstrom, Gentry, and Melwani (1989) used gender and self-described political involvement to subdivide the "analysis" and "debate-only" groups. If respondents were female, exposure to the Gergen-Shields analysis seemed to dampen their reactions, regardless of level of political involvement. For males, exposure to the analysis seemed to dampen reactions only for those with low involvement.

Lowry et al. (1989) used an experimental methodology similar to that used by the Ferguson group at Florida. The Lowry study concentrated on the first Bush-Dukakis debate—the debate with perhaps the *least* clear winner-loser verdict. University of Southwestern Louisiana communications students were assigned to one of five groups: (1) a *control* group, which watched the debate only; (2) an *"interpersonal"* group, which watched the debate and then discussed the debate among themselves for 10 minutes; (3) the *ABC* group, which watched the debate and subsequent ABC analysis; (4) the *CNN* group; and (5) the *CBS* group. One great advantage of this study is that it matched differences in what the analyses said with measures of audience responses, in a way roughly similar to what our studies will be able to do. The most interesting difference between the analysis programs was that ABC reported a poll showing that 45% believed Dukakis won the debate, compared with 36% who said Bush did. Lowry et al. say the poll report led to a much greater—and clearer—verdict favoring Dukakis than was found on either of the other two analyses, and—fortuitously—the poll results were repeated by Peter Jennings moments before the ABC group filled out its questionnaires. Interestingly, the ABC group was the *only* one in which a majority said that Dukakis had won the debate.

CONCLUSION

Apart from 1976, support for the existence of a news verdict effect more often comes from anecdotal use of quasi-tracking polls than it does from carefully controlled research findings. None of this means that we do not believe there may be a news verdict effect. We do believe, however, that we need to use a better, more sensitive, design to give a news verdict effect a fair chance to show itself. In fairness to our predecessors, we should say that financial constraints often crippled previous efforts to get definitive results about verdict effects.

Both the October 5 Quayle-Bentsen debate and the October 13 Bush-Dukakis debate seem prime candidates for a media verdict effect, since media verdicts following each debate seem clear (see Chapters 3 and 4 for descriptions of these verdicts). The September 25 debate between Dukakis and Bush seems less promising as a candidate for a verdict effect, given the very short life span of the poll-based ABC verdict.

In any case, we believe that the present study has more of the strengths and fewer of the design weaknesses of the previous research literature. The project combines simultaneous content analysis of media coverage in the 1988 campaign with a short time-series survey research design. Chapter 2 provides a more detailed discussion of our research design.

NOTES

1. Bush campaign manager James Baker told ABC's Brit Hume on the ABC evening news, just before the debate, "I think the debates, as I said earlier, have a way of freezing campaigns, and we've been preparing [for the debate], as has been the Dukakis campaign. Once the debate is over, we'll be free to resume campaigning across the length and breadth of this country."

2. For example, after the Quayle-Bentsen debate, ABC's "Nightline" was the vehicle for its post-debate analysis. Multiple references were made on the program to campaign organizations' efforts to exert "spin control" over news verdicts through the use of "spin doctors." The ABC program also had an interesting, though brief, discussion of the effects of next-day newscasts' replaying of certain sound bites and not others on impressions formed by voters—especially on those who did not watch the debate itself. Both the CBS and NBC analyses programs

the same night gave great attention to the same topics, not to mention the same networks' analysis programs after the second Bush-Dukakis debate.

3. One of the authors had a revealing experience concerning this point. During the Ford-Carter campaign, Lemert had assigned his Reporting I class to "cover" what later was to become the infamous "Eastern Europe fiasco" for Ford. Assigned to turn in their news stories in the early morning after the debate, not a single one of the 16 students mentioned Ford's remark about Eastern Europe in her/his story. Since it was a class assignment—and they were taking notes—one must conclude that they were at least as motivated to watch the debate carefully as were most other American viewers. Later discussion with the class suggested that these university juniors and seniors lacked enough background on modern European history to recognize the significance of Ford's remark. Because of the early deadline for their news stories, none of them had watched a post-debate analysis program, so their stories were based on the debate itself, not any subsequent analysis.

REFERENCES

Bothwell, R. K., and J. C. Brigham. 1983. Selective evaluation and recall during the 1980 Carter-Reagan debate. *Journal of Applied Social Psychology* 13:427–442.

Chaffee, S. H., and J. Dennis. 1979. Presidential debates: An empirical assessment. In *The past and future of presidential debates*, ed. A. Ranney, 75–101. Washington: American Enterprise Institute for Public Policy Research.

Cheney, R. B. 1979. The 1976 presidential debates: A Republican perspective. In *The past and future of presidential debates*, ed. A. Ranney, 107–136. Washington: American Enterprise Institute for Public Policy Research.

Comstock, G., S. Chaffee, N. Katzman, M. McCombs, and D. Roberts. 1978. *Television and human behavior*. New York: Columbia University Press.

Davis, M. H. 1982. Voting intentions and the 1980 Carter-Reagan debate. *Journal of Applied Social Psychology* 12:481–492.

Deaver, M. 1988. Sound-bite campaigning: TV made us do it. *Washington Post*, October 30, C7.

Engstrom, E., J. Gentry, and G. Melwani. 1989. *Evidence for differential effects on males and females in the wake of post-debate analyses*. Paper presented to the annual meeting of the Committee on the Status of Women, Association for Education in Journalism and Mass Communication, August, Washington, D.C.

Fazio, R. H., and C. J. Williams. 1986. Attitude accessibility as a moderator of the attitude-perception and attitude-behavior relations: An investigation of the 1984 presidential election. *Journal of Personality and Social Psychology* 51:505–514.

Ferguson, M. A., B. A. Hollander, and G. Melwani. 1989. *The "dampening effect" of post-debate commentary: The Bentsen-Quayle debate*. Paper presented at annual meeting of the Political Communication Division of the International Communication Association, May, San Francisco.

Geer, J. G. 1988. The effects of presidential debates on the electorate's preferences for candidates. *American Politics Quarterly* 16:486–501.

Graber, D. A. 1988. *Processing the news: How people tame the information tide*, 2d ed. New York: Longman.

Hagner, P. R., and L. N. Rieselbach. 1978. The impact of the 1976 presidential debates: Conversion or reinforcement?" In *The presidential debates: Media, electoral, and policy perspectives*, ed. G. F. Bishop, R. G. Meadow, and M. Jackson-Beeck, 157–178. New York: Praeger Publishers.

Hershey, M. R. 1989. The campaign and the media. In *The election of 1988: Reports and interpretations*, ed. G.R. Pomper, R. K. Baker, W. D. Burnham, B. G. Farah, M. R. Hershey, E. Klein, and W. C. McWilliams, 73–102. Chatham, N.J.: Chatham House.

Horvath-Niemeyer, P. S., and M. A. Ferguson. 1989. *Effects of post-debate analyses on biased processing: The Bentsen/Quayle debate*. Paper presented at annual meeting of the Theory and Methodology Division, Association for Education in Journalism, August, Washington, D.C.

Jamieson, K. H. 1988. For televised mendacity, this year is the worst ever. *Washington Post*, October 30, C1, C2.

Just, M., A. Crigler, and L. Wallach. 1990. Thirty seconds or thirty minutes: What viewers learn from spot advertisements and candidate debates. *Journal of Communication* 40 (Summer):120–133.

Katz, E., and J. J. Feldman. 1962. The debates in the light of research: A survey of surveys. In *The great debates*, 1st paperback edition., ed. S. Kraus, 173–223. Bloomington: Indiana University Press.

Kraus, S. 1988. *Televised presidential debates and public policy*. Hillsdale, N.J.: Lawrence Erlbaum Associates.

Lang, G. E., and Lang, K. 1978. The formation of public opinion: Direct and mediated effects of the first debate. In *The presidential debates: Media, electoral and policy perspectives*, ed. G. F. Bishop, R. G. Meadow, and M. Jackson-Beeck, 61–80. New York: Praeger Publishers.

Lemert, J. B. 1981a. *Does mass communication change public opinion after all? A new approach to effects analysis*. Chicago: Nelson-Hall.

Lemert, J. B. 1981b. *Simple reductionism in the study of media effects: How we got there, and are we stuck with it?* Paper presented at the annual spring conference, Mass Communication and Society Division, Association for Education in Journalism, March 21, Kent, Ohio.

Lemert, J. B., W. R. Elliott, K. J. Nestvold, and G. R. Rarick. 1983. Effects of viewing a presidential primary debate. *Communication Research* 10:155–173.

Lowry, D. T., J. A. Bridges, and P. A. Barefield. In press. The effects of network television "instant analysis and querulous criticism" following the first Bush-Dukakis debate. *Journalism Quarterly*.

McLeod, J. M., Z. Pan, S. W. Sun, and K. Hein, 1989. *To know them is to what? Media influences on knowing and feeling in the 1988 election campaign*. Paper presented at annual meeting of Theory and Methodology Division of the Association for Education in Journalism and Mass Communication, August, Washington, D.C.

Nielsen Media Research. 1989. Nielsen measures presidential debates. November 1988.

Patterson, T. A. 1980. *The mass media election: How Americans choose their president*. New York: Praeger Publishers.

Payne, J. G., J. L. Golden, J. Marlier, and S. C. Ratzan. 1989. Perceptions of the 1988 presidential and vice-presidential debates. *American Behavioral Scientist* 32: 425–435.

Petty, R. E., and J. T. Cacioppo. 1981. *Attitudes and persuasion: Classic and contemporary approaches*. Dubuque, Iowa: Wm. C. Brown.

Rosenberg, W. L., and W. R. Elliott. 1987. Effect of debate exposure on evaluation of 1984 vice-presidential candidates. *Journalism Quarterly* 64:55–64.

Rouner, D., and R. M. Perloff. 1988. Selective perceptions of outcome of first 1984 presidential debate. *Journalism Quarterly* 65:141–147, 240.

Sears, D. O., and S. H. Chaffee. 1979. Uses and effects of the 1976 debates: An overview of empirical studies. In *The great debates: Carter vs. Ford, 1976*, ed. S. Kraus, 223–261. Bloomington: Indiana University Press.

Sigelman, L., and C. K. Sigelman. 1984. Judgments of the Carter-Reagan debate: The eye of the beholders. *Public Opinion Quarterly* 48:624–628.

Smith, W. E. 1989. *The shrinking sound bite: Two decades of stylistic evolution in television news*. Paper presented to the Association for Education in Journalism and Mass Communication, August, Washington, D.C.

Steeper, F. T. 1978. Public response to Gerald Ford's statements on Eastern Europe in the second debate. In *The presidential debates: Media, electoral, and policy perspectives*, ed. G. F. Bishop, R. G. Meadow and M. Jackson-Beeck, 81–101. New York: Praeger Publishers.

Stein, M. L. 1988. Discouraging negative political ads: *Washington Post* columnist says press should do a better job of it. *Editor & Publisher*, December 3, 15.

Sussman, B. 1988. *What Americans really think: And why our politicians pay no attention*. New York: Pantheon Books.

Walker, C. E. 1979. Discussion following R. B. Cheney paper. In *The past and future of presidential debates*, ed. A. Ranney, 134. Washington, D.C.: American Enterprise Institute for Public Policy Research.

Wall, V., J. L. Golden, and H. James. 1988. Perceptions of the 1984 presidential debates and a select 1988 presidential primary debate. *Presidential Studies Quarterly* 18:541–563.

2

STUDY DESIGN AND RATIONALE

Research does not just happen. It is the result of careful planning to insure that the goals of the research can be met within the budgetary and time constraints allotted to the project. This project was planned over several years, beginning with an earlier study on presidential primary campaign debates (Lemert, Elliott, Nestvold, and Rarick 1983). Since that original study, we have had time to develop a plan for continued investigation. We designed our research to help us determine the effect of media verdicts and debate exposure on the responses of the public.

In this study we combined two research designs, both familiar to researchers in mass communication. The first methodology, *content analysis*, has been defined by Kerlinger (1973, 525) as "a method of studying and analyzing communications in a systematic, objective, and quantitative manner to measure variables." Our second methodology, *survey analysis*, used telephone interviewing techniques to gather information from the subjects in our study on a day-by-day and an aggregated (sometimes the various survey time points are combined) basis.

There are obvious reasons for using both surveys and content analysis. Foremost among them is that during a political campaign, individuals do more than respond to *media*. They respond to media *content:* to newspaper stories, television commercials, magazine articles, radio talk shows, and television commentary. When analyzing something as complex as a televised presidential candidate debate and post-debate commentary, it is necessary to integrate media content with how people respond to that content.

While this approach may seem obvious, it is not often followed by researchers. Typical media content analysis studies tend to tell us what was written about candidates, what candidates said, or what was said about them. Only rarely do they tell us what readers, viewers, and listeners found interesting or how they reacted to the content.

Effects studies, particularly those using survey techniques, often use approximate measures of media exposure to determine how media influence people's political orientations. (How many hours of television do you watch on an average night? How many days per week do you read the newspaper?) We believe that the best way to determine how the media influence political cognitions, attitudes, and behaviors is to find out more specifically what is being read, what is being watched, and what is being listened to.

We have attempted to improve somewhat on typical political communication research by looking at both elements, the content of the campaign and public's orientation toward the campaign. By integrating television newscasts and post-debate analysis with public evaluations of the candidates, we hope to present an understandable analysis of both how the media respond to the debates and how and whether the fall presidential and vice-presidential debates and post-debate analyses influence the public.

THE CONTENT ANALYSES

Content analysis is one of the most common of research methodologies in mass media research. It has a long history and has been a mainstay of mass media research since at least the late 1920s.[1] The systematic collection, coding, analysis and interpretation of the way the media responded to the 1988 presidential campaign provide useful information about those aspects of the campaign the media select as important and about the consistency or inconsistency in the way various media outlets elect to cover campaign events, especially the debates. In addition, by going back and looking at media coverage of the 1976 Carter-Ford debates, the 1980 Reagan-Carter debate, and the presidential and vice-presidential debates of 1984, we are able to see what, if any, changes have resulted in the ways the print and broadcast media have elected to analyze and discuss candidate debates.

We conducted three content analyses of the way the media have covered presidential debates. The first study, presented in Chapter 3, analyzed evening newscast coverage of the fall presidential debates, beginning with the 1976 campaign. Our second content analysis, presented in Chapter 4, focused on immediate post-debate analysis of the same debates, providing valuable information on the way these news specials create verdicts about candidate performance in the debate. The final debate study, which is presented in Chapter 5, analyzed verdicts in the news about the debates as political institutions. Taken together, these three analyses provide a broad portrait of the relationship between debates and media content.

Study I: Television News Coverage of the Debates

In the first of three content analytic studies (discussed in Chapter 3), network evening newscast coverage of the presidential debates since 1976 was examined. Newscasts by ABC-TV and CBS-TV were analyzed for the first and fourth nights after each debate. Such an approach allowed us to determine not only the immediate network response and judgment about the debate but possible later changes or reaction stories spinning off from the debate. For the 1976, 1980, and 1984 debates, tapes from the Vanderbilt News Archives were used. For 1988, all ABC and CBS network newscasts were recorded in Eugene.

The content coders looked at the "evaluative statements" made during the newscasts. Evaluative statements were those based on judgments or evaluations which made a reference to the debaters, either implicit or explicit. For example, some statements within stories—indeed some entire stories—made reference only to the campaign (e.g.,"Bush will not run a kinder and gentler campaign"). These were not included in the analysis. But the following statement would have been included as a unit of analysis: "Dukakis knows *after last night* a lot of people will say the election is over." The italicized section here would imply a reference to the previous night's debate.

Coding became a two-step process. First, two of us determined what statements were to be included in the analysis and coded those statements. Another verified the inclusion of the statement in the analysis. Typically, disagreement on the inclusion of the unit occurred when a coder did not include a statement rather than when one was included erroneously. In these cases, the statement was added to the analysis.

Each evaluative statement was then coded for statement source (specific journalist making the statement), coverage emphasis (issues, tactics, performance, etc.), media self-consciousness (role of the media in establishing a debate verdict), object of the verdict (candidate, candidates), direction of the verdict (positive, negative, neutral), pre-debate performance expectations, object of the pre-debate expectations, importance of the debate, network, year, which debate, placement (reporter's taped story or anchor's studio story), and the number of days after the debate. Cross-tabulations and Chi-square analyses were used to interpret the findings. A total of 1,256 evaluative statements were coded.

Study II: The Content of Post-Debate Analysis

The second content analytic study (presented in Chapter 4) looks at the post-debate analysis portion of television's coverage of the debate. Post-debate analysis potentially provides the viewer with an "instant" verdict and interpretation of the outcome of the debate. As such, it merits special consideration in any study of debate influence.

All available post-debate analysis programming from ABC, CBS, and NBC was analyzed. This effort resulted in data collected from the first two Ford-Carter debates in 1976, the debate between Jimmy Carter and Ronald Reagan in 1980, the three presidential campaign debates of 1984 (two Reagan-Mondale, one between vice-presidential candidates Bush and Ferraro), and the three 1988 presidential campaign debates, two between Michael Dukakis and George Bush and one between vice-presidential candidates Dan Quayle and Lloyd Bentsen. Tapes of the post-debate analysis for 1976, 1980, and 1984 were gathered from the Vanderbilt University television news archive; the 1988 post-debate analysis was conducted from tapes made by the researchers. A total of 9 hours and 45 minutes of videotape was reviewed.

Evaluative statements were again the unit of analysis for this study. A total of 24 content categories were used to classify each statement, divided into groupings around the evaluation of the debate (to be discussed in Chapter 5) and the debaters. Verdicts about the rival debaters are the focus of this study, reported in Chapter 4. Some 2,302 evaluative statements were analyzed.

Study III: The Debates as Political Institutions

The third content analysis (presented in Chapter 5) looks at the debates as American political institutions and uses the same videotaped data set from Chapter 4. The unit of analysis was the assertion or declarative statement about the debate. Each statement was coded according to the direction of the verdict on the debate as an institution, importance of debates, conflict level, interest/excitement, new information and insights, comparisons with the 1960 "great debates," informativeness to voters, and references to debate sponsors or format.

In addition to the television content study, we also examined reactions of broadcasters and print media to the withdrawal of the League of Women Voters from sponsorship of the 1988 debates. This part of the chapter is more qualitative and anecdotal than the formal content analysis.

Central to this chapter is this question: Do journalists undercut the legitimacy of the presidential debates? We look at this question by using a number of different indices.

Study IV: The Debates in the Larger Context of the Campaign

In the final content analysis (presented in Chapter 11) we used a qualitative approach to analyze how the debates fit in with the rest of the campaign. By studying material from television network newscasts—particularly coverage by ABC and CBS—and materials from the Vanderbilt Television News Index and other media sources on the 1988 fall campaign, we were able to focus on debate strategies used by the candidates and how these strategies reflected overall campaign strategies. In addition, we compare the relative news attention the debates and presidential campaign ads received in each campaign since 1976.

THE SURVEY ANALYSES

Survey analysis also has a long history as a mass communication research methodology. Whereas content analysis provided us with the opportunity to determine what was being said and written, survey analysis allowed us to determine how the public responded to what was seen and read.

There are a variety of ways of conducting survey research. Surveys can be conducted by telephoning and interviewing the subjects for the survey, by mailing self-administered questionnaires to respondents, by giving intact groups (such as a class of students) questionnaires to complete, or by having interviewers question subjects in a face-to-face situation. In our surveys, we telephoned randomly selected subjects in each of the three study locales and administered a questionnaire lasting approximately 20 minutes.

Surveys can also be administered at a single point in time, over several days or a longer time period. In many cases, where time itself is not an important variable, the information collected over several days of interviewing is aggregated into a single grouping for analysis. When time is an important variable, as it is for some of our analyses, particularly those presented in Chapters 6 through 8, the analysis is referred to as a *time-series analysis*.

Mass communication research has tended to rely on single-time-point studies or on designs which rely on fairly simple two-time-point models. To be generalizable, such studies assume that the conditions at the time of data collection remain relatively constant over time. As Davis and Lee (1980) have noted, such assumptions do not necessarily hold. For instance, they use the example of exposure to media violence and aggressive response. At certain points in an individual's life, such exposure might increase the likelihood of violence; at a different age, however, exposure to violence would not be related to an aggressive response. Because of the relatively infrequent use of time-series studies in mass communication research, this technique needs some explanation.

Although mass communication research provides few examples of time-series studies, the studies are informative and provide new insight into the way the mass media operate in contemporary society. For our purposes, the most important of the time-series studies are those looking at political campaigns. Finn (1987) interviewed a panel (same subjects interviewed at multiple time points) of students during five weeks of the 1984 political campaign. Eighty-seven students who were U.S. citizens of voting age were interviewed during the last four weeks of the presidential campaign and one week following the election. Finn measured his subjects' media use and support for political candidates (presidential, U.S. Senate, gubernatorial). Subjects who changed their opinion regarding candidates were asked about the information leading to that change. Finn found that interpersonal information was relatively unimportant and that information received from broadcast sources tended to be image-oriented and biased.

Finally, there are some time-series studies tied directly to presidential and vice-presidential campaign debates. Sears and Chaffee (1979) reviewed 32 audience studies of the 1976 debates between candidates Ford and Carter. Of the 32 studies, 19 involved time-series designs using two and five points. Generally, these were panel studies with responses collected before and after one or more of the debates. Typical of these studies is the one by Dennis, Chaffee, and Choe (1979). Respondents in this four-time-point panel design (N = 164) were interviewed just before the first 1976 presidential candidate debate, between the first and second debates, after the last debate but before the election, and after the election. Their findings suggested that debate exposure increased the importance of issue positions as a predictor of voting decisions.

Only one study, by Miller and MacKuen (1979), collected data on a day-by-day basis. They found evidence of shifts in assessments of the images of both candidates around the three debates and concluded that these effects were relatively short-term, lasting approximately two days.

Types of Time-Series Designs

A time-series or longitudinal design is defined as any research design in which data related to the research problem is collected at two or more time points (Stanford 1989). There are three general types of time-series or longitudinal designs (Wimmer and Dominick 1989).

Panel studies. Panel studies utilize designs in which the same subjects are interviewed at multiple time points. The prototype panel study for mass communication research was conducted during the 1940 presidential campaign between Democratic candidate Franklin Roosevelt and Republican Wendell Wilkie (Lazarsfeld, Berelson, and Gaudet 1948). Every fourth house in Erie County, Ohio, was visited, resulting in a pool of approximately 3,000 potential subjects. From this group, four groups of 600 were selected. Three of these groups served as controls, with subjects in them interviewed only once. The fourth group, called the "main panel," was interviewed in June, July, August, September, October, and November. Whenever subjects changed the way they intended to vote, detailed records were kept. This innovative design allowed the researchers to tie changes in voting intention to changes in campaign events. At the time, the results seemed to indicate that the majority of people changed little during a political campaign.

Cohort Analysis. Another form of longitudinal design uses samples of cohorts, individuals "who have experienced the same significant life event within a given period of time" (Wimmer and Dominick 1989, 196). Using cohorts, it would be possible to compare individuals born during or before November of 1954 (who would be of voting age in 1972) with individuals born after November of 1954 (who would not vote for president until 1976 at the earliest) to determine differences between groups which had experienced the sequence of events known as "Watergate" with voters for whom "Watergate" had less serious implications.

Trend Studies. The trend study looks at different samples drawn from the same population at multiple time points. The best known of these types of studies are the public opinion polls of firms such as the Roper and Gallup organizations. Such studies have proven valuable in determining the influence of media coverage of issues on public opinion and of the influence of specific events on public attitudes toward politics. Generally, trend studies chart changes in public opinion regarding an issue or candidate over the time period of the study.

Our study, which also looks at trends and involves the interviewing of separate samples of individuals selected from the same population, provides an example of what Cook and Campbell (1979) have described as a simple interrupted time-series (SITS) design. The design is diagrammed in Figure 2.1, which illustrates how a simple time-series study can be organized. In this particular model, there are eight data collection points (O_1 to O_8) and an intervention, "X," taking place between O_4 and O_5. For us, the intervention would be the political debate. The analysis of this design involves investigating differences in the measured variables before and after the intervention. Some of the possible outcomes are illustrated in Figure 2.2 (Kelly and McGrath 1988).

Possible Time-Series Outcomes

Figure 2.2a illustrates the type of graph that would result if the interruption (the "X") had no effect at all. Here the graph continues to

$$O_1 \quad O_2 \quad O_3 \quad O_4 \; X \; O_5 \quad O_6 \quad O_7 \quad O_8$$

Figure 2.1
Simple Interrupted Time-Series Design

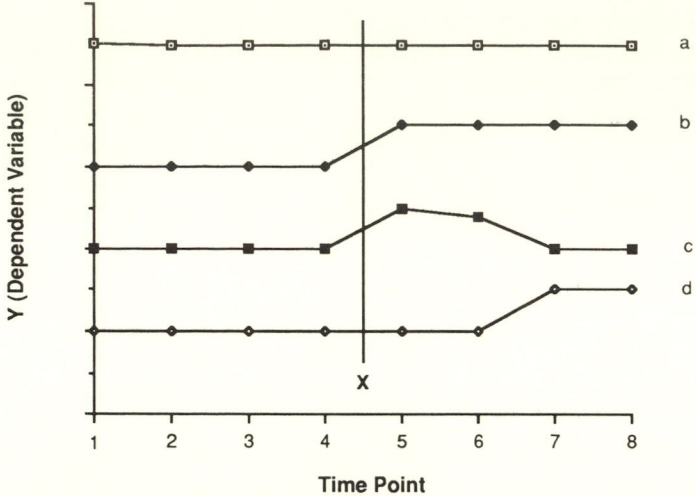

Figure 2.2
Possible Time-Series Outcomes

be as flat after the "X" as it had been before it. In 2.2b, however, another possible outcome is demonstrated. Here there is an abrupt change taking place between O_4 and O_5 that continues through O_8. The "eyeball" interpretation would be that the intervention had an effect which was maintained through time. Figure 2.2c provides the type of outcome we think we are very likely to find, a change that takes place after the interruption but decays over time. Figure 2.2d shows what a delayed effect might be like. We might anticipate such a delay in response if something mentioned in a debate were somehow to become a major news story two days or so after the debate.

It might help to look at a real-life example of what time-series data can look like and why it is necessary to use more than one time point in making judgments about the influence of a single event such as a debate. First, the graph in Figure 2.3 shows the Gallup Poll results for candidate preferences for Richard Nixon and John Kennedy at two points during the 1960 presidential campaign: on September 25, 1960, just before the first presidential candidate debate, and on October 12, just over two weeks after the September 26 debate. Just looking at these numbers might indicate that Kennedy had benefited considerably from the debate, increasing his approval from 46% to 49%, while Nixon saw his lead disappear as he fell from 47% support to 46%. If this were the sole basis for evaluating the influence of the debate, then it seems quite possible that Kennedy had benefited from a four-point shift: three points added to his own number while Nixon lost one point.

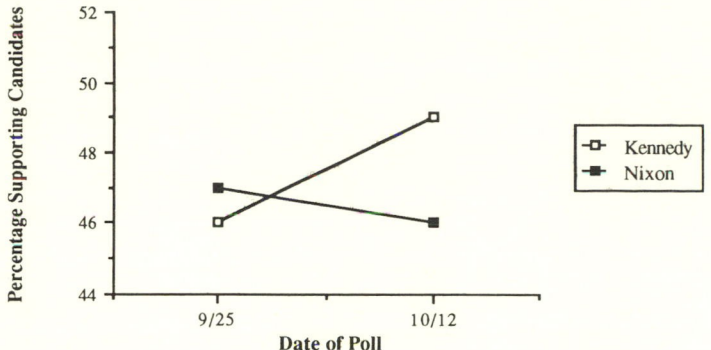

Figure 2.3
1960 Candidate Preferences Just Before and Just After the First Presidential Debate on September 26, 1960

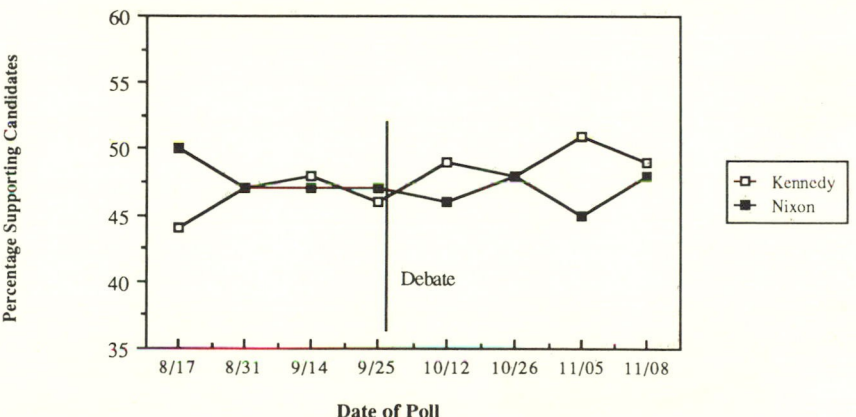

Figure 2.4
1960 Candidate Preferences Before and After the First Presidential Debate on September 26, 1960

But, such an interpretation would be too simple. The graph presented in Figure 2.4 illustrates the pattern of candidate support over a longer time period. From the graph it is apparent that the biggest drop in Nixon's support took place before the debate, between August 17 and August 31, when his support decreased from 50% to 47%. At the same time, Kennedy was gaining in support, improving from 44% on August 17 to 48% on September 14. After the debate, the tendency was for Kennedy's support to continue to improve somewhat while Nixon's moved up and down. After the election, the two candidates were again close together. What this demonstrates, quite simply, is that more data points make interpretations more complex, but they also make interpretations more accurate and reflective of the process that is taking place.

In our own time-series design, diagrammed in Figure 2.5, we used eight time points specific to the first presidential debate on September 25, 1988, four time points specific to the vice-presidential candidate debate on October 5, and seven time points for the second presidential candidate debate on October 13. In addition to the data collection points shown here, we also collected information from our subjects immediately after the primary elections in each state and on November 6, 1988, just before the election. The interviews in the spring provide a baseline measure before the fall campaign began; the November 6 interviews provide a "summing up" measurement—long after the debates but very close to Election Day (November 8).

In effect, we conducted three simple interrupted time-series designs. The first, beginning on September 22, 1988, involved measurement on eight successive nights, three before the September 25 presidential candidate debate, one on debate night, and four after the debate until September 29.

The second series started on October 4, the night before the vice-presidential candidate debate, and continued on October 5, 6, 9, 11, and

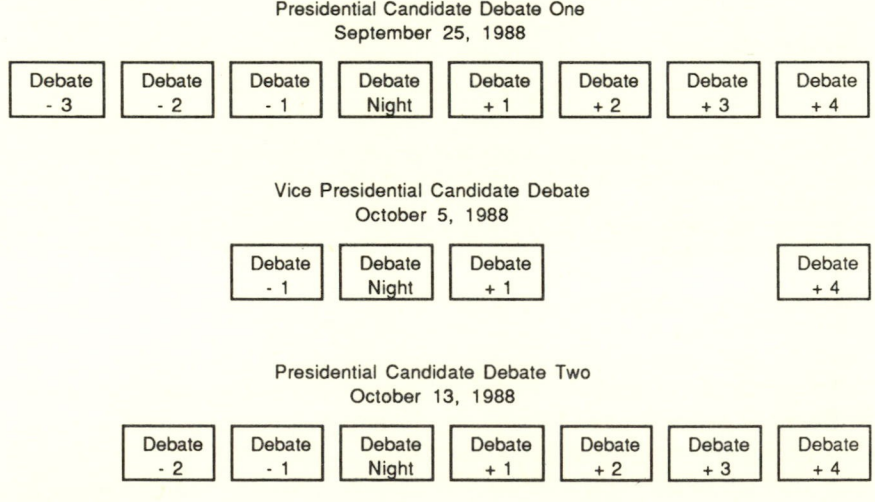

Figure 2.5
Time-Series Analysis Design for the 1988 Presidential and Vice-Presidential Debates

12. The third series began on October 11, two nights before the second presidential candidate debate, and continued for seven nights through October 17. Over the three interviewing periods, a total of 19 samples were interviewed. The analysis of each of these designs is presented in Chapters 6 (first presidential debate), 7 (vice-presidential debate), and 8 (second presidential debate). Utilization of this type of design, we hoped, would allow us to track not only the influence of the debate itself on debate nights (survey data were collected immediately after each debate) but also of any verdicts rendered in post-debate analysis or by the press later, as was the case with Gerald Ford's statement about Soviet domination of Eastern Europe in the 1976 Carter-Ford debates (Steeper 1978).

Advantages and Disadvantages of Time-Series Designs

Advantages. There are numerous advantages to using a time-series design, even one with as few as two time points. However, the more time points used in collecting data, the stronger the design and the more sophisticated the possible analysis. Among the specific advantages the day-by-day time-series design we have used are:

- One can link voter reactions to specific events as they occur and be able to trace the possible impact of such events on the public's attitudes, cognitions, and behaviors. In our studies, particularly in the study of the vice-presidential debate presented in Chapter 7, the use of time-series data allowed the careful tracking of people's open-ended responses to questions asking them to recall stories about the debates. Through comparisons of subjects' responses before and after the debate, it was possible to see the influence of media coverage of the debate on the way the public interpreted the candidates' debate performance.

- Day-by-day interviewing in a time-series design also takes advantage of people's immediate recall. The greater the delay between an event and interviewing, the greater the chance of inaccurate recall. It is important to be able to use people's most recent and most accurate memories.

- There are also advantages in using the type of study we have designed over "tracking polls" or "trend studies." While our study may be similar to such studies, there are important differences. First, tracking polls and trend studies usually focus on a single independent variable, time, and one dependent variable, although—as ours is—they often are built around some form of intervention. In our study, which relied on data contained in detailed questionnaires administered to each subject during the telephone interviews, we were able to gather information concerning a variety of dependent variables, including evaluations of the candidates as debaters, the winners of the debate, open-ended evaluations of debate performance, candidate image, recall of news stories about the debate, debate issues that might influence the election, the probability of voting for each candidate, and who the subjects would vote for at the time of the interview, as well as media use and demographic information.

Unlike most trend studies, we were able to bring a number of variables to bear on the question of debate and verdict influences, using models that are significantly more complex than those usually encountered in trend studies. From a theoretical perspective, this approach encourages a better understanding of the issues involving the debate, post-debate analysis, and the political process.

• Perhaps most importantly, time-series studies allow us to make far stronger cause-and-effect statements than it is possible to do with single time-point studies. By recording when an event took place and comparing the public's attitudes, cognitions, and behaviors before and after that event, we are in a much better position to state whether or not it is reasonable to say that the event "caused" the measured attitudes, cognitions, and behaviors.

• When the data are collected using a panel design, the problems of subject mortality (people dropping out of the survey) and test sensitization (learning what to expect from a questionnaire because they have already seen the questions on a previous questionnaire) can be critical. By using separate cross-sections of subjects each interviewing day in our design, we eliminated the problems of mortality and sensitization.

Disadvantages. If time-series studies have such advantages over static designs, then why are they not used more frequently? There are a number of reasons, several of which are suggested below:

• *Expense.* It is much less expensive to conduct a survey on a single night or over a relatively small number of nights where time is not an important consideration. Our study, which involved interviewing 1,915 subjects over the three debate time series—not to mention the spring and November 6 interviews—was significantly more expensive than typical mass communication investigations, when a relatively small number of subjects are interviewed. Time may be great as a variable, but time is money, especially in research.

• *Complexity of statistical analysis.* The analysis of time-series data can be extremely complex. Analysis is made even more complex because the typical time-series study requires at least 50 data points before the use of complex analytical models begins to make sense. While a discussion of the methods for long-term time-series analysis is left to more detailed treatments (Davis and Lee 1980; Cook and Campbell 1979; McDowall, McCleary, Meidinger and Hay 1980; McCleary and Hay 1980; Lewis-Beck 1986; Simonton 1977), such treatments usually assume data collected as a panel design and, if not a panel, require many more time points for intelligent analysis than would have been appropriate for our study.

Our approach to the problem was to use Multiple Classification Analysis techniques to determine the influence of the debate and post-debate analysis on our dependent variables. Such a statistical model seems to fall within the guidelines suggested for parallel quasi-experimental designs by Cook and Campbell (1979).

Our Survey Design

The Locales. Surveys on each night were completed in three communities: Philadelphia, Pennsylvania; Eugene-Springfield, Oregon; and Carbondale, Illinois.

Philadelphia, Pennsylvania, is a major Eastern city with an urban population of 1.7 million. It is the fourth largest media market in the country. Traditionally, it votes for the Democratic presidential candidate. Interviews in the Philadelphia area were conducted by the Drexel University Survey Research Center.

Eugene, Oregon, is a medium-size community with approximately 110,000 residents in the Eugene-Springfield area. Eugene is home to the University of Oregon, one of Oregon's two major state universities. Politically, Eugene tends to be liberal and heavily involved in environmental issues. Springfield is a blue-collar community of 47,000, adjacent to Eugene. Interviews were coordinated through the School of Journalism at the University of Oregon.

Carbondale, Illinois, is a rural community in Southern Illinois with a permanent population of approximately 25,000. This figure excludes many of the approximately 24,000 students enrolled at Southern Illinois University at Carbondale. The surrounding area is rural, with farming, mining, and tourism the major industries. Interviewing was coordinated through the Mass Communication Research Center in the School of Journalism at Southern Illinois University.

The Samples. At each survey site, we used random digit dialing (RDD) techniques to select respondents. Random digit dialing techniques have become standard in telephone surveying, because they allow access to unlisted as well as listed numbers. The technique for selecting the numbers varies but usually involves the random assignment of digits to prefixes selected from local telephone directories and exchanges. Table 2.1 provides the number of subjects interviewed at each location by the time of interview.

Interviews. The procedure we followed was the same for each interview locale. Normally, interviewing would begin at 7:00 P.M. and continue until 10:00 P.M. Paid interviewers, often graduate students, were recruited and trained at each site. For the surveys conducted around each of the debates, interviewers began calling immediately upon completion of the debate and continued as long as possible. Because of the time zone differences, this sometimes meant that interviews in Philadelphia continued until 11:00 P.M. and in Carbondale until 10:30 P.M.

When interviewers reached potential subjects on the phone, they asked to speak to the person in the house who was at least 18 and whose next birthday was closest to the date we called. Such a technique helps to balance between male and female respondents. When no adult was available, interviewers attempted to find an appropriate time to call back.

Table 2.1
Number of Interviews, by Locale and Time

Interviewing Cycle	Eugene	Philadelphia	Carbondale	Total
Post-Primary Interviews	153	77	129	359
First Presidential Debate				
September 22	37	19	35	91
September 23	36	20	40	96
September 24	38	19	39	96
September 25 (Debate)	52	22	37	111
September 26	42	33	40	115
September 27	33	21	39	93
September 28	42	24	28	94
September 29	41	16	45	102
Total	321	174	303	798
Vice Presidential Debate				
October 4	35	21	34	90
October 5 (Debate)	49	2	27	78
October 6	30	25	27	82
October 9	40	26	43	109
Total	154	74	131	359
Second Presidential Debate				
October 11	44	20	34	98
October 12	38	24	26	88
October 13 (Debate)	36	21	21	78
October 14	38	55	39	132
October 15	37	51	36	124
October 16	39	49	38	126
October 17	41	30	41	112
Total	273	250	235	758
November 6 Interviews	54	21	29	104
Overall Total	955	596	827	2,378

Busy signals and no answers were recorded and attempts were made to contact these individuals later that night. When possible, at least two call-backs were attempted. Business establishments were excluded unless the individuals answering the phone indicated they had time to answer the questions. In Eugene, one interview actually was done with a man who answered a pay telephone, but generally numbers for pay phones were recorded as "no answers." Answering machines pose a unique problem.

We treated them as "no answer" responses and, when possible, attempted at least two call-backs. A copy of the interview used for the first presidential debate is included in the Appendix. The interview took between 20 and 30 minutes.

The Survey Analyses

Survey research results are presented in five of our chapters. These chapters rely variously on time-series designs or on "aggregate data analysis" (where measures across several time periods are combined).

Study I: The first presidential debate, September 25, 1988. The first survey results are presented in Chapter 6. Here the time-series analysis is of the first presidential debate period beginning on September 22, three nights before the September 25 debate, and continuing through September 29, four nights later. The primary variables of interest in this study include ratings of the candidates as debaters, open-ended evaluations of candidate debate performance, perceptions of the debate winner, candidate image, probabilities of voting for the candidates, and actual voting choice at the time of the interview. A total of 798 subjects were interviewed over the eight nights of the survey.

Study II: The vice-presidential debate, October 5, 1988. The time-series analysis of the survey data for the vice-presidential debate is presented in Chapter 7. Here, the interviewing period included the night before the October 5 debate, the night of the debate, the next night (October 6), and October 9, 11, and 12. A total of 546 respondents were interviewed. In this particular study, the emphasis was on open-ended responses regarding what people remembered from the news about the vice-presidential debate, open-ended responses evaluating vice-presidential candidates Bentsen and Quayle's performance during the debate, issues raised in the debate, voting choice, vice-presidential candidate ratings as debaters, and voting probability *if the vote was for the vice-presidential candidate alone.*

Study III: The second presidential debate, October 13, 1988. The analysis of the time-series data for the second presidential debate is presented in Chapter 8. Interviewing began on October 11, two nights before the debate, and continued through October 17. A total of 758 subjects were interviewed over the seven nights of the survey. In this study, the primary emphasis was on the influence of the debate and post-debate analysis on the ratings of the candidates as debaters, open-ended descriptions of the candidates' debate performances, candidate image, perceived importance of issues raised in the debate, candidate voting probabilities, and voting choice.

Study IV: Debates as a political institution. In Chapter 9 we look at how people evaluate the debates as political institutions. In this chapter information is presented showing how the audience for presidential candidate debates has decreased considerably since the 1960 Kennedy-Nixon debates. The majority of the analysis involved looking at our subjects' responses to a series of questions about the debates as a political institution. Subjects were combined across the various interviewing periods (aggregate) for this analysis. Most analyses were based on the total sample for the fall campaign, though some comparisons were made with the spring primary surveys.

Study V: The audience responds to the campaign ads. The final survey study is presented in Chapter 10. This time, the purpose was to look at how individuals responded to the ads of the campaign. Data collected during the primary, over the debate interviewing period, and just before the election (on November 6), were used. We looked at whether people recalled ads as positive or negative, at the relationship between exposure to political ads and agreement with statements such as, "There's too much mudslinging in the campaign," and the relationship between exposure to negative ads and the probability of voting for the candidates.

DATA ANALYSIS

The Content Analysis

In reporting the results of the content analysis studies, we relied primarily on cross-tabulations and percentages to summarize and present our findings. Statistical interpretations were made using the Chi-square statistic.

The Time-Series Analysis Model

We borrowed parts of the logic of time-series analysis suggested by Ostrom and Simon (1989). We accepted their position that the most important factor between an event (in our case the debate) and the public's response to it is the number of days elapsed between the event and the interview. The most important factor in measuring the impact of an event on the public is to look at the public response immediately before and immediately after the event. Our design made it possible to look at the public's response before the debates, immediately after the debates, and up to four nights after a specific debate. To analyze these influences, we opted for Multiple Classification Analysis and other appropriate techniques (Chi-square), depending on the measurement level of the dependent variable.

Implicit in each of our time-series analyses was one basic hypothesis: Public perceptions and orientations toward presidential candidates are influenced by exposure to campaign debates and, particularly, by the interpretations presented in post-debate analysis of the debates by television networks.

The Aggregate Data Survey Model

When we analyzed the data taken before the debates (after the primaries), during the debates, and after the debates (November 6, 1988), we combined many of the measures into single variables which would allow us to look at how the debates themselves and campaign ads were viewed by the audience (Chapters 9 and 10).

CONCLUSION

In this chapter we have attempted to lay out the way we went about our study. In an innovative manner, we think, we have combined traditional content analysis and survey research with a time-series design to provide us with a powerful base for investigating the impact of the debates and post-debate analysis on our various samples of individuals. Where necessary, additional details of the research methods are presented within each chapter.

NOTE

1. Fortunately, there are a number of useful introductions to content analysis (Wimmer and Dominick 1987; Stempel 1989a; Stempel 1989b) and more advanced texts on the subject (North, Holsti, Zaninovich, and Zinnes 1963; Krippendorff 1980; Weber 1985) for those needing more detail on the method.

REFERENCES

Cook, T. D., and D. T. Campbell. 1979. *Quasi-experimentation: Design & analysis issues for field settings*. Chicago: Rand McNally.

Davis, D. K., and J. Lee. 1980. Time-series analysis models for communication research. In *Multivariate techniques in human communication research*, ed. P. R. Monge and J. N. Capella, 429–454. New York: Academic Press.

Dennis, J., S. H. Chaffee, and S. Y. Choe. 1979. Impact on partisan, image, and issue voting. In *The great debates: Carter vs. Ford, 1976*, ed. S. Kraus, 314–330. Bloomington: Indiana University Press.

Finn, S. 1987. Electoral information flow and students' information processing: A computerized panel study. In *Communication yearbook 10*, ed. M. L. McLaughlin, 517–532. Newbury Park: Sage.

Kelly, J. R., and J. E. McGrath. 1988. *On time and method*. Newbury Park: Sage.

Kerlinger, F. N. 1973. *Foundations of behavioral research*, 2d ed. New York: Holt, Rinehart and Winston.

Krippendorff, K. 1980. *Content analysis: An introduction to its methodology.* Beverly Hills: Sage.

Lazarsfeld, P. F., B. Berelson, and H. Gaudet. 1948. *The people's choice: How the voter makes up his mind in a presidential campaign,* 2d ed. New York: Columbia University Press.

Lemert, J. B., W. R. Elliott, K. J. Nestvold, and G. R. Rarick. 1983. Effects of viewing a presidential primary debate. *Communication Research* 10:155–173.

Lewis-Beck, M. S. 1986. Interrupted time series. In *New tools for social scientists: Advances and applications in research methods,* ed. W. D. Berry and M. S. Lewis-Beck, 209–240. Beverly Hills: Sage.

McCleary, R. M., and R. A. Hay, Jr. 1980. *Applied time series analysis for the social sciences.* Beverly Hills: Sage.

McDowall, D., R. McCleary, E. E. Meidinger, and R. A. Hay, Jr. 1980. *Interrupted time series analysis.* Beverly Hills: Sage.

Miller, A. H., and M. MacKuen. 1979. Informing the electorate: A national study. In *The great debates: Carter vs. Ford, 1976,* ed. S. Kraus, 269–297. Bloomington: Indiana University Press.

North, R. C., O. R. Holsti, M. G. Zaninovich, and D. A. Zinnes. 1963. *Content analysis: A handbook with applications for the study of international crisis.* Evanston: Northwestern University Press.

Ostrom, C. W., Jr., and D. M. Simon. 1989. The man in the teflon suit? The environmental connection, political drama, and popular support in the Reagan presidency. *Public Opinion Quarterly* 53:353–387.

Sears, D. O., and S. H. Chaffee. 1979. Uses and effects of the 1976 debates: An overview of empirical studies. In *The great debates: Carter vs. Ford, 1976,* ed. S. Kraus, 223–261. Bloomington: Indiana University Press.

Simonton, D. K. 1977. Cross-sectional time-series experiments: Some suggested statistical analyses. *Psychological Bulletin* 84:489–502.

Stanford, S. W. 1989. Statistical designs in survey research. In *Research methods in mass communication,* 2d ed., ed. G. H. Stempel, III, and B. H. Westley, 173–199. Englewood Cliffs: Prentice Hall.

Steeper, F. T. 1978. Public response to Gerald Ford's statements on Eastern Europe in the second debate. In *The presidential debates: Media, electoral, and policy perspectives,* ed. G. F. Bishop, R. G. Meadow, and M. Jackson-Beeck, 81–101. New York: Praeger.

Stempel, G. H., III. 1989a. Content analysis. In *Research methods in mass communication,* 2d ed., ed. G. H. Stempel, III, and B. H. Westley, 124–136. Englewood Cliffs: Prentice Hall.

Stempel, G. H., III. 1989b. Statistical designs for content analysis. In *Research methods in mass communication,* 2d ed., ed. G. H. Stempel, III, and B. H. Westley, 137–149. Englewood Cliffs: Prentice Hall.

Weber, R. P. 1985. *Basic content analysis.* Beverly Hills: Sage.

Wimmer, R. D., and J. R. Dominick. 1987. *Mass media research: An introduction,* 2d ed. Belmont, Calif.: Wadsworth.

3

NETWORK TELEVISION NEWS COVERAGE OF THE DEBATES: 1976 to 1988

Conventional wisdom about news coverage of presidential debates suggests that stories in the aftermath of the debates have an impact on consumers of that information. Assertions to this effect:

. . . Journalists take on the powerful role of interpreter of the debate, providing meaning and a framework for interpreting an otherwise incomprehensible and esoteric event. (Meadow 1987)

Given the arcane nature of most debate questions and answers, the audience tends to be in the position of a theater-goer attending a preview and saying, "I can't wait to read the reviews so I'll know what I thought about this." (Greenfield 1980)

And as we mentioned in the introduction, several factors suggest that the post-debate verdict effect intuitively makes sense: voter reliance on the quick media "fill-in" on the debate; increasingly lower campaign attention and interest; the fall-off of debate viewing after the first debate; and lack of voter ability to recognize candidate mistakes when they occur during the debates (Lemert 1981 and Graber 1988). We have also already suggested how, during the last several debate cycles, individual presidential campaigns have attempted to reduce the amount of candidate risk by controlling the rules and format of the debates. This, in the eyes of some researchers, has turned the debate into nothing more than glorified "whistle-stop speeches" (Meadow 1983). It has also meant ambiguous

debate outcomes, forcing voters to rely on the news media for "clarification."

Given the potential for a verdict effect, we thought it was important to
devote several chapters to the way in which network television news has
covered presidential debates since 1976. In this chapter we ask the
following questions about early-evening network news: What have television network journalists been saying about the presidential debates? How
have they reported presidential debates? What differences exist in how
individual networks cover the debates? And, finally, what was the nature
of debate coverage by network television journalists in 1988?

BACKGROUND

Presidential debates have become institutionalized since 1976 to the
extent that we not only expect them to be held but we also expect
candidates to participate in them, and we expect debate formats to exist
a certain way. On the other hand, as we have noted elsewhere (Lemert
et. al. 1989), the quantity of research on presidential debates has been
inconsistent after the swell of interest in the 1976 debates. This is
especially true for content studies of debate news coverage.

The studies that do exist, however, seem to share a consistent finding:
Even when the debates are heavily issue-oriented, subsequent coverage
is "decidedly less so" (Sears and Chaffee 1979, 228.) For example,
content analyses of the coverage of the 1976 debates show news media
coverage of the debate devoted approximately 40% to issues, while issue-
related comments from the candidates themselves made up approximately 80% of the televised debates (McLeod et al. 1979; Miller and
McKuen 1979). And less than one-fifth of network television news coverage of the first Carter-Ford debate was devoted to issues (Sears and
Chaffee 1979; Miller and McKuen 1979). Instead, the research shows, the
news media in the fall of 1976 focused on the "hoopla" of the debates,
covering them in much the same way they would have covered other
portions of the campaign. In addition, coverage tended to focus on who
"won" the debates, debate performance, and candidate competence and
personality.

Other media-content research surrounding the 1976 debates has primarily been agenda-setting research (see Becker et al. 1979; McLeod et al.
1979; Jackson-Beeck and Meadow 1979; Gadziala and Becker 1983.)
These studies, like most agenda-setting research, attempt to show relationships between what the media deem important as debate issues and
what the public believes is important, although in one case the researchers
were also interested in candidate agendas (see Jackson-Beeck and
Meadow 1979). In any event, the agenda-setting research, by its nature,
assumes the existence of issue orientation from the debates and subse-

quent media coverage, if not predominance. In fact, what we have seen from previous research on debate coverage suggests that this assumption is misguided.

Since 1976, as research on debate effects and debate-coverage effects has lessened, a parallel decline has occurred in research on the content of news coverage of the debates. Still, two studies supply strong anecdotal evidence that the media coverage of the only debate between Jimmy Carter and Ronald Reagan focused on "winners and losers" and relied heavily on polls and political analysts to determine who "won" (see Berquist and Gordon 1981; Meadow 1983). Berquist and Gordon also assert that media coverage before the debates affects verdicts in that it creates expectations about potential winners and losers (1981, 125–129). In their impressionistic essay on media coverage of the debates, Diamond and Friery (1987) find similar themes. In addition, they say that media coverage of the debates focuses on judgments of the debates themselves (that is, whether they were dull or exciting).

Our objective in this chapter is to combine the impressions and notions people have suggested about news coverage of presidential debates to see if discernible patterns exist in the coverage. Our purpose was to test these notions empirically and to discover whether changed patterns have developed in the way presidential debate verdicts manifest themselves in the news. We were interested in the following questions:

- Do verdicts from television news coverage of the 1984 and 1988 debates focus more on performance and tactics and less on issues than does coverage of the 1976 and 1980 debates?

- Do verdicts from television news coverage of the 1984 and 1988 debates come from polls to a greater extent than do verdicts from 1976 and 1980?

- Were the networks relying more heavily in 1976 and 1980 on their own journalists for verdicts and less on political insiders than in 1984 and 1988?

- Have the networks shown awareness of their own influence over the years? That is, has media self-consciousness increased since 1976?

- What differences exist between the networks in how they have covered the debates?

- What differences exist among correspondents in how they have covered the debates?

- Does the incumbent party get more verdict attention from network television news than the "out" party?

- Are the verdicts accompanied by self-consciousness on the part of the media?

- What role do pre-debate expectations play?

We think it is important to take stock of these questions and issues now as televised presidential debates and their format become institutionalized. At least one fall debate has been held since 1976 and, in the last two elections, debates have occurred during the primaries. We therefore are reaching the point at which the public expects debates to occur and candidates to debate regardless of whether they want to.

Concomitantly, the public may expect the news media to provide information about the debates that they may not be able to get from the debate themselves (see Jackson-Beeck and Meadow 1979). If a pattern exists that indicates, for example, that issue coverage about the debates has lessened since 1976, changes in debate coverage and possibly in the debates themselves may be necessary. Likewise, the domination of coverage that deals with performance at the expense of issue coverage may have public policy implications.

THE DEBATES WE STUDIED

To compare network news coverage of the presidential debates since 1976, we analyzed newscasts from ABC and CBS that ran the night following a debate and the fourth night after the debate. We relied on the Vanderbilt News Archives for tapes from 1976, 1980, and 1984; we taped all ABC and CBS network newscasts during the 1988 fall campaign.

The rationale for choosing the next night is obvious: We expected the debate to dominate that newscast. (Our expectations largely were met.) The rationale for also analyzing newscasts from four nights hence was threefold: First, we believed there would be lingering effects from news verdicts on the previous debates. Second, history suggested there might be delayed, or firmer, verdicts later in the week than the night after the debate. And third, reactions to the verdicts themselves often have consequences that take a few days to play out.

For example, in 1984 Ronald Reagan by most accounts lost his first debate with Walter Mondale. But a comment from a White House doctor to the effect that Reagan seemed alert during the debate "for a man his age" helped trigger several days worth of debate-related coverage, including stories on new Reagan campaign strategies for the second debate. It took journalists a couple of days to pull out all the staff and campaign reactions.

Our choice of CBS and ABC newscasts was predicated first on the financial limitations on the number of tapes we could order from Vanderbilt. Then, once we had to choose two networks, we left NBC out on the basis of impressions and potential influence. That is, we observed throughout the primary and political convention season differences among the three networks in the way they covered the candidates, particularly George Bush. For example, CBS seemed most critical of Bush, ABC the least critical, and NBC somewhere in between. And, at the time of our selection, CBS had the highest ratings among the three network newscasts. The combination of the ratings and the impressions took NBC out of the picture.[1]

Primarily for financial reasons, we limited ourselves to the first two Carter-Ford debates of 1976 and the only Carter-Reagan debate of 1980. But our analysis includes all the debates from 1984, including the debate between George Bush and Geraldine Ferraro, and all the 1988 debates, including the vice-presidential debate. (For more on the variables used and analyses employed for this content analysis and the one reported in Chapters 4 and 5, see Chapter 2.)

RESULTS

In several subsections of this chapter we have discussed possible explanations for our findings immediately after reporting the findings. In other portions of the chapter, however, we have delayed an explanation until the next section of the chapter. We did this, as the reader will see, because for many of the findings we report, a major theme exists that may provide an explanation for several sets of results.

Focus of Network Debate Coverage, 1976–1988

Have verdicts from television news coverage of the 1984 and 1988 debates focused more on performance and tactics and less on issues than coverage of the 1976 and 1980 debates? Yes. The data in Table 3.1 indicate a continuous decline, from 1976 to 1984, in the proportion of issue coverage from ABC and CBS. In 1976, for example, about 38% of the statements about the first two Carter-Ford debates pertained to issues. (Most studies of the coverage of that debate estimated the amount of *time* devoted to issue coverage as 40%.) By 1980 the percentage of newscast statements about issues had dropped by more than half, and the percentage continued to drop with coverage of the 1984 debates. Issue coverage of the 1988 debates leveled off from 1984, but remained less than 10% of all coverage.

The decline in issue coverage during the last two sets of debates has accompanied an increase in the percentage of statements devoted to tactics, competence, and previous record. The proportion of tactics coverage has doubled from 1976 to 1988; the percentage of coverage devoted to competence to govern has increased fivefold in the same period; and the proportion of previous record coverage has increased in every year. Meanwhile, coverage devoted to performance increased through 1984, but dropped with coverage of the 1988 debates.

Sources of Presidential Debate Verdicts, 1976–1988

Verdicts from television news coverage of the 1984 and 1988 debates do come from polls to a greater extent than do verdicts from 1976 and

Table 3.1
Focus of Television News Coverage of Debates

	Year			
Focus of Statement	1976	1980	1984	1988
Issues	38.4%	18.8%	5.2%	5.7%
Debate performance	44.5%	54.2%	61.9%	46.3%
Tactics	12.7%	15.3%	20.4%	25.9%
Competence to govern	1.6%	0.0%	2.5%	8.1%
Previous record	1.6%	3.5%	7.4%	9.7%
Other	1.2%	8.3%	2.7%	4.3%
(N)	(245)	(144)	(446)	(421)

Chi-square = 250.078, df = 15, p < .001

1980, with one disclaimer (see Table 3.2). In 1980 about one-fifth of all statements in coverage of the Carter-Reagan debate were about polls, no doubt because of the telepoll that ABC sponsored following the debate. Because in this study we made no distinction when coding between statements about the telepoll and statements concerning scientific polling, we believe that, in fact, 1984 and 1988 television news stories about the debate relied more heavily on polls than on other sources once the 1980 telepoll is excluded.

Despite not having made the distinction between statements about telepolls and those about random-sample polls, we could and did attempt to answer the question another way: by controlling for the network on which the stories ran. In other words, for 1980 we also looked only at CBS poll stories, in the aftermath of the debate. Looking only at these stories, we find that 8.7% of news verdicts for the 1980 debate came from polls. We conclude, then, that the networks have relied on polls to an increasing extent since 1976.

No clear trend emerges on the question of whether the networks increasingly relied more heavily for verdicts on their own journalists or on political insiders. Certainly the data in Table 3.2 show relatively more reliance on politically elite sources than journalists in 1980 and 1984, but the discrepancy in 1988 was not as great. In fact, the percentage of

Table 3.2
Source of Television News Coverage of Debates

Source of Statement	Year			
	1976	1980	1984	1988
Journalist	37.6%	20.8%	26.3%	32.8%
Poll	3.3%	20.1%	10.1%	11.2%
M-O-S/Viewers*	10.2%	0.7%	1.1%	1.2%
Political elite	44.9%	53.5%	57.8%	47.5%
Crowd	2.4%	4.2%	3.8%	4.8%
Deferred verdict	1.6%	0.0%	0.9%	2.6%
(N)	(245)	(144)	(446)	(421)

Chi-square = 108.517, df = 15, p < .001

* M-O-S refers to "man on the street"; "viewers" refers to those who watched the debates on television. This category includes statements from non-elites who were interviewed after watching a debate. Typically, the interviews occurred after the respondent had watched at home or in some public place, such as a bar or a meeting hall.

statements from journalists increased from 1984 to 1988, while the proportion of statements from political insiders decreased.

Two other interesting results show up in Table 3.2. Verdicts no longer come from in-home viewers and persons in the street as much as they did in 1976. And 1988 saw an increase in the proportion of statements that deferred a verdict by implying that only time would tell who won, although these statements made up a small percentage of the overall coverage. Still, it indicates an increase in the number of times the networks were hedging their calls.

Media Self-Consciousness in Debate Verdicts

Table 3.3 indicates that media self-consciousness has increased since 1976. The percentage of statements indicating the media's own awareness of their potential influence and role in the campaign went from 4.9% in 1976 to 8.8% in 1988. The 13.2% of media self-conscious verdicts in 1980 can again be attributed to the ABC telepoll and an awareness by the

Table 3.3
Media Self-Consciousness, by Year

Media Self-Consciousness	Year			
	1976	1980	1984	1988
Yes	4.9%	13.2%	7.4%	8.8%
No	95.1%	86.8%	92.6%	91.2%
(N)	(245)	(144)	(446)	(421)

Chi-square = 9.011, df = 3, p < .05

network that the technique itself had become a story. Again, controlling for the network and removing ABC from the analysis lend further support to the notion that media self-consciousness has increased since 1976. Taking into account only statements from CBS in 1980, we find that only 4.2% of them indicate self-consciousness. In 1984, 6.9% of verdicts from CBS contained media self-consciousness; in 1988, 12.5% did.

Differences Between ABC and CBS in Presidential Debate Coverage

We performed analysis to test differences between ABC and CBS in three areas: the sources they relied on in debate coverage, the direction of the verdicts in their debate coverage, and the existence of media self-consciousness in their debate coverage. Only with respect to sources did we find differences between the two networks. Table 3.4 shows that ABC has relied more on its own journalists than has CBS, but less on political elites and polls (even when we included the 1980 telepoll). The two networks are similar in the direction of the verdicts that occur in their coverage: Nearly half the statements for both networks are negative; a little more than a third are positive, with the rest neutral. CBS and ABC are equally self-conscious about their coverage since 1976. In the case of each network, more than 9 of 10 statements do not contain a reference to the spin doctors or the potential effects of the media on the campaign. But differences do emerge when we look at each year and compare the networks on media self-consciousness. For example, in 1980 ABC tended to demonstrate more self-consciousness, but as mentioned above, that is primarily attributable to its telepoll following the first Carter-Reagan debate.

Table 3.4
Source Differences Between Networks in Debate Coverage

Source	Network	
	ABC	CBS
Journalists	36.9%	25.0%
Poll	7.9%	12.1%
MOS/Viewers	3.8%	2.1%
Elite	47.6%	54.0%
Crowd	2.9%	4.7%
Deferred	1.1%	2.0%
(N)	(559)	(700)

Chi-square = 29.711, df = 5, p < .001

What is more striking is the difference in 1988 between ABC and CBS. All but one of the 37 evaluative statements in our analysis that contained media self-consciousness aired on CBS in 1988, and no device such as the ABC telepoll existed on CBS in 1988. Perhaps the network was more acutely aware of its role than it normally would have been because of the February 1988 showdown between Dan Rather and George Bush.

Comparison Among Individual Network Correspondents

We coded each evaluative statement for the individual who made the statement, including as values twelve network correspondents,[2] a category for other network correspondents not among the twelve, and a category for non-journalists, who usually if not always appeared in sound-bite segments of stories. We were interested in differences among the correspondents primarily in two areas: the sources they used in stories and media self-consciousness.

Table 3.5 lists the eight correspondents included in the analysis who had the most statements. For each correspondent, we have rank-ordered the first three sources. In almost every instance, the correspondents rely on an elite source, a poll, or their own judgments in making the evaluative statements. The only noticeable difference among this group of correspondents is CBS's tendency to rely on its main field correspondents

Table 3.5
Who Journalists Use As Sources in Debate Coverage

| | Source | | | |
Journalist	Crowd	Elite	Journalist	Poll
Rather*		32.5%	28.8%	35.0%
Cronkite		48.4%	35.5%	12.9%
Morton		41.9%	36.3%	17.7%
Stahl		34.3%	38.9%	23.1%
Schieffer	7.3%	69.5%	15.9%	
Donaldson	3.9%	48.1%	42.9%	3.9%
Hume	11.8%	35.3%	50.0%	
Jennings		34.1%	46.3%	19.5%

*   The percentages reported for Dan Rather include two years when he was a correspondent (1976 and 1980) and two years when he was CBS's main anchor (1984
and 1988). The percentages for Walter Cronkite are for 1976 and 1980 only. The
percentages for each journalist do not sum to 100% because only the top three
sources are included in the table. For Donaldson, "crowd" and "poll' tied for third
with 3.9% each.

(Rather in 1980, Stahl and Morton in all years) to give poll results in
stories.

Table 3.6 shows the media self-consciousness of the individual correspondents. That is, the data indicate the extent to which the correspondents acknowledge the potential influence they have as individuals and
the media have collectively on the debates, debate verdicts, and the
election process as a whole.

Sam Donaldson and Brit Hume of ABC show the least self-consciousness of all the correspondents we name, while Dan Rather and Peter
Jennings show the most. At first blush, one would think that the Rather
and Jennings self-consciousness stems from their "figurehead" anchor
positions. Both might want to protect themselves and their ratings by
showing a sensitivity to the potential for media influence. But, interestingly enough, the greatest proportion of Rather's media self-conscious
statements within a given year comes in 1980 when he was covering the
election from the field, not the anchor desk. Still, Rather displayed media
self-consciousness nearly a fifth of the time in debate stories in 1988, just
months after his contentious interview with George Bush.

Table 3.6
Self-Consciousness Among Journalists in Debate Coverage

| Journalist | Media Self-Consciousness | | N |
	Yes	No	
Rather	16.3%	83.8%	80
Cronkite	9.7%	90.3%	31
Mudd	15.4%	84.6%	13
Morton	11.3%	88.7%	124
Stahl	12.0%	88.0%	104
Schieffer	8.5%	91.5%	82
Hume	0.0%	100.0%	34
Donaldson	2.6%	97.4%	77
Reasoner	0.0%	100.0%	11
Jennings	17.1%	82.9%	41
Other correspondents	10.2%	89.8%	323
Non-journalists	2.4%	97.6%	335

Verdict Attention: Incumbent Party vs. "Out" Party

Does the incumbent party get more debate verdict attention than the challenging party? And are there shifts in focus from one debate to the next? Table 3.7 clearly shows the Republicans being the greater focus of debate verdicts, even in 1980, when the Democrats were the incumbents. A probable explanation was the intense media curiosity about Ronald Reagan: who he was, what he believed, how "safe" he would be if elected.

The tables also indicate different patterns of verdict attention, depending on the year. For example, in 1976 networks focused their attention evenly after the first debate between Gerald Ford and Jimmy Carter. Following the second, however, they focused heavily on Ford, probably due to the so-called Eastern European gaffe.

In 1984 the focus on both candidates increased with each debate,

Table 3.7
Object of Debate Verdicts, by Year

Year/Debate	Both	Republican	Democrat	N
		Object of Verdict		
1976*				
Carter-Ford #1	61.8%	18.0%	20.2%	89
Carter-Ford #2	5.2%	76.1%	18.7%	155
1980				
Carter-Reagan	19.0%	50.7%	30.3%	142
1984*				
Mondale-Reagan #1	4.8%	58.6%	36.5%	249
Ferraro-Bush	11.4%	56.8%	31.8%	88
Mondale-Reagan #2	19.3%	63.3%	17.4%	109
1988*				
Dukakis-Bush #1	14.4%	42.5%	43.2%	146
Bentsen-Quayle	10.9%	55.1%	34.0%	147
Dukakis-Bush #2	5.5%	48.4%	46.1%	128

*   For the 1976 debates, Chi-square = 105.118, df = 2, p < .001; for the 1984 debates, Chi-square = 26.131, df = 4, p < .001; for the 1988 debates, Chi-square = 10.364, df = 4, p < .05

seemingly at the expense of the Democratic candidate. In 1988 the focus on both candidates decreased with each debate, and we see a departure from the aforementioned concentration on Republican candidates in the first and third debates, both between the presidential candidates. The concentration on the Republican candidate in the second debate, between the vice-presidential candidates, comes from the performance of Dan Quayle.

The verdicts from subsequent newscasts on Quayle's performance were mostly negative. Nearly three-fourths (72.9%) of the statements about Quayle's performance were negative, while 22.9% were positive and the rest neutral. Conversely, 71.8% of the statements about Democratic candidate Lloyd Bentsen were positive, while 23.1% were negative.

For the debates between the two 1988 presidential candidates, verdict direction switched in the second debate. That is, 61.8% of the verdicts on George Bush in his first debate with Michael Dukakis were negative and 38.2% were positive. But in the second debate between the two, 55.9% of statements about Bush were positive and 22% were negative. On the other hand, more than half the statements about Dukakis's first debate performance were positive (51.6%), while more than half following the second presidential debate were negative (55.2%).

Pre-debate Expectations: Were They Fulfilled? At Whom Were They Directed?

In more than two-thirds of the statements, network news coverage indicated no sign of expectations attached to the debates. But in cases where the coverage indicated either high or low expectations about the debate, the expectations were generally unmet. For example, when the statements indicated that pre-debate expectations had been high, they often led to a negative candidate verdict. On the other hand, when expectations had been low, the plurality of the verdicts were positive (see Table 3.8).

Not surprisingly, pre-debate expectations were usually directed at the candidates of the Republican Party. Intuitively, this seems to make sense, considering that they have been the incumbent party in three of the four years analyzed (see Table 3.9).

Direction of Verdicts and Media Self-Consciousness

Intuitively one would think that when journalists deliver a negative verdict, they would be filled with a sense of self-consciousness about

Table 3.8
Fulfillment of Pre-Debate Expectations

Expectations	Direction of Verdict			
	Positive	Neutral	Negative	N
High	20.3%	12.6%	67.0%	182
Low	57.6%	6.7%	35.7%	210
None	36.0%	17.6%	46.4%	866

Chi-square = 72.664, df = 4, p < .001

Table 3.9
Object of Pre-Debate Expectations

	Object of Expectations			
Expectations	Republican	Democrat	Both	N
High	53.8%	34.1%	12.1%	182
Low	11.1%	56.0%	32.9%	207

Chi-square = 16.938, df = 2, p < .002

what they are saying. In fact, our data show a different situation. Nearly 9% of positive verdicts are media self-conscious, while just more than 5% of negative verdicts are (see Table 3.10a). At first we thought this might be due to a reliance on spin doctors as elite sources giving positive assessments of their candidates. But further analysis, controlling for the source of the verdict, indicated elite sources were no more likely to make positive statements that were media-conscious than they were to make negative ones.

What can explain this apparent anomaly? One possibility is the timing of the verdict: Media self-consciousness is much greater for all types of verdicts the day after the debate than four days after (see Table 3.10b). Apparently, the media consensus that builds over time further emboldens journalists and makes them less worried about media effects and spin doctors. (Recall the prototypical scenario of debate verdicts portrayed in Chapter 1.)

CONCLUSION

The data presented here give a strong indication of the direction network news debate coverage has been headed and where the emphasis of debate verdicts now lies. The networks have never emphasized the issue component of the debates and have focused primarily on the performance component of the debates since 1976. But their emphasis on issues during the last three sets of debates has actually become subordinated to additional categories of coverage, particularly tactics and strategy coverage. And scientific polls as sources of debate verdicts have become more common than they were in 1976 and 1980. Finally, the media's self-awareness of their own role in the presidential debate process, though not high, has increasingly manifested itself since 1976.

One main reason for our findings is the desire by journalists to appear

Table 3.10a
Verdict Direction, by Media Self-Consciousness

Verdict Direction	Media Self-Consciousness		
	Yes	No	N
Positive	8.7%	91.3%	470
Neutral	15.3%	84.7%	190
Negative	5.3%	94.7%	599

Chi-square = 19.458, df = 2, p < .001

Table 3.10b
Media Self-Consciousness One Day and Four Days After the Debate

	Media Self-Consciousness		
	Yes	No	N
One day after	9.0%	91.0%	1124
Four days after	0.8%	99.2%	118

Chi-square = 9.397, df = 1, p < .005

objective or impartial. The increase in polls as sources of verdicts certainly reflects the advances in polling technology available to the networks since 1976 and the increase in their overall use by the media throughout the campaign. But we also believe that polls are a way in which journalists attempt to take themselves out of the verdict-rendering process. We would even make the argument that in 1976, when polling technology was not as sophisticated and accessible to the networks, verdicts based on person-in-the-street interviews and "living-room polls" provided yet another way for journalists to attribute affect-laden statements to others and to maintain the appearance of impartiality.

If that is, indeed, the case, network journalists have simply exchanged one way of reporting on feedback for another. Regardless of the technique, the essence is that journalists have bought into the conventional wisdom on debate verdicts and have become sensitive to the perception that they directly influence campaigns by calling debaters "winners" or "losers." And even though a poll may have some influence, it provides the news organization with a way to remove itself from direct responsibility for involvement.

The deferred verdict works in much the same way. By suggesting that "only time will tell" who won the debate or that "voters will be the ultimate judges," journalists not only remove themselves from the verdict-rendering process, they suspend the process altogether. More often than not, however, network news operations have been willing to analyze the debates. As our results indicate, the analyses have focused less on issues and more on tactics and performance increasingly over the last four elections. Again the appearance of impartiality and objectivity plays a role. As one researcher has suggested, reporting on tactics "lets reporters maintain the necessary appearance of impartiality and balance" that in-depth reporting on candidates' issue positions would not allow (see Hershey 1989, 98).

In addition, stories about what is going on behind the scenes of campaigns are much easier to do than are discussions of complex issues and candidate positions on issues. Stories about the machinations of campaigns allow journalists to appear investigative without expending the time and resources necessary for a true investigative report.

Concern over the appearance of impartiality may also explain the media's growing self-consciousness of their own role and influence in the debates. Here the media attempt to demonstrate their impartiality by commenting on their own performance. With a collective voice, the media (the networks in the case of our study) seem to be saying, "We know that the way we cover the debates doesn't serve the public as well as it should. We know we're being used by the spin doctors and that's not right. But revealing our foibles and downfalls will get us off the hook."

Media introspection may not assuage voters for whom the debates provide the only chance to see and hear the candidates for extended periods of time. Certainly voters who expect debates to be held, candidates to debate, and the media to provide clarification of what was said in the debates will find their expectations largely unfulfilled if the trends of network news debate coverage of the 1980s continue in 1992.

NOTES

1. In a more impressionistic analysis of network news coverage of the 1988 presidential campaign, Nimmo (1989) suggested a similar continuum for the television networks.

2. We chose the correspondents on the basis of personal observations about who covered the campaigns most often during the four elections we analyzed. The correspondents were Dan Rather, Walter Cronkite, Roger Mudd, Bruce Morton, Leslie Stahl, and Bob Schieffer of CBS, and Brit Hume, Sam Donaldson,

Harry Reasoner, and Peter Jennings of ABC. We also had values for John Chancellor and Tom Brokaw of NBC, but the limitations we mentioned earlier prevented us from analyzing NBC newscasts.

REFERENCES

Becker, L. B., D. H. Weaver, D. A. Graber, and M. E. McCombs. 1979. Influence on public agendas. In *The great debates: Carter vs. Ford, 1976*, ed. S. Kraus, 418–428. Bloomington: Indiana University Press.

Berquist, G. F., and J. L. Golden. 1981. Media rhetoric, criticism and the public perception of the 1980 presidential debates. *Quarterly Journal of Speech* 67:125–137.

Diamond, E., and K. Friery. 1987. Media coverage of presidential debates. In *Presidential debates: 1988 and beyond*, ed. Joel Swerdlow, 43–51. Washington: Congressional Quarterly Press.

Gadziala, S., and L. B. Becker. 1983. A new look at agenda-setting in the 1976 election debates. *Journalism Quarterly* 60:122–125.

Graber, D. 1988. *Processing the news: How people tame the information tide*, 2nd ed. New York: Longman.

Greenfield, J. 1980. *Playing to win: An insider's guide to politics*. New York: Simon & Schuster.

Hershey, M. R. 1989. The campaign and the media. In *The election of 1988: Reports and interpretations*, ed. G. M. Pomper, 73–102. Chatham, N.J.: Chatham House.

Jackson-Beeck, M., and R. Meadow. 1979. The triple agenda of presidential debates: Media, electoral, policy perspectives. *Public Opinion Quarterly* 43:173–180.

Lemert, J. B. 1981. *Does mass communication change public opinion after all?* Chicago: Nelson-Hall.

Lemert, J. B., W. L. Rosenberg, W. R. Elliott, J. M. Bernstein, and K. J. Nestvold. 1989. *Impact of the Bentsen-Quayle debate and of news "verdicts" about the debate—a time-series analysis*. A paper presented to the annual meeting of the American Association for Public Opinion Research, St. Petersburg, Fla.

McLeod, J. M., J. A. Durall, D. A. Ziemke, and C. R. Bybee. 1979. Reactions of young and older voters: Expanding the context of effects. In *The great debates: Carter vs. Ford, 1976*, ed. S. Kraus, 348–367. Bloomington: Indiana University Press.

Meadow, R. G. 1983. Televised campaign debates as whistle-stop speeches. In *Television coverage of the 1980 presidential campaign*, ed. W. C. Adams, 89–102. Norwood, N.J.: Ablex.

Meadow, R. G. 1987. A speech by any other name. *Critical Studies in Mass Communication* 4:207–210.

Miller, A. H., and M. MacKuen. 1979. Informing the electorate: A national study.

In *The great debates: Carter vs. Ford, 1976*, ed. S. Kraus, 348-367. Bloomington: Indiana University Press.

Nimmo, D. 1989. Episodes, incidents, and eruptions: Nightly network TV coverage of candidates '88. *American Behavioral Scientist* 32:464–478.

Sears, D. O., and S. H. Chaffee. 1979. Uses and effects of the 1976 debates: An overview of empirical studies. In *The great debates: Carter vs. Ford, 1976*, ed. S. Kraus, 223–261. Bloomington: Indiana University Press.

4

CANDIDATE VERDICTS IN POST-DEBATE ANALYSIS PROGRAMS

Once a presidential debate has concluded, one of the first opportunities for reaction comes in the post-debate analysis programs that air on the same broadcasting networks that carried the just-completed debate. Such analysis not only gives journalists their first opportunity to evaluate the debate but may also provide members of the public their first chance to reflect on what they have just seen and/or heard.

As the post-debate analysis programs unfold, journalists, politicians, campaign supporters, and members of the public present their comments, evaluations, and verdicts. Thus begins the process of confirming, changing, reshaping, adjusting, fine-tuning, undermining, upsetting, or reinforcing the opinions of the voters. These post-debate programs concern themselves heavily with two topics—(1) evaluations and discussions of presidential debates as political institutions (this aspect of the post-debate analysis programs will be covered in Chapter 5), and (2) the performance of the candidates in the debate. Candidate performance—especially televised verdicts about performance—will be the focus of this chapter, which covers post-debate analysis programs from 1976 through 1988.

Diamond and Friery (1987) report that one aspect of debate performance—"television style" and/or actual physical presentation qualities and abilities on camera—is an important part of post-debate analysis by journalists:

Our own analysis of . . . network television coverage in each of the debate years reaffirms that media discussion of the images projected and dissections of the candidates' physical appearance and gestures constitute a major part of the coverage following a debate.

This chapter, however, will be concerned with a much broader range of candidate performance than just physical appearance. Here are questions we will discuss:

- Do the three major networks (ABC, CBS and NBC) differ to any significant degree in how favorable their verdicts are about candidates' performances in debates?

- Where do the verdicts come from? The journalists on the programs? Politicians? Campaign workers? Members of the public who are interviewed? Other sources?

- How often are debaters evaluated in terms of the pre-debate goals of their respective campaign staffs?

- How often did the analysis refer to the ability of the debaters to perform on television—their television style? Has emphasis on television style grown over time?

- In the 1988 debates, how did Bush, Dukakis, Bentsen, and Quayle fare in the post-debate analysis programs? Did verdicts about Bush and Dukakis change from their first to their second debate? Clearly, answers to these questions are very relevant to survey tests of the impact of any such verdicts (Chapters 6, 7, and 8).

- When did references to "spin doctors" or similar partisan supporters become a noticeable topic of discussion on the analysis programs? Are particular networks more prone to carrying candidate verdicts issued by spin doctors? When they do, are spin doctors' verdicts usually positive, for their candidate, or usually negative, against the opposition candidate?

These are some of the questions we will attempt to answer in this chapter as we examine the post-debate news specials on ABC, CBS, and NBC. We will examine the 1988 fall debates, plus those in 1984, 1980, and 1976 (including the vice-presidential debates in 1988 and 1984). This type of extensive, detailed analysis of the post-debate programs has not been included in prior presidential debate research projects. Bits and pieces of such analyses have been done, but certainly not on this scale.

Lowry, Bridges, and Barefield (in press) conducted an experimental study following one debate in 1988 (the first Bush-Dukakis debate). In their evaluation of the television network post-debate analysis, they found that (1) the networks carried more positive than negative verdicts ("assertions") about both candidates, (2) subjects who watched both the debate *and* a network post-debate analysis program were less inclined to call Bush the winner of the first debate than were subjects who had viewed the debate only, and (3) those same subjects who watched both the debate and the analysis evidenced more favorable movement toward Dukakis than toward Bush, as compared with subjects in the control group who viewed the debate only.

However, the Lowry, Bridges, and Barefield study did not include detailed content analysis of the post-debate programs on the networks. This is the type of analysis that is needed in order to try to determine *why* network post-debate analysis programs (along with television newscasts and other post-debate media reporting) may play a role in voters' perceptions of candidates. Our study, as reported in this chapter on candidate verdicts and in Chapter 5 on the debates as an institution, provides the type of detailed documentation of network post-debate programming that is necessary in order to try to connect content with political effects.

METHODOLOGY

We examined all available general election campaign post-debate analysis programming on the ABC, CBS, and NBC television networks following the first two Ford-Carter presidential debates in 1976 (September 23 and October 6), the single Carter-Reagan debate in 1980, all three debates in 1984 (two Reagan-Mondale debates and one vice-presidential debate between Bush and Ferraro), and all three debates in 1988 (two Bush-Dukakis debates and the one vice-presidential debate between Quayle and Bentsen).

In 1976 and 1980 this post-debate analysis programming included a few comments by network anchors immediately following each debate, along with a longer program—usually presented about 30 minutes later. In 1984 all three networks presented their post-debate analysis programs immediately following each debate. In 1988 some of the post-debate analysis was immediate, while some was presented later the same evening. Tapes of the programming from 1976, 1980, and 1984 were secured from the Vanderbilt University Television News Archive, while taping of all video materials from 1988 was done by the authors. Twenty-five network post-debate analysis programs (as well as the brief immediate post-debate comments), a total of 9 hours and 45 minutes of network analysis programming, were coded.

The mean length of each network post-debate analysis program was 23 minutes. Program length was quite consistent across both networks and years, ranging between 20 and 23 minutes per program, with one notable exception. In 1980, following the only debate in that campaign between Carter and Reagan, ABC presented its post-debate analysis on Ted Koppel's "Nightline" program, resulting in a 70-minute post-debate analysis production—two and a half times the average length of such network programs.

As with the content analysis of network newscast verdicts (Chapter 3), units of analysis were evaluative statements made during the post-debate analysis programs. The statements—or verdicts—which became units referred either to the debaters themselves (candidate verdicts) or to the debate as an institution. This chapter will examine the candidate verdicts, while Chapter 5 will analyze verdicts pertaining to the debates as political institutions. Data for both Chapters 4 and 5 come from the same data set generated from the 25 post-debate analysis programs, with all coding for both chapters done by the same two coders at the University of Oregon.

RESULTS

The 25 network post-debate analysis programs for the four presidential election years produced 2,302 separate units, or verdicts.

The evaluative statements were coded for eight different sources: (1) journalists—program anchors, reporters, or correspondents from the network or from other media; (2) public reaction from a standard public opinion survey; (3) public reaction from a phone-in poll conducted by the network; (4) reactions from members of the public in locations away from the studio debate, such as the traditional "man on the street" (MOS) interview, or interviews with living room viewers; (5) reactions from the studio debate audience; (6) named elites, including politicians, campaign officials, and others; (7) unnamed elites, such as "staff"; (8) reactions from post-debate rallies or crowds; and (9) implied verdicts ("to be determined") from the public.

Debate Verdicts Over Four Presidential Election Years

How were the 2,302 separate verdicts categorized among the nine different possible sources? The majority of such verdicts, of course, are made by journalists—the anchors and other journalists who are covering and reporting the debates, and who feel qualified to make a judgment—as shown in Table 4.1. Nearly two-thirds of all verdicts (both candidate and institutional verdicts) included in post-debate analysis programs have journalists as the source.

In 1988, journalists accounted for more than 62% of all such verdicts on the three major television networks. This proportion of journalist-generated verdicts was consistent over the years of the study, with one exception—1980. That year was somewhat unusual, with regard to this study, in two ways: (1) Since Carter and Reagan had only one debate that fall (and there was no vice-presidential debate), the network post-debate analysis programming consisted of only three programs, one from each network; and (2) the long, special edition of "Nightline" used by ABC-TV for its post-debate analysis enabled that network to run a special 900-

Table 4.1
Source of Post-Debate Network Analysis Verdicts, by Year

Source	1976	1980	1984	1988
Journalists (N=1371)	64.2%	46.2%	63.6%	62.2%
Public Opinion Survey (N=18)	--	.2%	.7%	1.7%
Phone-in Poll (N=34)	--	6.9%	--	--
Man-in-Street/Living Room (N=106)	6.6%	2.8%	4.9%	4.6%
Studio Audience (N=58)	4.3%	4.5%	.8%	2.1%
Named Elite (N=546)	16.6%	28.0%	25.6%	22.2%
Unnamed Elite (N=55)	2.6%	4.7%	.5%	2.7%
Rally/Crowd (N=28)	3.2%	2.0%	.8%	.1%
Implied (N=86)	2.6%	4.7%	3.2%	4.3%
TOTAL (N=2302)	15.2% (349)	21.4% (493)	33.1% (761)	30.4% (699)

Chi-square = 244.099, df = 24, p < .001

number viewer phone-in poll, with the viewer responses presented during the program. The result on ABC was a lower percentage of time devoted to verdict discussion by journalists, offset by a large number (34) of candidate verdicts (amounting to nearly seven % of all network post-debate verdicts that year) credited to that single program's phone-in poll. (The three networks did not use that 900-number technique in any of the other post-debate analysis programs in any other year. ABC's 1980 phone-in "poll" technique met virulent criticisms from the polling industry and members of the American Association for Public Opinion Research, an organization of commercial and academic pollsters.)

Table 4.1 also shows the beginning of the use of standard public opinion polling data during the network post-debate analysis programs. Although the phone-in poll conducted by ABC in 1980 was really an aberration in the seeking of public opinion for inclusion in post-debate analysis programs (not used before by ABC, CBS, and NBC during such programs and not used since), the networks (primarily ABC) have begun to increase their use of standard public opinion polling techniques for use on post-debate programs. While no such data were evident in 1976, the networks began using such survey-generated information in 1980 and have been increasing their use of it since, with nearly 2% of all verdicts in the 1988 post-debate analysis programs coming from standard public opinion surveys. ABC's more prominent interest in such data gathering is evidenced by the fact that of the 18 verdicts (all candidate-related) tabulated from the use of public opinion surveys, 16 came from ABC, two from CBS, and none from NBC.

The politicians who are interviewed following the debates (specific campaign staffers and managers—the people who are the most outspoken in their opinions of who won or lost a debate) receive significant amounts of time on the network post-debate programs, and, as a result, are the second largest category of verdict sources. In 1988, named elites accounted for 22.2% of all such verdicts, almost exactly the 23% average of such sources over the four election years of the study. Despite 1988's concern about "spin doctors" on these programs, the kind of people who were trying to control the spin generally were present as often as before on these programs.

So the networks continue to give air time to political elites from both parties following presidential and vice-presidential debates, even though the unbridled partiality of such elites often is so blatant as to render their comments and candidate verdicts about as far from being newsworthy as could be imagined. For example, on October 11, 1984, on NBC's post-debate analysis program following the Bush-Ferraro vice-presidential debate, NBC correspondent Roger Mudd did a segment with Democrat Steve Engleberg, issues director for the Ferraro campaign, and Dean Burch, senior political adviser for Bush. In beginning the segment, Mudd referred to the two advisers as Democratic and Republican "handlers," and then asked them "to raise your right hands and swear to tell the truth, the whole truth, and nothing but the truth." Engleberg and Burch dutifully raised their right hands, and the interview was on. At one point, Engleberg said, "I think Mrs. Ferraro won the debate hands down, unquestionably." Mudd's reaction: "Hands down? Okay." And then Mudd chuckled. At the conclusion of the segment (for which nearly anyone could have scripted the answers the two gave to Mudd's questions), Mudd said, "I'm going to get indictments for perjury on you two guys," followed by lots of laughter from all three. It is difficult to see what such interviews (and all networks use them on these types of programs) contribute in terms of meaningful information or evaluations in post-debate analysis programs.

Object of Verdicts

This chapter is devoted to the evaluation of the specific candidate verdicts made during the post-debate analysis programming. Nearly 85% of all verdicts identified from such programs were candidate-specific; slightly more than 9% of the verdicts pertained only to the issue of the debates as an institution; and 6.2% of all the verdicts referred to both the debate as an institution and to specific candidates (see Table 4.2). The data for both 1988 and 1984 involved programs following three debates—two presidential and one vice presidential. In both years the number and percentages of candidate verdicts in the post-debate analysis programs were nearly the same: in 1988, 88.8% (621 verdicts), and in 1984, 88.0% (670 verdicts).

The major change since 1976, shown in Table 4.2, has been whether the evaluative statements have been about the candidates or about the debate. Significantly more statements about debate(s) in general were made in the earlier years of 1976 (10%) and 1980 (16.8%) than were made in 1984 (7.1%) and 1988 (5.4%). By 1988 the presidential and vice-presidential debate pattern had begun to become established in the American political system. This seems to have resulted in far less discussion about such issues as the role of presidential debates in our political process than was the case in the earlier years of 1976 and 1980, when the subject of debates

Table 4.2
Year of Post-Debate Analysis, by Object of Verdict

	Object of Verdict		
Year (N)	Candidate(s)	Debate Itself	Both
1976 (349)	84.0%	10.0%	6.0%
1980 (493)	74.0%	16.8%	9.1%
1984 (761)	88.0%	7.1%	4.9%
1988 (699)	88.8%	5.4%	5.7%
Total (N)	84.7% (1949)	9.1% (210)	6.2% (143)

Chi-square = 64.638, df = 6, p < .001

was not as far removed from the long pause since the 1960 Kennedy-Nixon debates.

The three networks, by the way, were not carbon copies of each other regarding how much emphasis they placed on candidate verdicts or debates-as-institution verdicts. CBS and NBC *did* resemble each other: Both had almost exactly 90% candidate verdicts. But for ABC, during the four presidential years of the study, only 75.6% of the verdicts were exclusively about candidates, while 15.6% of the verdicts concerned the debate as an institution. (The remaining nearly 9% touched on both.)

Direction of Verdicts

All three networks *are* carbon copies of each other, however, when it comes to whether the candidate verdicts they have included in such programming are positive, negative, or neutral (see Table 4.3). For all candidate verdicts tabulated, the average for all three networks was 48.6% positive, 31.6% negative, and 19.8% neutral, with very little difference among the networks. Thus, we have no evidence that one network or another is more positive or negative toward presidential and vice-presidential candidates. Indeed, the three networks were nearly identical in their pattern of presenting five favorable comments or evaluations of candidate performance for every three negative or unfavorable ones.

Slightly more variation in this ratio can be seen over the past four presidential debate years when one examines it by individual years. In 1988, candidate verdicts were 44.4% positive, 34.2% negative, and 21.4% neutral. These figures compare with prior years as follows:

Table 4.3
Direction of Candidate Verdicts on Network Analysis Programs

Network (N)	Direction of Verdict		
	Positive	Neutral	Negative
ABC (701)	48.4%	20.1%	31.5%
CBS (786)	50.1%	18.9%	31.0%
NBC (595)	47.0%	20.5%	32.5%
Total	48.6%	19.8%	31.6%
(N)	(1014)	(412)	(658)

Chi-square = 1.415, df = 4, NS

- 1984—53.4% positive, 29.2% negative, and 17.2% neutral.
- 1980—49% positive, 30% negative, and 21% neutral.
- 1976—45.7% positive, 32.8% negative, and 20.3% neutral.

In terms of the direction of candidate verdicts, the main deviation from the typical pattern was in 1984, during Reagan's second presidential campaign, when he was running against Mondale and the vice-presidential candidates were Bush and Ferraro. In the analyses following the three debates that year, the verdicts were significantly more positive and less negative, with fewer being neutral.

Source of Verdicts

Who issues those positive candidate verdicts? And who are the sources of the negative ones? Do network journalists (and other reporters and editors who make comments on the programs) issue fewer positive verdicts than political elites? After all, do not these elites have a vested interest in making their candidates look good?

Table 4.4 shows where the pro and con evaluations of the debaters come from. Negative comments regarding the candidates come more often from the journalists themselves; 36% of their comments are negative, while slightly more than 43% are positive. This should not be surprising, given that the three networks have had some very outspoken individual analysts/commentators assigned to do political reporting, such as ABC's Sam Donaldson, Brit Hume, and Jeff Greenfield; CBS's Dan Rather, Roger Mudd (also later for NBC), Bruce Morton, and Leslie Stahl; and NBC's John Chancellor and Andrea Mitchell. The outspoken, challenging, querulous side of these journalists has frequently come through, resulting in a near (but not quite) balance of positive versus negative comments during the programs—certainly more in the direction of "balance" than for any other source. Perhaps the very nature of the journalist as objective observer, even in highly partisan environments such as the aftermath of major political debates, drives the anchors, reporters, and commentators toward avoiding being labeled or seen as particularly pro or con. The result, in any case, is the near balance of candidate verdicts shown in the table. Journalists also provided nearly 60% of *all* candidate verdicts tabulated.

Candidate verdicts from named elites—politicians, candidate staffers, and other campaign and party officials—comprised 25% of all candidate verdicts, and were overwhelmingly favorable. When elites had the chance to comment following the debates, they were much more concerned about boosting the stock of their candidate(s) than they were about denigrating the opposition. While they did not exactly hesitate to describe the opponent in unfavorable terms (30% of their comments), nevertheless

Table 4.4
Source of Favorable/Unfavorable Candidate Verdicts

	Direction of Verdict		
Source	Positive	Neutral	Negative
Journalists (N=1220)	43.2%	20.8%	36.0%
Public Opinion Survey (N=17)	64.7%	17.6%	17.6%
Phone-in Poll (N=20)	80.0%	20.0%	--
Man-in-Street/Living Room (N=100)	61.0%	15.0%	24.0%
Studio Audience (N=53)	62.3%	11.3%	26.4%
Named Elite (N=511)	60.1%	9.2%	30.7%
Unnamed Elite (N=52)	61.5%	7.7%	30.8%
Rally/Crowd (N=28)	85.7%	3.6%	10.7%
Implied (N=83)	3.6%	94.0%	2.4%
TOTAL (N)	48.6% (1014)	19.8% (412)	31.6% (658)

Chi-square = 390.438, df = 16, p < .001

they were twice as inclined to try to leave a positive impression of their candidate in the minds of the viewers. Perhaps what is happening here is that the last thing these elites want to do is leave a *neutral* impression. This two-to-one ratio of favorable to unfavorable verdicts was almost exactly the same even when the elites were *not* named. (Unnamed elites usually were staff members or campaign supporters.)

The +60% positive verdict pattern also holds true for evaluative statements coming from, or attributed to, the studio audience, man/woman on the street/in the living room, or in standard public opinion polls taken in the immediate aftermath of a debate. For each of these sources, however, the undecided or neutral element rises in comparison with the verdicts issued by elites, who can be expected to be more polarized in their assessment of the candidates. The nearly totally neutral grouping of verdicts in the "implied" category generally resulted when the journalist declared that public reaction was still undetermined, unknown, or "yet to come."

With regard to whether journalists evoked pre-debate goals of the respective campaign staffs and then assessed the candidates in terms of those goals, the data indicate no real change over time. In the four election years included in the study, the debaters were assessed in terms of such pre-debate campaign staff goals 22% of the time, with no significant differences among the four election years.

The Role of "Spin Doctors"

What about those "spin doctors"—those partisans trying to influence media verdicts and, through the verdicts, American public opinion? Actually, the attempt by campaign managers and staffers, political party officials, and politicians to persuade the media—and thereby the public—that their candidate is better (or the other candidate is worse) is not what is unique. This has been going on for decades in politics in this country and elsewhere. What *is* unique or new is what the technique is now called ("spinning" or "spin doctoring") and, perhaps, the aggressiveness with which those who try to "put a favorable spin" on the media reporting of a political race or event in that race. This aggressiveness has become especially noticeable during the immediate aftermath of presidential and vice-presidential debates, when armies of spin doctors, it seems, materialize in front of journalists—especially network television reporters—ready, willing, and able to give strong opinions of who won and who lost.

Direction of Spin Doctor Verdicts. In our study of verdicts arising from the three television networks' post-debate analysis programs, we sought to gather some data about spin doctors: the degree to which the media tell us spin doctors are present, and what type of spinning goes on. We wondered how the journalists were handling the spinning. Did they call attention to it, perhaps in an effort to declare their own independence and objectivity?

In the great majority of verdicts identified in this study, the media did not call attention to spin doctoring. But in nearly 10% of the verdicts, it was identified as such (see Table 4.5). In those 10% of the verdicts, we categorized the spin doctor references in either of two ways: (1) "campaign spin" or (2) "media spin."

We defined references to *campaign* spin as those in which journalists noted that campaigners had made deliberate efforts to influence media and public verdicts about a debater's performance. In earlier years, this

Table 4.5
Candidate Spin Doctor Verdicts

Reference to "Spinning" (N)	Direction of Verdict		
	Positive	Neutral	Negative
No Reference (1874)	49.5%	18.8%%	31.6%
Campaign (153)	39.9%	24.2%	35.9%
Media (51)	49.0%	31.4%	19.6%
Total	48.8%	19.5%	31.7%
(N)	(1014)	(406)	(658)

Chi-square = 10.793, df = 4, p < .05

took the form of warnings or very quick discounting statements, such as Walter Cronkite once saying, after performance appraisals by a Democrat and a Republican, that the party officials pretty much said what was expected and that there were not any surprises from their statements. In 1988, however, appraisals and warnings were, in general, much more self-conscious, accompanied by explicit labels using terms like spin control, spinners, and spinnees. Underlying these kinds of references was the notion—not always explicitly articulated—that the media are spinnees, victims, or objects, just as the public is.

We defined references to *media* spin as those references to the impact or effects of media-borne verdicts, including effects of "quickie" polls in the media on later polls and effects of media interpretations in the aftermath on later public reactions. In general, media spin references were those in which there was a shift to either explicit or implicit references to the media as an actor or causal agent in the process, not as mere objects, victims, or spinnees. Media spin references were about news media interpretations of debate performance that might affect outcomes of such key aspects of the campaign as post-debate polls or even the election itself.

The listing of candidate verdicts given a spin doctor label included three times as many campaign as media spin references. And this campaign spinning was nearly equally divided between positive and negative references. But the same was not the case when spinners brought into the discussion the way the media would evaluate the outcome. In those media spin cases, the sources of the reference to media were much more concerned about the positive image or perception of candidates, apparently feeling that favorable media reaction would come from a discussion of a candidate's positive traits rather than reference to the opponent's negative qualities.

"Spinning" Over Time. The 1988 election year was the first real campaign "year of the spin doctor." Although there had been references to this form of attempted influence—either specifically or indirectly— since 1976, a sudden and very large jump in this type of reference, as included in the networks' post-debate analysis programs, took place in 1988 (Table 4.6). A nearly three-fold increase in spin doctor references occurred from 1984 to 1988. Of all verdicts identified in the post-debate analysis programs in 1988, more than 17% contained a reference to

Table 4.6
Spin Doctor References, by Year and Network

	By Year	
Year (N)	Campaign "Spin"	Media "Spin"
1976 (12)	2.5%	1.2%
1980 (35)	6.8%	1.7%
1984 (44)	3.5%	2.7%
1988 (116)	14.3%	3.2%
Total (N)	75.4% (156)	24.6% (51)

Chi-square = 11.298, df = 3, p < .025

	By Network	
Network (N)	Campaign "Spin"	Media "Spin"
ABC (62)	5.8%	3.0%
CBS (90)	9.3%	2.0%
NBC (55)	6.9%	2.3%
Total (N)	75.4% (156)	24.6% (51)

Chi-square = 5.332, df = 2, NS

spinning. The big increase over prior years was in campaign spin references, made mostly by journalists.

While the identification of spinning as a means of attempting to influence opinion remained fairly low until 1988, the trend has been upward in the labeling of such references since 1976. There was no significant difference among the networks regarding references to spinning in post-debate analysis programs over the four general election campaign years of the study. However, ABC—apparently very cognizant of the increased spinning activity in 1988 and apparently having questioned the value of spinning in its coverage—included this statement, by Peter Jennings, at the end of the final 1988 presidential debate on October 13:

There are some things we want to avoid in this next half-hour. If you're going to look for the candidates' representatives to tell you again what a wonderful job this man did, this is not the place. Our focus tonight will be on what the candidates needed to accomplish, and whether they did.

And, true to its word, ABC did not present any coverage even remotely resembling spin doctoring—not a single comment by a politician, campaign staffer, or other partisan individual in the entire post-debate program. Only journalists were called upon for their expertise, evaluations, opinions, and comments.

But aside from ABC's action following the last Bush-Dukakis debate, the networks in 1988 included a great variety of spin doctor segments, or what one network described as "a visit to spin alley," in the post-debate programs. All of the networks carried some readily identifiable spin segments in which politicians or campaign staffers praised their party's debater and/or attempted to downplay the other debater's efforts. In other words, the difference was not that elites were not quoted; the difference was in how often in 1988 the interviews were referred to as spin doctoring. If anything (see Table 4.1), elites were sources of verdicts somewhat more often in 1988 than in 1976, and almost as often as in 1980 and 1984.

To indicate the extent of this type of information carried on the programs in 1988, out of a total of more than 160 minutes of news in the networks' post-debate programs, more than 28 minutes were devoted to identifiable spin doctor segments. This is 17.5% of the programs' total news time. Every program (with the exception of the ABC program on October 13) carried one or more spin doctor segments. The average post-debate program's news hole in 1988 was 20 minutes, and the average amount of time (identified either directly or indirectly as spin doctoring) per program totaled 3.5 minutes. Here are some of the remarks by journalists as they dealt with spin doctoring on the programs:

- Jeff Greenfield of ABC—"The instant the debate ended, campaign operatives descended [on the press corps] with lines concocted before the debate, with the predictability of locusts."
- Tom Brokaw of NBC—"There was so much spinning it's a wonder that the Civic Auditorium didn't go into orbit."
- Lisa Myers of NBC—"As you know, the spin doctors often have to do a little bit of acting after each debate in order to tell how good a job their guy did, even if he wasn't that great."
- Dan Rather and Leslie Stahl of CBS—(Rather was setting up a report by Stahl.) "As soon as a debate is over," said Rather, "the candidates' handlers—and don't they have a lot of them—go on non-stop spin patrol." Stahl added, "Frankly, it's getting a bit like a broken record."

Journalists' References to "Spinning." In 1988 Rather and Stahl, especially, along with Sam Donaldson of ABC, were regular users of the spin doctor terminology as they reported the post-debate activity (see Table 4.7 for an indication of the network journalists who most frequently refer to spin doctoring. Not all journalists are listed by name, only those most frequently identified with this descriptive form).

Table 4.7
Number of Journalists' References to Spin Doctors, by Journalist

Journalist (N)	Number of References	
	Campaign "Spin"	Media "Spin"
Rather (24)	16	8
Stahl (13)	12	1
Donaldson (11)	10	1
Jennings (9)	3	6
Brokaw (7)	6	1
Morton (7)	6	1
Hume (7)	4	3
Other Journalists (61)	54	7
Non-Journalists (68)	45	23
Total	156	51

As an indication of how one network reported and presented spin doctor information in 1988, here is what CBS did after the Bentsen/ Quayle debate. Following an opening segment during which anchor Rather discussed the debate with correspondents Bob Schieffer and Bruce Morton, Rather moved to a lengthy (more than four minutes) segment which he introduced this way: "From the moment Dan Quayle and Lloyd Bentsen left this stage, their handlers have been on what's called spin patrol, trying to talk up their man and influence the way the press reports what happened here." Leslie Stahl then begins the piece: "The spinning here tonight was even more intense than it was after the first presidential debate. We reporters were more than just spun tonight, we were twirled, we were twisted, we were Cuisinarted. Here was the scene in the press room after the debate." Six short soundbites follow, representing both parties and both candidates, with each bit damning or praising either Bentsen or Quayle. Stahl again: "They called it spin alley, a huge corridor set up specifically for the Republican and Democratic armies to launch their waves on hordes of willing reporters who circled around one, then the other spin doctor, for a good quote. The selling of Quayle and Bentsen was frenetic and furious." Then four more sound bites for or against the debaters. Finally, Stahl wraps up the piece: "Ridiculous. It's a sausage factory. There's all of this pressure and persuasion on reporters' work. . . . Will what happened here tonight work? We'll all have to wake up and read the papers in the morning."

Journalists question the spinning, even though most put up with it, and the networks cover it live. As Michael Oreskes of the *New York Times* said on the CBS post-debate analysis program following the first presidential debate in 1988:

It's not that long ago that we used to throw people like this out of the press room for interfering with our work. Well, now they come down here, now they make a lot of noise and say a lot of things, but we write this debate. We cover the story. And that's what we're gonna do tomorrow.

And Mark Nelson of the *Dallas Morning News* had this comment on CBS following the final presidential debate of 1988: "We don't believe everything we hear from these guys." Then later he added, "I hope in '92 we'll have a spin-free zone in the filing [journalists'] center."

The Issue of Debate Performance

How about the issue of "television presence"—the smoothness or stiffness of the debaters while on television? Has this aspect of verdicts changed over time? The data appear to indicate that the perceived *negative* differences in "television presence" verdicts between opposing candidates are becoming more pronounced. Here are the data, for the four election years since 1976, of the general trend toward an increase in candidate verdicts (as percentages of all candidate verdicts coded in the study) in which one candidate was described as less relaxed, or "stiffer," than the other: 1976—2.9%, 1980—3.4%, 1984—6.0%, and 1988—6.0%. On the other hand, there is no similar pattern, either up or down, of candidate verdicts in which one candidate was described as smoother, or "looser," than the other: 1976—7.2%, 1980—6.1%, 1984—8.2%, 1988—6.6%.

Verdicts About the 1988 Debaters

What were the candidate verdicts about the 1988 debate performances of Bush, Dukakis, Bentsen, and Quayle? What type of change, if any, was evident in such verdicts for the two presidential candidates from the first to the last debate? What was the extent of any negative perceptions of the debate performances of the two vice-presidential candidates?

It may very well be true that the several content analyses done for this book could stand on their own as contributions to the research literature on the debates. Nevertheless, content analyses of candidate verdicts serve an important second purpose: We need to be able to document what the media were saying about the rivals in each of the three 1988 debates in order better to connect media themes and messages to our survey data. In fact, part of the power of our overall research design is our ability to link what was happening in the media environment to what was happening, over time, in our survey responses. We therefore turn now to a series of tables documenting performance verdicts about Bush, Dukakis, Quayle, and Bentsen in their respective debates.

Bush vs. Dukakis I and II. Table 4.8 presents a comparison of verdicts reached after the first Bush-Dukakis debate with those reached after their second meeting. The table shows a dramatic swing in the direction of verdicts given the Republican and Democratic contenders in post-debate analysis programs that were only two and one-half weeks apart. At the conclusion of the first Bush-Dukakis debate on September 25, 1988, the evaluations of Bush's performance were so negative that even Jim Baker, Bush's campaign manager, while he gamely stated on ABC, "I think it was a clear win for the vice president," took pains to point out that "the vice president of the United States is not a professional debater, he has not been a professor at Harvard, he's not a lawyer," as he tried to do damage control in the aftermath of the Bush performance. Verdicts about Dukakis in the first debate on the other hand, were overwhelmingly positive, in marked contrast to those about Bush. On ABC, for example, some of the journalists' evaluations of Bush went like this:

Table 4.8
Presidential Candidate Verdicts

Following 1st Presidential Debate, September 25, 1988

	Direction of Verdict		
Debater (N)	Positive	Neutral	Negative
Bush (76)	42.1%	9.2%	48.7%
Dukakis (67)	70.1%	11.9%	17.9%
Both (59)	28.8%	55.9%	15.3%
Total	47.8%	23.6%	28.6%
(N)	(96)	(48)	(58)

Chi-square = 66.741, df = 4, p < .001

Following 2nd Presidential Debate, October 13, 1988

	Direction of Verdict		
Debater (N)	Positive	Neutral	Negative
Bush (67)	76.1%	11.9%	11.9%
Dukakis (72)	36.1%	13.9%	50.0%
Both (68)	22.1%	51.5%	26.5%
Total	44.2%	25.5%	30.3%
(N)	(92)	(53)	(62)

Chi-square = 69.990, df = 4, p < .001

- Brit Hume—(in comparing Bush's presentation at the Republican convention to his just-concluded debate performance)—" . . . the Vice President was not nearly as comfortable, not nearly as relaxed, not nearly as much in command of the situation."
- Jeff Greenfield—"Bush was . . . occasionally meandering in his language, . . . occasionally resorting to the old Bush, kind of almost treating English as a second language."

In contrast, ABC reporters had this to say about Dukakis:

- Sam Donaldson—"Dukakis did what he had to do, and that is come across as a credible candidate for the presidency. . . . He was calm, he was cool, he projected a knowledge of his own positions."

- Jeff Greenfield—"Dukakis' biggest plus was being here, seeming to be equal with the Vice President, and a far more eloquent close than George Bush, which I for one would not have expected."

The references to Dukakis scoring points for just being in the debate indicate the importance, at least in the eyes of network journalists, that national prime-time debate appearances have for challengers, especially lesser-known ones. But regardless of what prompted Dukakis' overwhelmingly favorable debate performance verdicts, our study data indicate that it was apparent by the end of the three network post-debate analysis programs on September 25 that the viewing public had been given a strong positive evaluation of Dukakis in contrast to a much more negative evaluation of Bush.

Let us segue now to October 13, 1988, the evening of the second Bush-Dukakis debate, and the aftermath of that debate, as examined by our analysis of the post-debate programs on the three major networks, shown in the second part of Table 4.8. The huge flip-flop in debate performance verdicts about Bush and Dukakis, in comparison with the conclusion of their first debate just two and one-half weeks earlier, is obvious. Favorable verdicts for Bush nearly doubled, to 76.1%, while negative verdicts of his debate performance dropped precipitously from 48.7% (after the first debate) to only 11.9%. Dukakis' second debate performance, on the other hand, resulted in positive verdicts of only 36.1%, even lower than for Bush after the pair's first debate, while the Democratic challenger's negative verdicts nearly tripled, to 50%—which was also a higher percentage than was recorded for Bush after the first debate.

Thus, the viewing public got an entirely different picture of the two candidates from these October 13 analysis programs, as, for example, these comments from journalists on ABC's program:

- Sam Donaldson—". . . unlike the last debate, it was the Vice President who was most aggressive tonight. Dukakis . . . tonight too often . . . was on the defensive."

- Jeff Greenfield—"One of the most interesting questions that was asked [was] who are your heroes? Dukakis mostly listed abstractions. . . . It took him a long time to come up with a name. . . . It's that kind of problem that the Dukakis people have been wrestling with with their candidate all through the campaign, [he is] good at abstract matters but does not have the instinct to relate at a personal level."

- Sam Donaldson again—"[Dukakis] . . . doesn't inspire great passion in his crowds, or, I suppose, in the television [audience] tonight."

• Brit Hume—"My sense is that he [Bush] was much looser tonight than he was in the first debate. I thought he was looser at the beginning . . . but he seemed much more comfortable, much more confident."

As far as the post-debate analysis was concerned, for the viewing public the Bush-Dukakis debate performance turnaround was complete. From the end of the evening of the first debate, when Dukakis was, in evaluative terms, the winner, and Bush the loser, Bush had emerged with an overwhelmingly stronger final debate performance, and the general election was less than one month away.

The sharp Dukakis switch on the post-debate programs from strong positive to negative echoed the same type of flip-flop for then-President Ford in 1976 between the first and second debates that year, from a positive ratio of 77.8% to 16.7% after the first debate, to a negative ratio of nearly two to one in news specials following the second debate. (Fellow debater Carter, while benefiting from the Ford drop, did not see much change in post-debate verdicts pertaining to him that year following the first two debates: his positive reading remained in the mid-60s for both debates, and his negative percentage remained in the low 20s following both debates.)

In 1984 the decrease in favorable post-debate analysis verdicts for Mondale between his first and second debates with Reagan also was marked, although not as pronounced as for Dukakis in 1988. The changes downward for Mondale in 1984 were: first debate—73.3% positive, 14.3% negative; second debate—58.3% positive, 31.3% negative. (In comparison with the Mondale decrease in favorable verdicts in 1984, President Reagan enjoyed a solid change from negative to positive that year [although somewhat less of a switch than the Bush reversal in 1988] in post-debate analysis verdicts: first debate—36.6% positive, 50.5% negative; second debate—61.3% positive, 35% negative.)

The Vice-Presidential Debaters. Let us turn now to verdicts in post-debate news analysis about Bentsen and Quayle. Two things probably stand out in the memories of nearly all viewers of that vice-presidential debate on October 5, 1988: (1) the dramatic, instantly famous rejoinder by Bentsen following Quayle's effort to compare himself to the late President Kennedy when JFK was still in the Senate, "Senator, you're no Jack Kennedy"; and (2) the big debating win that Bentsen scored over Quayle in that face-to-face confrontation.

And our study data from the three network news specials certainly indicate, as far as candidate verdicts were concerned, that it was indeed a big win for Bentsen (see Table 4.9). While there were twice as many candidate verdicts about Quayle alone as about Bentsen alone on the three networks, the majority of the Quayle verdicts were negative, by a margin of 57.3% to 37.9%. In fact, no 1988 debater had as many negative

Table 4.9
Vice-Presidential Candidate Verdicts

Following Vice Presidential Debate, October 5, 1988

Debater (N)	Direction of Verdict		
	Positive	Neutral	Negative
Quayle (124)	37.9%	4.8%	57.3%
Bentsen (62)	75.8%	--	24.2%
Both (48)	10.4%	70.8%	18.8%
Total	42.3%	17.1%	40.6%
(N)	(99)	(40)	(95)

Chi-square = 152.980, df = 4, p < .001

verdicts about him as did Quayle. But for Democratic candidate Bentsen, it was a huge positive performance, by a more than three-to-one margin in verdicts. And one interesting fact about the evaluations of Bentsen's performance was that *all* the verdicts about him were either positive or negative; not a single verdict about Bentsen was neutral in the data gathered from the three post-debate programs.

The differences between the Bentsen and Quayle performances in the debate were picked up quickly by the journalists who covered the event.

- Bruce Morton (CBS)—"I thought Bentsen came across . . . in this debate as a teacher and Quayle as a student. Quayle seemed to get lost once or twice . . . and there were other times when he seemed to wander off the perception path."

- Bob Schieffer (CBS)—"That certainly was the moment in this debate (the Bentsen JFK retort). It seemed to just kind of knock the wind out of Senator Quayle. . . . I think Senator Bentsen zinged him on that one."

- Bruce Morton again—"I think the Dukakis people are going to be very happy with Lloyd Bentsen. He did seem calm, assured; his sentences presented better than Senator Quayle's. They are going to be able to say, I think, our man won the debate."

- John Chancellor (NBC)—"I don't think as a debater he (Quayle) did terribly well. . . . I think that Bentsen looked like the sorrowful uncle talking to the wayward nephew."

- Andrea Mitchell (NBC)—"Quayle had more difficulty answering what he would do if he were vice president, and tragedy struck."

• Ken Bode (NBC)—"He said he'd say a prayer and call a staff meeting, but he didn't say much what he'd do after that."

The few positive verdicts awarded to Quayle were far enough in between that at one point CBS's Dan Rather had this back-handed compliment for Quayle: "Both sides going into this said the bar over which Senator Quayle had to get was pretty low. Did he get over it? It seems to me he did." Added CBS's Bruce Morton, "Quayle certainly did better than the low expectations Republican spin doctors had tried to set for him. . . . In fact he's had so much negative press, and the Republicans this past week have tried so hard to say, listen, if he gets his own name right, he's had a terrific evening." Perhaps, given the low advance expectations set for Quayle by the Republican spin doctors, he performed admirably in the debate (at least in the eyes of his handlers and in the comments by journalists who were reporting on the interviews with the handlers) by garnering as many positive candidate verdicts as he did.

CONCLUSION

Candidate verdicts make up the overwhelming portion of evaluative statements included in post-debate analysis programs on the three major television networks. These programs are the opportunities for the network journalists to analyze the just-concluded debate, to give individual judgments of who did well and who did poorly, and to sample public opinion in some way to try to determine how the debate was received by the general public, to present opinions of other (non-network) journalists regarding the debate, and to air the so-called "spinning" or partisan statements by supporters of the candidates.

In 1988 there were some major shifts in direction of candidate verdicts following the two presidential debates, as measured from the networks' post-debate analysis programs. The documenting of those shifts in candidate verdicts plays a key role in this research study's measurement and analysis of the effect that media-generated verdicts have on the voting public.

Candidate verdicts on the post-debate programs are primarily positive or favorable to the candidates, with the positive verdicts outweighing the negative by a ratio of 5 to 3. Nevertheless, in 1988, negative verdicts were prominent on the following occasions: (1) on October 5, Dan Quayle received a majority of negative verdicts; (2) on September 25, George Bush received a plurality of negative verdicts, and (3) on October 13, Michael Dukakis received a plurality of negative verdicts.

It will be interesting to see, as we look ahead to the presidential election campaign of 1992, if the spin doctor activity that was so often reported in 1988 will continue to be a significant part of the process of trying to influence public opinion via the news media. Will activity by spin doctors be more on offense or on defense? Will more attention be devoted to media spin? Perhaps the television networks, recognizing spinning for what it is—an overt effort on the part of partisan politicians and political managers to influence a campaign—will consider the final 1988 debate example of ABC-TV in eliminating such material from the key post-debate programs. Even without the benefit of spin doctors, of course, the public will have a great wealth of data to choose from as it wends its way down the road to the next presidential election campaign.

REFERENCES

Diamond, E., and K. Friery. 1987. Media coverage of presidential debates. In *Presidential debates: 1988 and beyond*, ed. J. L. Swerdlow, 43–51. Washington, D.C.: Congressional Quarterly, Inc.

Lowry, D. T., J. A. Bridges, and P. A. Barefield. In press. The effects of network TV "instant analysis and querulous criticism" following the first Bush-Dukakis debate. *Journalism Quarterly*.

5

JOURNALISTS AND THE IDEA OF PRESIDENTIAL DEBATES

In this chapter, we examine news treatment of the debates as political institutions in our society. Both quantitative and anecdotal answers will be presented to such questions as:

- Do journalists reduce the importance of presidential debates to how a debate will affect the chances of the candidates?
- When journalists cover the debates, how often does the usefulness of a debate to *voters* figure in their coverage?
- When the debates themselves become the focus of verdict-laden coverage, are network journalists themselves more negative than the people they interview about a debate?
- What changes have taken place, over time, in media treatment of the debates as political institutions?

DEBATES' ROLE IN LEGITIMIZING POLITICAL INSTITUTIONS

As suggested in Chapter 1, the existence of televised presidential debates probably contributes to the legitimacy of the election process, though we do not know of any direct empirical tests of that argument. There is evidence that debates tend to legitimize certain political institutions such as Congress and the Supreme Court (see Dennis and Chaffee 1978; Chaffee and Dennis 1979), but less evidence that their joint appearance in debates lends "acceptability" to *both* candidates. Debates apparently *do* reinforce voters' loyalties to their *favored* candidate, but—if anything—they may make the opponent *less* acceptable to partisans of the other side (Dennis and Chaffee 1978). When the "other" candidate wins, good feelings among "losing" voters toward the new president probably depend more on the perceived legitimacy of the election itself, plus such ceremonies as the inauguration, coupled with the accretion of press coverage which takes for granted the right of the new president to hold office. However, there is some evidence that viewing the debates may lead to legitimacy for both candidates when we look at independent voters (Dennis and Chaffee 1978).

As for the debates' role in legitimizing the election process itself, the question hardly seems to have been asked. Certainly, a nationally televised debate, carried out in the open with most voters watching, would seem to be made to order to create a sense of voter involvement and system openness. Some writers (e.g., Lemert 1981a) have suggested that the debates stimulate greater voter turnout than otherwise would be the case. Presumably, one way turnout could be stimulated might be through legitimization of the electoral process. However, the more plausible route to higher turnout may be through the debates' widely documented effect of reinforcing voter loyalties, since such a reinforcement effect almost certainly increases the individual's motivation to participate (Lemert 1981b, especially 93–101).

Would the existence of televised presidential debates always lead to a greater sense of system openness? Obviously not: It would be easy to imagine scenarios where a debate—and perhaps news treatment of that debate—convinced potential voters that the whole process was a sleazy fraud. In other words, only if the debates themselves were seen as an open and fair test of the candidates would the debates have a chance to lend legitimacy to the election process. It would seem to follow, then, that (assuming debates are held) *if the institutional legitimacy of the debates is threatened, then eventually the legitimacy of the election process itself also may be threatened.* Inasmuch as Chapter 9 presents survey results bearing on voter support for the debates, the reader may wish to look at that chapter after this one. Here, we concentrate on news treatment of the debates as political institutions.

LEGITIMIZING THE DEBATES THEMSELVES

Certainly the most commonly used justifications for holding presidential debates involve their benefits in reminding voters of their civic responsibilities and informing them about the issues, the candidates, and the campaign. There is considerable evidence that they do, but also marked disagreement about what to make of that evidence.

The Debates as "Teacher"

- Some writers, in noting that both attention to, and learning from, debates tends to be concentrated among those who are already relatively well informed, question whether the debates should even be held if all they do is widen "knowledge gaps" among the population (see especially Bishop, Oldendick and Tuchfarber 1978).
- However, Lemert, Elliott, Nestvold, and Rarick (1983) found that citizens who said they would not otherwise have watched a Republican debate during the 1980 primaries showed a surge in interest after induced exposure. Even more important, *they showed continued learning of new information even after they believed the study had been completed*. What this implies is that even accidental exposure to debates can increase both interest and learning. In another study, after they had controlled for interest, education, and other motivational factors that would tend to enhance a "knowledge gap," Miller and MacKuen asserted flatly, "The 1976 presidential debates produced a better-informed electorate than would have existed if the debates had not been held. Watching the debates increased the level . . . of information that *all* citizens had about the candidates. . . ." (1979, 290; emphasis added).

We have emphasized here the two extremes in the literature on learning from the debates, one saying that whatever learning takes place is only among the already informed and motivated, and the other saying that the high visibility of fall debates means that, inevitably, some people with low motivation will be exposed to, and learn from, televised debates. These extremes still tend to agree that people do learn from viewing the debates. The difference between them boils down to a disagreement about whether *more* people learn more than they otherwise would have.

In contrasting these two extremes, we should not lose sight of the fact that much of the debates effects literature reliably finds audience learning from presidential debates. (See Sears and Chaffee [1979] and Katz and Feldman [1962] for reviews of much of this research; also see Kraus [1988] for an extensive bibliography of more recent research and Jamieson and Birdsell [1988, Chapter 5] for an extended analysis of what can be learned from, and revealed by, debates).

If debates enhance voter knowledge, and if society values this contribution to the electoral process, one research question we need to ask in this portion of our study is whether news coverage stresses these positive effects of the debates.

Other Contributions Made by Debates

In an incisive analysis, Jamieson and Birdsell (1988, Chapter 5) argue that debates can benefit voters by, among other things, representing a threat that forces candidates to think through some of the decisions they will have to make as president, thus giving voters two better-prepared presidential candidates than they otherwise would have had. As threat, debates may also reduce demagoguery and manipulation. "In a world in which . . . sitcoms lure voters from political substance, a world in which spot ads and news snippets masquerade as significant political fare, a world in which most citizens believe that it is better to receive information than to seek it, debates are a blessing" (Jamieson and Birdsell 1988, 161). Again, we need to ask whether news coverage often considers such matters.

NEWS AND THE IDEA OF DEBATES

We think that analysis of media treatment of the institutional aspects of presidential debates is overdue. Despite the fact that in Chapter 1 we bemoaned the paucity of adequate and recent candidate verdict studies, by contrast with the vacuum in institutional analyses, we are absolutely awash in candidate verdict studies!

In their brief review of how the media covered the debates prior to 1988, Diamond and Friery imply that voters and viewers are the forgotten participants when journalists cover the debates: ". . . The media—and especially television—must focus on what the debate can do for the public and not on what it can do for any specific medium [or other elite group]" (1987, 51). Yet, if the voter/viewer is the forgotten participant in this televised event, one of the principal rationales and justifications for holding debates—their value to voters—also gets lost in the shuffle, and thus an occasion for legitimization of the debates also is missed in news coverage.

On the other hand, Kraus seems to imply that a *lack* of news coverage about negotiations concerning the format and rules of presidential debates *protects* the legitimacy of the debates: "Both from the candidates' point of view and from the League's [of Women Voters, the debate sponsor in 1976, 1980, and 1984], it would have been bad publicity to let the public know that candidates have control over negotiations, and furthermore that they are even able to keep the fact of that control secret" (1988, 45). According to Kraus, (1) *sponsors* fear leaks will lead to cancellation; (2) *broadcasters* "fear some sort of retribution" (1988, 45), and (3) *candidates* and their representatives fear everything and anything that could cost them the election. Thus, a kind of conspiracy of silence envelops those on the inside of the negotiations concerning how the debates will be run. Yet, outside the negotiations, there is no shortage of critics with credentials to tear apart the format and ground rules, once announced. *If* they had been asked to do so by the news media. But are they asked?

In 1988 even the League of Women Voters joined the ranks of those critics when the League turned down the Commission's invitation to sponsor the final Bush-Dukakis debate. In this chapter, we look at how the League's October 3 blast at candidate control was covered by the news media, and we compare that coverage with network television treatment of similar criticisms made by its own correspondents and anchors.

So a case can be made either that the media support or that they detract from the legitimacy of the debates. Or perhaps even that they do both. This chapter presents a combination of quantitative content-analytic data and a qualitative sample of print and broadcast discussion of the debates. We begin with the content analysis of post-debate news specials from 1976 to 1988.

DEBATES IN POST-DEBATE NEWS SPECIALS

The first part of this chapter looks at the same data set we used in Chapter 4:

- 1976—first and second Carter-Ford debates.
- 1980—the single Reagan-Carter debate.
- 1984—all three debates, including Ferraro-Bush.
- 1988—all three debates, including Bentsen-Quayle.

We were able to obtain and content-analyze all network post-debate news analyses that were broadcast after the nine debates listed above. With only two exceptions,[1] each of the three networks did a post-debate analysis program after each of the above debates. Even when there was no post-debate show, as such, each network had a two-to-three-minute wrap-up in the period immediately after the "live" debate itself. All these wrap-ups—typically done "voice-over" while candidates, their families, the panel, and guests chatted on stage—were included in our content analysis.

Our units of analysis were assertions or declarative statements about the debates. Sometimes the same sentence could produce multiple verdicts about both the debate and candidates. At the other extreme, sometimes it took several sentences to produce a single unit. In general, however, the number of units was very directly related to the amount of time each news special was given by the network. The same coders who did the coding for results in Chapter 4 also coded the results for this part of Chapter 5. For more detail about methodology, see Chapters 2 and 4.

Are Voters the Forgotten Participants?

The debates are framed primarily in terms of their importance to the candidates, not to voters, as shown in Table 5.1. When the verdict is

Table 5.1
Importance of Debate, by Object of Verdict

| Object of Verdict (N) | Importance of Debate to | | | |
	Candidates	Voters	Both	Not Important
Candidates (1842)	79.3%	5.0%	14.6%	1.1%
Debate (140)	15.7%	55.7%	18.6%	10.0%
Both (120)	44.2%	14.2%	31.7%	10.0%
Total	73.0%	8.9%	15.8%	2.2%
(N)	(1535)	(187)	(333)	(47)

Chi-square = 568.071, df = 6, p < .001

about candidates, the debate almost always is seen as important—and that importance usually relates to the ambitions of the candidates. Based on the numbers of cases for each row in Table 5.1, almost all verdicts (87.6% of them) took as their exclusive object the candidates. Less than 7% of the time was the debate the exclusive focus of a verdict.

Further, note that the debate is said to be unimportant more often (10% of the time) when the debate itself becomes a focus of the verdict. In other words, *it is easier for a debate to be described as "important" when the consequences for the candidates are at issue.* In fairness, however, we should also point out that, on the rare occasions when the debate itself is the object of the verdict, more than half the time it is described as *important to voters.* Unfortunately, from the viewpoint of media support for the debates as an institution, importance to voters is neither mentioned nor implied very often in these post-debate news specials.

As Table 5.2 shows, over time the undiluted emphasis on importance *to voters* actually has declined, with the exception of an upsurge from 1976 to 1980 that prevents the decline from being drawn as a straight line downward. The single Carter-Reagan debate was the only time in which the exclusive emphasis on candidates' fortunes fell below an almost constant 77%. Since 1980 also was the only year there was just one debate between the Democratic and Republican contenders, perhaps the networks were led to stress the debate's importance to voters a little more than usual, on the rationale that voters with questions about the candidates had only one chance to view them in something approximating a

Table 5.2
Whether (and to Whom) Debate Important, by Year of Post-Debate Analysis

Year (N)	Importance of Debate to			Not Important
	Candidates	Voters	Both	
1976 (277)	77.3%	13.0%	6.5%	3.2%
1980 (454)	57.9%	15.9%	23.1%	3.1%
1984 (722)	77.7%	5.8%	14.0%	2.5%
1988 (659)	76.6%	5.7%	16.8%	0.9%
Total	73.0%	8.9%	15.8%	2.2%
(N)	(1535)	(187)	(333)	(47)

Chi-square = 103.599, df = 9, p < .001

"spontaneous" situation. Consistent with this explanation about 1980 is the fact that no other single debate received the amount of news special time—or had the number of assertions about it—that the 1980 debate did.

On the other hand, though, ABC's Reagan-Carter post-debate analysis show lasted 70 minutes, almost double the *combined* length of the other two networks' 1980 analyses. Significantly, the reason that ABC show lasted 70 minutes was a decision to stay on the air with a phone-in tally on who won the debate. This rather notorious (to pollsters) ABC attempt to promote and use its 900-number phone-in poll produced, as part of the apparent effort to promote phone calls, numerous statements by ABC's correspondent and two anchors that the number of phone calls was "remarkable." Since the phone calls were from potential voters, each such comment was recorded as saying the debate was important to voters (and, sometimes, to both voters and candidates). In any event, the unique nature of the single Carter-Reagan confrontation and ABC's emphasis on its phone-in poll probably combined to produce the apparent anomaly of a 1980 surge upwards in voter importance references.

Table 5.3 compares the importance attributed to the debates by journalists, political elites, and other sources of verdicts. Before we examine this and later tables that use the same categories of sources, we need to define our terms. The *journalists* include a few newspaper reporters interviewed by network journalists but overwhelmingly are network correspondents, analysts, and anchors. In the case of George Will, who acted as an analyst for ABC, we coded him as a political elite after the

Table 5.3
Whether (and to Whom) Debate Important, by Source

| | Importance of Debate to | | | |
Source (N)	Candidates	Voters	Both	Not Important
Journalists (1218)	80.5%	5.7%	10.1%	3.7%
Political Elites (580)	79.3%	6.7%	13.8%	0.2%
All Others (304)	31.2%	25.7%	42.8%	0.3%
Total	73.0%	8.9%	15.8%	2.2%
(N)	(1535)	(187)	(333)	(47)

Chi-square = 391.428, df = 6, p < .001

second Reagan-Mondale debate. (Will had helped prepare Reagan for that debate and, when this conflict of interest was later discovered, was heavily criticized by other journalists for trying to have his cake and eat it. We felt that in the case of this debate, at least, Will could not be regarded as acting in the role of a journalist. In all other cases, Will was coded as a journalist.)

Political elites include both named and unnamed "insiders": campaign officials, party officials, senators, representatives, and the like. Overwhelmingly (by roughly a 10-to-1 ratio) these people were named—and usually featured in a sound bite.

Other sources include feedback from the audience at the debate (interviews and/or sounds of applause or laughter), phone-in or standard public opinion surveys, interviews with panels of voters, crowd reactions to candidates at post-debate rallies, and so on. What these other sources have in common is that they all were both reactive and purportedly more representative of non-elites.

We can now see in Table 5.3 that both journalists and elites focused their attention on what the debate did for—or to—the candidates' ambitions. The main difference between elites and journalists was that journalists were more likely to say the debates were not important, though even the journalists rarely said this. "Other" sources concentrated on the debate's usefulness to voters much more than did both journalists and political "insiders."

What Aspects of Debate Were Emphasized?

Another way of looking at the institutional aspects of debate coverage is to consider what aspect of the debate was emphasized in each statement. We have already seen that candidates, not the debate itself, usually were the exclusive objects of verdicts. But candidates as objects are multidimensional; was it their issue stands, their tactics, their prior records, or what? Presumably, an emphasis on the candidate's prior record or policy views would imply greater usefulness to voters than would an emphasis on performance or tactics.

In Chapter 3 we saw that the early evening network newscasts had shown a tremendous drop (from 38% in 1976 to just above 5% in 1984 and 1988) in their focus on issues. So even if the reader is not familiar with the literature on election campaign coverage, it will come as no surprise that the post-debate shows also gave short shrift to issues coverage (Table 5.4). Very few of the statements concerned issues, candidates' competence to govern, or their prior records. Just as with the evening news shows, candidate performance statements dominate, followed by statements about the tactics used by the debaters. Tactics, of course, bear directly on debate performance as well.

Overall, the post-debate analysis shows did not emphasize issues as much as the evening newscasts did. Nevertheless, when we look more closely at *changes* in post-debate emphasis over time, we see that 1988 saw even less emphasis than usual on policy issues, but somewhat more

Table 5.4
Aspect of Debate Emphasized, by Year

Year (N)	Issues in Debate	Candidate Perfor-mance	Debate Tactics	Compe-tence to Govern	Candi-dates' Prior Record	Debate Itself	Other
			Aspect Emphasized				
1976 (347)	9.8%	56.5%	19.0%	2.0%	1.2%	11.5%	0.0%
1980 (492)	8.1%	51.4%	15.2%	3.3%	0.8%	19.5%	1.6%
1984 (762)	9.6%	62.6%	15.0%	3.4%	0.7%	8.7%	0.1%
1988 (699)	6.2%	60.9%	17.7%	5.0%	2.1%	7.7%	0.3%
Total (N)	8.3% (190)	58.8% (1352)	16.5% (379)	3.7% (84)	1.2% (28)	11.1% (256)	0.5% (11)

Chi-square = 91.429, df = 18, p < .001

emphasis on matters of competence—largely the "Quayle issue." In fact, more than half of the competence references in the three 1988 debates came after the single Quayle debate. As we have seen before and will again, the question of Quayle's competence cuts across both the post-debate survey responses (Chapter 7) and the content analyses results (Chapters 3 and 4, as well as this one).

Interestingly, journalists (1.8%) were *less* likely than political elites (6.5%) and others (6.1%) to emphasize candidate competence. What this may mean is that journalists used sound bites from others to say this. Among all their statements, the journalists were far *more* likely (19.9%) than the elites (13.5%) and others (7.6%) to emphasize debaters' tactics. They were also more likely than the other two groups of sources to emphasize the debate itself (data not tabled; Chi-square = 98.707, 12 df, p < .001).

Verdicts about the Debate Itself

We have already seen that the debates themselves rarely were at the focus of the post-debate programs. When they were, however, what were debate verdicts like? They included statements about the importance (or lack thereof) of a given debate to the campaign or to voters, criticism or praise of the "quality" of the debate, or comments about the debate's ground rules or format. (Comments about debate format/sponsorship were also coded separately, because it was conceivable that a debate verdict could be positive even though, embedded in it, was a negative comment about format—for example, "Despite the rules, the debate panel was able to extract clear answers from the candidates.")

Over the years, when post-debate analysts reached verdicts about debates, have those verdicts become more negative or more positive? Table 5.5 shows that, overall, no statistically significant shifts have occurred. But look at the positive verdict column. In 1976, the first year after presidential debates had resumed, half the verdicts about the debates were favorable. By 1988 only slightly more than a third of the verdicts were favorable, and for the first time there were more negative than positive verdicts. Despite the fact that the overall test does not reach statistical significance, when 1988 is compared with all the previous years combined, the downward slide in positive verdicts does reach acceptable levels of statistical significance. Apparently 1988 was relatively unique in its low level of positive verdicts about the debates.

Who was most likely to present negative verdicts about the debate(s)? Over the entire time span, it was journalists (Table 5.6). Political elites may have been close to the journalists on the negative end, but they were midway between journalists and other sources on the high end. The other sources were by far the most positive and least negative. It is very much

Table 5.5
"Verdict" About the Debate Itself, by Year

Year (N)		Verdict	
	Positive	Neutral	Negative
1976 (56)	50.0%	12.5%	37.5%
1980 (118)	52.5%	15.3%	32.2%
1984 (95)	47.4%	22.1%	30.5%
1988 (75)	34.7%	24.0%	41.3%
Total	46.8%	18.6%	34.6%
(N)	(161)	(64)	(119)

Chi-square = 8.723, df = 6, p < .20, overall.
Chi-square = 5.067, df = 1, p < .05, when "Neutral" and "Negative" combined and 1976, 1980 and 1984 combined.

Table 5.6
"Verdict" About the Debate Itself, by Source

Source of Verdict (N)		Verdict	
	Positive	Neutral	Negative
Journalists (238)	39.5%	22.3%	38.2%
Political Elites (56)	50.0%	14.3%	35.7%
All Others (50)	78.0%	6.0%	16.0%
Total	46.8%	18.6%	34.6%
(N)	(161)	(64)	(119)

Chi-square = 25.709, df = 4, p < .001

in order here to remember that these "other" sources purportedly were the people for whom the debates were being held: viewers and voters.

Major changes seem to have taken place over time in how favorably journalists evaluated the debates. In 1976, journalists' verdicts about the debates were at least as positive (actually, slightly more) as either elites' or others'. But by 1980, journalists' verdicts were considerably less positive and more neutral and negative, and they remained that way in 1984 and 1988. In 1976, 59% of journalists' debate verdicts were positive, compared with 39% in 1980, 41% in 1984, and only 26% in 1988.

Criticisms of Format or Sponsor

We have already implied that there would be more verdicts about the debates than there would be commentary praising or criticizing debate format, ground rules, or sponsorship. All told, there were only 147 references to format, ground rules, or sponsorship out of the 2,302 statements coded. Of the 147, very few of the references were to the debate sponsor, even though in 1988 the League of Women Voters had sharply criticized its rival, the Commission on Presidential Debates, as being a "front" for the candidates. This criticism occurred on October 3, 1988—before two of the 1988 debates (and their post-debate analyses) had even taken place. We shall return to the matter of the League criticism later in this chapter.

In any case, almost all the references were to matters of format, not sponsorship—for example, whether follow-up questions were allowed, whether the candidates could or could not address each other directly, and so on. Some 57% of the references to debate format were criticisms of it, as one probably would expect. Only 26% were favorable. Often not included in our count of only 147 references, however, was CBS anchor Dan Rather's studious avoidance of the term "debate" to refer to what he preferred to call a "joint appearance." Obviously, there was an implied criticism every time Rather, who turned down an invitation to moderate one of the 1988 debates, replaced the term debate with the words "joint appearance."

In the following instance, however, Rather's statement *did* produce two entries as negative assertions about format: [Rather, voice over as Bush and Dukakis shake hands at end of September 25 debate] "Against the backdrop of a standing ovation and handshakes, the first of the presidential campaign debates or, if you prefer, joint appearances, or if you prefer, orchestrated, controlled news conferences, has come to a close." Interestingly, most of the other CBS newspeople continued to use the word "debate."

Notwithstanding Dan Rather's avoidance of the word "debate," we found no evidence that journalists were more likely than elites or other sources to criticize the format. However, *if* journalists criticized the format, it often occurred when a member of the debate panel returned to his or her "home" network and was interviewed by colleagues. It almost seemed as if journalists who were on the panels had finally been made to realize how constraining and frustrating the ground rules were, while many other journalists, with less ego involvement, did not bother as often to try to tell the world about those constraints.

In any event, journalists were no more—and no less—likely than other sources to criticize the format and ground rules. We can only speculate about motivations when journalists did address the format and ground rules. There also was not much evidence of any change, over time, in references to format or ground rules.

Did the Debate Provide New Information?

Another way to look at media support for the debates is to examine whether the analyses said that the debates had served their institutional purpose of providing voters with new information and insights about the candidates. Table 5.7 shows a falling off, over time, in readiness to say that the debates did *not* provide any new information or insights about the candidates or their policy views. This pattern in the table is true whether one includes or excludes the items ("Can't Code"), where no assertion about new information, or the lack of it, can be coded. Journal-

Table 5.7
Whether Debate Provided New Information, by Year

	Did Debate Provide New Information?		
Year (N)	Can't Code	Yes, It did	No, It Didn't
1976 (348)	71.3%	18.1%	10.6%
1980 (493)	73.8%	14.4%	11.8%
1984 (761)	73.6%	20.5%	5.9%
1988 (699)	77.4%	17.9%	4.7%
Total	74.5%	18.0%	7.5%
(N)	(1713)	(415)	(173)

Chi-square = 35.766, df = 6, p < .001, overall
Chi-square = 28.099, df = 3, p < .001, excluding the "Can't Code" entries

ists, however, were the most likely to say there was no new information provided by the debate (Table 5.8). Least likely to take such a negative view were political elites, with other sources closer to elites than to the journalists.

Did the Debate Reveal Genuine Differences?

Finally, whether or not *new* information is provided, were the debates characterized as having revealed genuine differences between the candidates, their tickets, or their programs? Clearly, this is another ostensible purpose of the debates, so we have another indirect indicator here of media support. Once again, we find (Table 5.9) evidence of changes over time in the distribution of statements about what the debate had contributed. One change is the shift, over time, from relatively unqualified assertions that *all* the differences between the candidates had been exposed and clarified to the assertion that *some* of the differences had been. The second major trend is the decline, from 1976–1980 to 1984–1988, in the proportion of outright denials that the debate had clarified any differences.

All this talk about trends over time should not distract us, however, from recognizing one stable and constant finding: In each year, more than three of every four statements about the debates had no implications whatever concerning one of the debates' most widely accepted purposes: to inform voters about the choice they soon would have to make. When we look at the sources of these statements, we find that journalists were

Table 5.8
Whether Debate Provided New Information, by Source

	Did Debate Provide New Information?		
Source (N)	Can't Code	Yes, It did	No, It Didn't
Journalists (1371)	74.6%	16.2%	9.2%
Political Elites (601)	69.7%	24.8%	5.5%
All Others (329)	82.3%	13.4%	4.3%
Total	74.5%	18.0%	7.5%
(N)	(1713)	(415)	(173)

Chi-square = 39.391, df = 4, p < .001, overall
Chi-square = 19.667, df = 2, p < .001, excluding the "Can't Code" entries

Table 5.9
Whether Debate Revealed Differences, by Year

Source (N)	Did Debate Reveal Differences?			
	Can't Code	Yes, All Differences	Yes, Some Differences	No, Debate Didn't
1976 (348)	77.9%	3.7%	11.5%	4.9%
1980 (492)	75.2%	4.3%	13.4%	7.1%
1984 (762)	76.4%	2.6%	18.0%	3.0%
1988 (699)	79.7%	1.6%	16.0%	2.7%
Total	77.7%	2.8%	15.4%	4.1%
(N)	(1787)	(65)	(355)	(94)

Chi-square = 34.837, df = 9, p < .001, for entire table
Chi-square = 29.108, df = 6, p < .001, when "Can't Code" excluded

Table 5.10
Whether Debate Revealed Differences, by Source

Source (N)	Did Debate Reveal Differences?			
	Can't Code	Yes, All Differences	Yes, Some Differences	No, Debate Didn't
Journalists (1371)	82.2%	1.4%	12.3%	4.1%
Political Elites (601)	67.2%	5.0%	23.6%	4.2%
All Others (329)	77.8%	4.9%	13.4%	4.0%
Total	77.7%	2.8%	15.4%	4.1%
(N)	(1787)	(65)	(355)	(94)

Chi-square = 72.613, df = 6, p < .001, for entire table
Chi-square = 17.920, df = 4, p < .01, when "Can't Code" excluded

the *least* likely source to say that the debate had revealed either some or all differences. However, this difference was due more to the fact that journalists did not as often even address the question, not because journalists more often denied that information about candidate differences was given in the debate.

Given the role of campaign insiders in these post-debate shows, it is no surprise to find them claiming that the differences they wanted to impress on the audience had been clearly shown in the debate. However, the fact that audience members ("other" sources) *also* were more likely than journalists to address whether all or some differences had been revealed suggests that the lower rates for journalists are not just the result of role differences between journalists and elites.

We turn now from the quantitative content analysis to two sets of qualitative/anecdotal descriptions and analyses. The first set concerns support for the debates as political institutions within the pages of two elite print media as well as within the pages of *Broadcasting*, the major trade publication of the broadcasting industry. The second set of observations is a case study of a major event in the history of presidential debates: the 1988 withdrawal of the League of Women Voters from any involvement in those debates. Once we have presented these qualitative analyses, we shall try to draw all the results together.

BROADCASTING, NEWSWEEK, AND THE *TIMES* WEIGH IN

Broadcasting magazine, a broadcasting industry trade magazine, typically represents the views of the television industry. It has not been reluctant editorially to express itself on the debates. For this analysis, *Newsweek* was chosen to represent the weekly news magazines and the *New York Times* to represent the elite newspaper press. We analyzed editorials and articles from all three publications from 1976 through 1988.

We concentrated on editorials and opinion columns where, we believed, we would more often find analyses and opinions addressing the value of presidential debates than we would in news stories. Still, in at least some cases we discovered evaluations of the idea of debates implicit in "straight" news stories, especially those in the two magazines.

Broadcasting

For the industry magazine, the format issue and the sponsorship issue were intertwined, not only with each other, but also with the issue of full First Amendment freedoms for broadcasters and the repeal of Section 315 of the 1934 Communication Act, the "equal time" provision. In 1960 Congress temporarily suspended Section 315 to allow the television networks to carry the Kennedy-Nixon debates without having to allow minor-party candidates to participate. In 1976, however, Congress failed to take similar action. Instead, an arrangement was reached whereby the networks could cover the debates as "bona fide" news events under the sponsorship of any nonpartisan organization (in this case, the League of Women Voters).

For broadcasters and their magazine "voice," this was a lose-lose situation. The industry lost what little leverage it had in negotiating with the candidates over such format issues as whether to allow the networks to use their own cameras in addition to the shared cameras, whether to allow audience reaction shots, and how to choose panelists. The industry lost as well on the broader issue of First Amendment rights, because Section 315 remained intact. Had 315 been repealed, broadcasters reasoned, the networks would have been able to cover the debates any way they wanted. As it was, *Broadcasting* editorialized, "the politicians . . . once again demonstrated their determination to manipulate broadcasting to their own ends, in outright contempt of its journalistic rights" ("Long shot" 1976).

Right after the first debate between Jimmy Carter and Gerald Ford (the one with the 27-minute audio gap) the networks and the magazine said, "We told you so." Had broadcasters been in charge, no gap would have occurred, the magazine said. Again, *Broadcasting* editorialized for repeal of Section 315, this time reasoning that the legal troubles caused by the rule far outweighed those that might result from its repeal ("Political device" 1976).[2]

In 1980, with Jimmy Carter refusing to debate third-party candidate John Anderson, *Broadcasting* found additional reason to decry the imposition of government regulation on television political coverage. Incumbent Carter wanted the first debate to include only himself and Republican Ronald Reagan and threatened to withdraw if the League of Women Voters allowed Anderson to take part. The League had established a criterion for Anderson's inclusion—a 15% standing in public opinion polls—that he ultimately met.

The political maneuvering that preceded the September 21 Anderson-Reagan debate detracted from the real issue, according to *Broadcasting*: Section 315 "unnecessarily complicates all arrangements for broadcast appearances by candidates" ("Rerun" 1980). Removal of the rule, the editorial argued, would allow broadcasters to deal with candidates directly rather than through the League of Women Voters. That might not eliminate all political manipulation, the editorial acknowledged, but it would make negotiations easier.

Section 315 not only was the root of the political manipulation problem, in the eyes of *Broadcasting*, it was also to blame for a debate format that allowed the candidates to evade questions and stick to entirely rehearsed responses. In an editorial following the Reagan-Anderson debate, the magazine praised the League of Women Voters for serving as third-party representative "with commendable tact and skill." Nevertheless, it said, the League's involvement was "an intrusion" that had allowed the candidates to dictate format rules that weakened the role of debates as providers of information to the public ("In the way again" 1980). Following the Carter-Reagan debate, a *Broadcasting* editorial once again praised the League, calling the debate "flawless." The editorial said the debate enlivened an otherwise dull campaign and demonstrated the value of debates in the election process. However, the magazine still maintained that the debates had been best executed in 1960, when Section 315 had been suspended ("Excess baggage" 1984).

These were the first signs that the magazine actually saw value in the debates. When, in 1983, the Federal Communications Commission interpreted Section 315 to allow broadcasters to sponsor debates as well as cover them, *Broadcasting* magazine's acceptance of the idea of debates increased. In fact, before the first 1988 debate, the magazine now saw the debates as "the most powerful and effective means of familiarizing a nation . . . with the men who would be president ("For the people" 1988)." Even so, the debates still had flaws in the eyes of *Broadcasting*. Following the first Reagan-Mondale debate in 1984, an editorial said the word "debate" was a misnomer, that instead they should be called "joint appearances." Make the candidates appear face to face, the editorial said ("Extra baggage" 1984). In 1988 a *Broadcasting* editorial criticized the use of spin doctors by the candidates: "It's no service to amplify babble unedited" ("Too much of a bad thing" 1988).

Newsweek

If the broadcasting trade magazine has viewed the debates primarily in the context of the industry's regulatory environment, *Newsweek* has focused mostly on what the debates mean to the candidates. Its debate coverage in all four election years has told the story more in terms of what strategies candidates used and who won a certain debate, rather than the information the voting public might have gotten from the debate.

In 1980, for example, when the candidates were wrangling over John Anderson's participation and the debates were actually in jeopardy, *Newsweek* suggested that not having the debates would be "the candidates' loss" ("Out of their League?" 1980, 21). Two weeks later, when Carter had decided not to debate with both Reagan and Anderson, *Newsweek* focused on how Carter's strategy would impact on Reagan, not on how voters' knowledge might be affected.

True, the magazine did wonder about "the future of Presidential debates in American politics" ("And then there were two" 1980, 25), but for whom was it concerned: the voting public, the politicians, or themselves and other media organizations? Apparently, not the voting public. When Anderson criticized Carter's withdrawal as an injury to the "right of [the] American people to hear, to know, to listen," *Newsweek* facetiously said Anderson was taking the "moral high ground" ("And then there were two" 1980, 25). And, after the Anderson-Reagan debate, when *Newsweek* asked who benefited from it, its answers had nothing to do with those who watched and everything to do with those who did—and did not—debate ("A boost for the stay-at-home" 1980).

Similarly, the magazine was brutally direct about who had the most to gain and lose from the Quayle-Bentsen debate. While conceding that, in theory, the debate was supposed to help voters decide who would make a better successor should something happen to the president, the magazine went on to say that, in practice, the debate was simply a question of how well Quayle would perform ("The veep showdown" 1988). As *Newsweek* has seen it, the candidates are not the only players in the debate game. The debates have been important to the media as well, especially when debates' potential for impact is great. For example, in the aftermath of the first Reagan-Mondale debate, the news weekly portrayed Mondale's surprisingly good performance as a way to make the campaign story better. The debate, in revitalizing the Mondale campaign, would inject some life into campaign news stories ("The great debate" 1984).

While *Newsweek* consistently has seen the debates as more important to the candidates and media than to the public, occasionally it indicated that voters had a stake in the debates. The voter stake, however, usually is tied to the candidate stake. For example, the importance for voters of the second Bush-Dukakis debate was tied to a need for *Dukakis* to demonstrate "some core of human emotion" ("Lectern to lectern" 1988, 139).

Generally speaking, *Newsweek* has never shown much reverence for the debates, which the magazine has called "the moral equivalent of the Friday night fights" ("The rise and fall of the age issue" 1984), equipped with a "pop-quiz format [that] discouraged the serious discussion of issues" ("Lectern to lectern" 1988, 120). "The form rewarded appearance over content, quickness over thoughtfulness. . . . Decisions turned on the quality of Richard Nixon's makeup, a slip of Gerald Ford's tongue, and the tilt of Ronald Reagan's head when he told Jimmy Carter, 'There you go again' " ("The rise and fall . . ." 1984, 109).

The *New York Times*

In sharp contrast, the *New York Times* always has viewed the debates as a way to focus voter attention on the candidates and the election, although it, too, has criticized debate flaws such as format and panelist selection. Overall, though, the *Times* and several of its columnists have strongly supported the idea of presidential debates, while expressing frustration over their unfulfilled potential.

In the aftermath of the first Ford-Carter debate, a *Times* editorial pointed out that the debates were really "joint appearances," more of an adaptation of "Meet the Press" than actual debates. But, the editorial said, they do perform a service by giving voters first-hand exposure to candidates, an important difference from second-hand news accounts. The editorial also criticized the debates' "show-business" character and the candidates' rehearsal and concern with grooming. Nevertheless, the editorial said, "in their paradoxical way . . . the mass-audience debates drop the shield of managers and any contrivance. . . . Character, integrity, compassion, intelligence—or lack of them—do have a way of showing through" ("Lights-camera—candidates!" 1976).

The flap over John Anderson's participation in the 1980 debates produced several *Times* editorials addressing not only the politics of letting Anderson debate but also the implications for the presidential debates as institutions, if the dispute were to disrupt them. In typical even-handed fashion, the *Times* acknowledged that Jimmy Carter's skipping any debate with Anderson may have been a politically smart thing to do "if one thinks debates are an issue solely for politicians to decide" ("An empty chair" 1980, A18). Three days later, the paper said it understood Carter's position, although it did not agree with it:

There is an objective, neutral, public value to televised debates. They may not be debates at all, only elaborate panel shows. Political scientists may argue about how decisive they are. But what is beyond question is that Americans pay attention to them. . . . ("Running against . . ." 1980, A18)

Later, when Anderson was excluded from a second debate because he no longer met the League's requirement that he have a minimum of 15% support in the polls, the *Times'* editorials took shots, first at the League of Women Voters for excluding Anderson and, second, at Ronald Reagan for refusing to debate Carter unless Anderson were also present. But in both editorials, underlying the criticism was the notion that "[t]elevised debates are very much in the public interest" ("Why not . . . 1984, A26"). "Presidential debates offer an opportunity available nowhere else in the endless American electoral campaign" ("A naked look . . ."1980, A30).

The public benefit from debates was a theme the *Times* would echo in 1984 and 1988. And even when its editorials found flaws in the debates, the *Times* also seemed to find some value within the flaws:

- Although they weren't true debates, they "provide something that transcends winning and losing: a sterling forum for discussing issues." ("Rabbits and reality . . . 1984," E20)
- Even though spin doctors put the focus on performance and emotions rather than issues, at least those spin doctors provide the public with "a range of judgments" from "students of politics." ("The debate and the spin doctors" 1984, E22)

Perhaps the only debate shortcoming to which the *Times* could not find some compensating public benefit was the debate format, especially the use of the journalist panel. The format so much inhibits spontaneity, the newspaper complained, that the public gets warmed-over stump speeches. The public would have learned more with a less-rigid format, perhaps one with a moderator and the candidates addressing each other rather than a panel of journalists ("Debates, domesticated 1988," and "Sure loser . . ." 1988). Still, the *New York Times* seemingly always believed what one of its editorial writers wrote in 1988: "Better debates than no debates" ("Debates, domesticated" 1988, A34).

THE LEAGUE BREAKS ITS SILENCE

From the resumption of the fall debates in 1976 until the fateful events of 1988, the League of Women Voters had been the sole sponsor of presidential debates. (The 1960 debates had been sponsored by each of the broadcast networks. Based on *Broadcasting's* editorials, we may conclude that the industry strongly resented being dislodged by the League.) For the first time since 1960, somebody besides the League was sponsoring a fall presidential debate. On September 25, the Commission on Presidential Debates, a creature of the two presidential campaigns, had sponsored the first Bush-Dukakis debate. Though the League had been offered no role in the September 25 debate, the two campaigns did offer the League the chance to sponsor the final Bush-Dukakis debate in Los Angeles. On October 3, after a week of testy, behind-the-scenes negotiations with representatives of the two campaigns and a weekend of discussion and reflection, the League of Women Voters announced that it was withdrawing from debate sponsorship.

Negotiations with the campaigns about sponsoring the October 13 Bush-Dukakis debate had been delayed until after the Commission-sponsored September 25 debate, League sources said. After the campaigns had invited League participation, it became quickly apparent to the League that the campaigns were so preoccupied with the first September 25 meeting that discussion of such prickly matters as who would choose members of the October 13 journalist panel could not take place until after September 25. Once negotiations began, League President

Nancy Neuman (1990) told one of the authors, the League had given up after a week of trying to reach an agreement with the campaigns.

At a Washington press conference on Monday, October 3, Neuman announced that the League had rejected the candidates' invitation to sponsor the Los Angeles debate. In vehemently rejecting the invitation, the League had publicly and openly raised issues and objections to campaign control for only the second time in its history of association with the fall presidential debates. The League asserted that the campaigns had presented it with a 16-page agreement between the campaigns with a "take it or leave it" demand. The agreement gave to the campaigns the right to pick the journalists on the panel, to control camera angles (a matter Richard Nixon had tried to control in 1960), and to prevent shots of one candidate reacting to the other. Panelists were not to be allowed any follow-up questions, either.

A comparison of the League's 1988 announcement with the only previous time it had done something like this leaves room for after-the-fact second-guessing, as we shall see. As debate sponsor in 1976, 1980, and 1984, the League had often battled behind the scenes with the campaigns over ground rules. As Kraus (1988) has pointed out, the League generally lost those hidden battles because the candidates had the ultimate trump card: No debate could be held without them.

Partly because of the League's own role in adhering to past silences *in advance* about debate formats and ground rules, there had always been relatively little information available in the popular media about the constraints imposed on presidential debates, although the League and other insiders often had written extensively about these problems in retrospective books, briefing papers, and other elite-oriented "insider" media. In fairness to the League, however, we should also say that, while it apparently had been willing to discuss with journalists the constraints imposed by the campaigns (those discussions taking place, with only one other exception, *after* that year's debates had been held) little or no news coverage had resulted.[3]

In the interview, Neuman (1990) conceded that, *before* the debates, "the only leverage we really have is going public [when the campaigns go too far in their demands]." She pointed out the League *had* gone public during the negotiations in 1984 when the campaigns had demanded the right to veto specific journalists as panel members. "It [that demand] stopped," she said, when the League went public about it. In a sense, then, 1988 could be regarded as the second time the League went public before the debates were over: "To me, there were a lot of First Amendment issues in 1988 that, I assumed, the media would pick up. I was wrong about that" (Neuman 1990).

In a second sense, however, the League's 1988 withdrawal announcement more closely resembled the League's previous retrospective efforts, from the point of view of journalists. *For, in the very act of withdrawing, the League had made itself "history" in the eyes of political journalists,* just as in previous years, those retrospective efforts to criticize campaign controls had evoked little press interest. As we shall see, when examining coverage of the League's withdrawal announcement, a dead giveaway that the League had become, in the minds of the journalists, "history" was journalists' preoccupation with whether the October 13 debate would go on anyway.

In 1984 the League went public *during* negotiations that had not been ended, but in 1988 the League declared that it had given up. In effect, then, the 1988 negotiations had *ended*, with no hope of renewal. In 1984 the League was still "alive" as a potential sponsor, with all the political power sponsors have; in 1988 it had already given up any prospect that it would wield that power. (In fairness to the League, however, the parallel with 1984 is not a perfect one. Unlike 1984, there was a substitute sponsor available: the Commission.) Ironically, with 10 days remaining before the final 1988 debate, the League was considerate enough about "inconveniencing" its rival that it sacrificed its one remaining bargaining chip, declaring its withdrawal far enough ahead of time to allow a smooth pickup of sponsorship by the Commission.[4]

In any event, one-day coverage of the League's October 3 criticism was given by the print and broadcast press, but there seemed to have been little interest shown in doing follow-up stories about these—or any other—format criticisms, with a revealing broadcast news exception to be noted shortly. Interestingly, editorial support for the League's position came from outside New York and Washington—such editorial voices as the *Oregonian,* the *Cincinnati Enquirer,* the *Denver Post,* the *Times-Picayune* (New Orleans), the *Dallas Morning News,* the *Chicago Tribune,* and the *Register-Guard* (Eugene-Springfield) weighed in with scathing editorial blasts at the campaigns, the Commission, and the debate ground rules.[5] However, follow-ups in the news generally were not common, with an occasional exception.[6]

CBS Coverage

Although its story was brief and was read by Dan Rather with little production, CBS gave perhaps the most sympathetic network treatment to the League's complaint. (Recall that Rather already had been studiously avoiding the term "debate" and using the term "joint appearance" instead.) Here's part of CBS' 34-second story:

The League . . . accused [both campaigns] of trying to "hoodwink" voters by imposing a format that would minimize real debate or spontaneity. It's the same format [in the October 13 debate] as the first Bush-Dukakis joint appearance, sponsored by what is called a bipartisan commission, a commission that in fact is controlled by the candidates." (CBS Evening News, October 3, 1988).

The rest of the brief story then shifted to whether the October 13 debate would be held anyway, implying that it would. This preoccupation with whether all scheduled debates would be held was characteristic of all the coverage the story received. The League was now, indeed, "history." There was no follow-up story on October 4. Instead CBS was preoccupied with doing advance stories about the October 5 Quayle-Bentsen confrontation.

ABC's Coverage

ABC did a much longer story (a minute and 52 seconds) and used a production package with reaction interviews and sound bites. Peter Jennings, in introducing the package, said the League had used "some extremely strong language" in withdrawing. Correspondent Barry Serafin paraphrased all of Neuman's complaints: "Neuman complained that the Bush and Dukakis campaigns, as in the first debate, insisted on controlling the format, the camera shots, and deciding on who would ask questions, and who would be in the hall."

There was no further development of these ideas. The only direct bite from Neuman was her two-sentence vow that the League would not be an "accessory to the hoodwinking of the American public." Reactions from Dukakis (a sound bite), the Bush campaign, and the Commission's Janet Brown (another bite) followed. Serafin's piece concluded with the reassurance that the Los Angeles debate would very likely be held anyway.

Jennings followed the Serafin piece with this rather muddy and ambiguous 9-second epilogue: "At one point today, all four of the television networks—ABC, CBS, NBC, and CNN—offered to sponsor the debate. No rules, no regulations were even discussed."

MacNeil-Lehrer's Coverage

Easily the most extensive broadcast coverage we saw was the nearly 11-minute interview conducted by Robert MacNeil with Neuman and with his own partner, Jim Lehrer, on their PBS show on the evening of October 3. Midway through the segment, Lehrer was brought on, as the moderator of the September 25 debate, to dispute Neuman's claim that the campaign-imposed rules had hamstrung the panelists.

In his usual careful manner, MacNeil gave Neuman plenty of chances to spell out all her objections to format and ground rules. But running under his questions was this unspoken perspective: Compared with what the League had already given up to the campaigns in 1976, 1980, and

1984, why are you so excited, *now*, about these concessions they wanted from you? "You can't in the end tell" men who are running for president "how to campaign for it, and I just wonder how you feel about that in this case," MacNeil asked Neuman. Later, MacNeil asked Neuman whether she felt "your ploy today to force a different kind of format . . . has now been defeated," since the debate would be held anyway—without the League.

Jeff Greenfield on "Nightline"

ABC's Greenfield, usually a thoughtful observer of campaigns, gave the League's withdrawal that very day just 34 seconds on his weekly 30-minute program about the campaign. After the "hoodwinking" bite from Neuman, Greenfield gave the now-familiar closing assurance that the October 13 debate would be held anyway. Almost all the program was devoted to items that apparently had already been produced and packaged as advance stories on the Quayle-Bentsen debate two nights later.

Prestige Newspaper Coverage

Both the *Washington Post* and the *New York Times* ran 11-paragraph stories October 4 under three-column headlines on the back pages of their news sections. The *Times* article, by David E. Rosenbaum, led with both the withdrawal by the League and the assurance that the final debate would be held as scheduled. The second paragraph used the Neuman quote about "becoming an accessory to the hoodwinking of the American people." Paragraphs 3,4,5, and 6 all concerned arrangements for the final debate, and the remaining paragraphs returned to the League's rationale for withdrawing.

The *Post* story, by Lloyd Grove, led with the League withdrawal announcement, but its second, third, and fourth paragraphs concerned arrangements for holding the final debate anyway. Interestingly, the *Post* story seemed more preoccupied with the question of whether the League would turn over its reservation of the Shrine Auditorium to the Commission, rather than with the League's fundamental criticisms of both campaigns' control of the Commission and of the debate ground rules.

Ironically, the same issue of the *Post* also carried a long, much more prominently displayed (page one, top left) story by David Hoffman, whose lead was about an order to an aide from Bush Campaign Manager James Baker to call the debate producer *during* the September 25 debate, asking moderator Jim Lehrer to shift the debate topic to foreign policy. This revealing juxtaposition at least did not escape the attention of the writer of a letter to the editor of the *Washington Post*, printed October 12: "[The page one story] emphasizes exactly the problem that led to the

League's withdrawal. . . . This is precisely what the League meant when it complained about the campaign's manipulations . . .'' (Boisvert 1988).

Meanwhile, back on that October 4 front page, Hoffman's story went on to say that the telephone incident illustrated Baker's ''trademark [of] disciplined political management.'' No connection was made in Hoffman's story to the League's complaint about the two campaigns' micromanagement of the debates. Also in that same October 4 issue, the *Post* editorialized that the League might have some good ideas about format, but in the last analysis the League's wish to have a say in debate rules was unrealistic. Thus, the League's withdrawal ''is an acceptance of reality.'' The Commission, the editorial said, is destined from now on to be the sole sponsor of fall presidential debates.

(Some of the intellectual justification for the Commission as sole sponsor was set forth by former Federal Communications Commissioner Newton Minnow and attorney Clifford M. Sloan in a paper written for the Twentieth Century Fund [1987]. Minnow-Sloan's paper purported to represent the consensus of those invited to a Harvard University forum on the future of the debates, a contention that at least two participants— Neuman and her colleague, Vicky Harian Strella (1990)—flatly deny.[7] The Minnow-Sloan argument, which was similar to the *Washington Post's* editorial of October 3, was that only an organization formed by the political parties had the clout to guarantee that whoever was nominated would debate. (In our final chapter, we shall return to the issue of who is best situated to sponsor the debates.)

Guess Who Talks about Format?

We said earlier in this chapter that journalists were no more likely than other sources to criticize the debate format, but there was one very revealing exception to that finding: *Whenever TV journalists were on the debate panel, they seemed very preoccupied with telling us the limits they had to cope with.* For example, while Jennings's October 3 evening news spent a minute and 52 seconds on the entire League withdrawal story, including extended reactions from the campaigns, panelist Jennings himself spent more time than that discussing format limitations with David Brinkley and James Baker on ABC's post-debate analysis show September 25: (Jennings to James Baker) ''You are the man who created this debate format in such a fashion that we reporters didn't have much of a chance to re-ask questions, but . . . why not, in Los Angeles, let them debate freely and without journalists present?''

Including comments by Baker and by Brinkley in response to widely separated questions from Jennings about the format, some *23 more seconds were spent on the problem of format when Jennings was a panelist than his newscast spent on the entire League withdrawal story.*

It was interesting to see as well that Jennings did not, in anchoring the October 3 story about the League, in any way connect his September 25 questions and concerns to the League withdrawal.

Another example from 1988 came on NBC's post-debate analysis of the final debate. NBC's Andrea Mitchell, complimented by anchor Tom Brokaw for her presence on the panel, shortly thereafter said the following: "Neither [Dukakis nor Bush] ever really answered the key questions [about the budget deficit] . . . . Try as we might, we didn't really get them off their program [programmed answers] . . . . As you know, Tom, because you were on last week's panel, how difficult it is to get around this format. And that, I think, is the overriding problem."

One of them, at least.

CONCLUSION

Ultimately, the existence of presidential debates contributes to the legitimacy of American presidential elections only if the debates themselves are seen as a fair and open opportunity for voters to gain insight and knowledge about the candidates. Therefore it is important to examine news media treatment of the debates as political institutions, regardless of whether one feels it is the "duty" of the news media to support the political legitimacy of presidential elections. One could also say that the question of the legitimacy of the debates is important, regardless of whether the elections themselves "deserve" to be legitimized.

The general impression created by both content analysis and qualitative accounts presented in this chapter is that media personnel were concerned about the institutional aspects of the debates primarily as those aspects affected *them* and the ambitions of other elites, not as they aided or harmed voters' decision-making processes. Increasingly, over time, the post-debate news analyses cast the importance of the debates in terms of candidate aspirations, not the needs of the voters. *Broadcasting* and *Newsweek*, each in its own way, tended to view the debates as opportunities for ambitious media, as well as for ambitious candidates. Only the *New York Times* seemed consistently aware of voters' needs and how the debates might serve them. When the League of Women Voters rejected the terms being imposed on it by the 1988 campaigns, journalists seemed far more interested in whether they would have another debate to cover than with whether the voters would lose anything in the bargain.

NOTES

1. In 1988 NBC was the only network not to have post-debate news "specials" on every debate. For the September 25 Bush-Dukakis debate, NBC resumed its

coverage of the Olympics after a brief wrap-up. The only other exception occurred on September 23, 1976, either because ABC did not do a news special following the first Ford-Carter debate or the ABC affiliate being taped at the Vanderbilt Television News Archives did not carry the program. Even in this case, however, we were able to analyze ABC's wrap-up.

2. The legal troubles that ensued from the 27-minute audio gap centered on the claim of independent candidates that if, in fact, the debate had been a "*bona fide* news event,'' the debate would have continued without television coverage.

3. In her telephone conversation with Lemert, Neuman generally remained committed to not publicly discussing demands made by the campaigns while the League was still negotiating as a potential sponsor of the debates, but seemed puzzled that journalists were not very interested in the same information after the debates were all over.

4. Neuman told Lemert that making the announcement in time to allow the debate to be put on by somebody else was an important reason for the timing.

5. Most of these editorials were packaged by the League and sent to the authors, so we cannot be sure how many other papers supported the League's action or opposed it.

6. Some columnists, such as Mary McGrory of the *Washington Post* (1988) strongly supported the League in follow-up pieces, and a few news stories followed as well, such as one in the *Boston Globe*, which also was part of the package sent by the League to the authors.

7. Neuman and Strella both were invited participants at the Harvard conference. Strella was the chief LWV staff person handling the debates in 1984 and debate negotiations in 1988. Each said many of the other participants disagreed with part or all of the Minnow-Sloan account of the consensus reached at the conference.

REFERENCES

And then there were two. 1980. *Newsweek*, September 22, 25.

Bishop, G. F., R. W. Oldendick, and A. J. Tuchfarber. 1978. The presidential debates as a device for increasing the "rationality" of electoral behavior. In *The presidential debates: Media, electoral and policy perspectives*, ed. G. F. Bishop, R. G. Meadow, and M. Jackson-Beeck, 179–196. New York: Praeger Publishers.

Boisvert, L. B. 1988. No wonder the League withdrew. Letter to the editor, *Washington Post*, October 12, A18.

A boost for the stay-at-home. 1980. *Newsweek*, October 6, 40–42.

Chaffee, S. H., and J. Dennis. 1979. Presidential debates: An empirical assessment. In *The past and future of presidential debates*, ed. A. Ranney, 75–101. Washington: American Enterprise Institute for Public Policy Research.

The debate and the spin doctors. 1984. *New York Times*, October 21, E22.

Debates, domesticated. 1988. *New York Times*, September 27, A34.

Dennis, J., and S. H. Chaffee. 1978. Legitimation in the 1976 U.S. election campaign. *Communication Research* 5:371–393.

Diamond, E., and K. Friery. 1987. Media coverage of presidential debates. In *The presidential debates: 1988 and beyond*, ed. J. L. Swerdlow, 45–53. Washington, D.C.: Congressional Quarterly, Inc.

An empty chair. 1980. *New York Times*, September 11, A18.

Excess baggage. 1980. *Broadcasting*, November 3, 106.

Extra baggage. 1984. *Broadcasting*, October 15, 98.

For the people. 1988. *Broadcasting*, September 12, 114.

The great debate. 1984. *Newsweek*, October 15, 30–34.

In the way again. 1980. *Broadcasting*, September 29, 90.

Jamieson, K. H., and D. S. Birdsell. 1988. *Presidential debates: The challenge of creating an informed electorate*. New York and Oxford: Oxford University Press.

Katz, E., and J. J. Feldman. 1962. The debates in the light of research: A survey of surveys. In *The great debates: Kennedy vs. Nixon, 1960*, ed. S. Kraus, 173–223. Bloomington and London: Indiana University Press.

Kraus, S. 1988. *Televised presidential debates and public policy*. Hillsdale, N.J.: Lawrence Erlbaum Associates.

Lectern to lectern. 1988. *Newsweek*, November 21, 139.

Lemert, J. B. 1981a. *Simple reductionism in the study of media effects: How we got there, and are we stuck with it?* Invited paper presented to the Spring Conference, Mass Communication and Society Division, Association for Education in Journalism, Kent, Ohio, March 21.

Lemert, J. B. 1981b. *Does mass communication change public opinion after all? A new approach to effects analysis*. Chicago: Nelson-Hall.

Lemert, J. B., W. R. Elliott, K. J. Nestvold, and G. R. Rarick. 1983. Effects of viewing a presidential primary debate. *Communication Research* 10:155–173.

Lights-camera-candidates! 1976. *New York Times*, September 24, A24.

Long shot. 1976. *Broadcasting*, August 30, 66.

McGrory, M. 1988. The League puts its foot down. *Washington Post*, October 6, A-2.

Miller, A. H., and M. MacKuen. 1979. Informing the electorate: A national study. In *The great debates: Carter vs. Ford, 1976*, ed. S. Kraus, 269–297. Bloomington: Indiana University Press.

Minnow, N. N., and C. M. Sloan. 1987. *For great debates: A new plan for future presidential TV debates*. New York: Priority Press Publications.

A naked look at the debate. 1980. *New York Times*, October 17, A30.

Neuman, N. 1990. Telephone interview with Lemert, March 8.

Out of their League? 1980. *Newsweek*, September 8, 21.

Political device. 1976. *Broadcasting*, September 27, 106.

Rabbits and reality in Louisville. 1984. *New York Times*, October 7, E20.

Rerun. 1980. *Broadcasting*, September 1, 74.

The rise and fall of the age issue. 1984. *Newsweek* special issue, November/December, 103–109.

Running against the television party. 1980. *New York Times*, September 14, E20.

Sears, D. O., and S. H. Chaffee. 1979. Uses and effects of the 1976 debates: An

overview of empirical studies. In *The great debates; Carter vs. Ford, 1976*, ed. S. Kraus, 223–261. Bloomington: Indiana University Press.
Sure loser in the debate: The format. 1988. *New York Times*, October 15, 30.
Too much of a bad thing. 1988. *Broadcasting*, October 17, 98.
The veep showdown. 1988. *Newsweek*, October 10, 40–41.
Why not debate now? 1984. *New York Times*, October 8, A26.

6

THE FIRST BUSH-DUKAKIS DEBATE: FACE-TO-FACE CONTACT

The first 1988 presidential candidate debate took place on September 25 between George Bush, the Republican, and Michael Dukakis, the Democrat. Its estimated audience of 100 million saw what most interpreted as an uneventful debate: no major slips, no major victories. What the audience did see—most of them for the first time—was the two candidates facing a potentially hostile panel of questioners, in new campaign territory where their usual shield of handlers, consultants, friends, and managers could not help.

Before this debate, the candidates initiated appropriate campaign strategies. *Time* magazine (Shapiro 1988) summarized Bush's basic strategy: to put Michael Dukakis on the defensive by attacking his patriotism, his stand on crime, and his position on national defense. Reports were circulating in the press about Bush's attempts to "lower expectations" of his debating skills by portraying Michael Dukakis as a professional debater who sharpened his skills as the moderator of public television's issue program, "The Advocates."

The timing and structure of the debates raised important questions for the candidates (Germond and Witcover 1989). The Dukakis team knew their candidate had been falling behind in the polls. Strong performance in a series of debates was his best hope for regaining voter support. They wanted four debates, three between the presidential candidates and one pairing their running mates. Bush's strategists, Jim Baker and Roger Ailes, saw the debates differently, as a possible threat. They wanted to limit the number of debates and to have the final debate as far from election day as possible, allowing time to correct any problems should the need develop. During the debate negotiations, they presented a "take it or leave it" offer to Dukakis's team; three debates to be held between September 25 and October 15. No exceptions. Dukakis's team agreed.

Pre-debate expectations among the members of the press ran high, particularly in response to their limited contact with the candidates. Shapiro (1988, p. 19) noted a period in September when George Bush went 13 days with only one press availability, and that lasted only 13 minutes! He summarized the hopes of many: "While debates are not an automatic panacea for pablum, seeing Bush and Dukakis at long last without their canned daily messages or scenic backdrops can only elevate the campaign."

Network hopes also were high. At CBS, Dan Rather, Bob Schieffer, and Bruce Morton discussed the difficulties faced by journalists as they attempted to cover the issues of the campaign. On the Friday before the Sunday debate, Dan Rather and Leslie Stahl pointed out that these "joint appearances" (Dan Rather did not refer to them as debates) "can help win or cost the election." They also commented on the role of the spin doctors, since what is said after such a "joint appearance" can be as important as the debate itself.

Carried live by the three commercial networks, CNN, and public broadcasting, the first debate had an audience of approximately 100 million. While it proved to be a ratings success, nothing unexpected happened during the debate. Both candidates stressed what they had emphasized in their campaigns. Hershey's (1989) content analysis of the debate showed that Dukakis tended to emphasize domestic programs—health care, drugs, housing, and the national debt—while Bush emphasized education. Bush repeatedly used references to Michael Dukakis's liberalism. At CBS, post-debate analysis focused on spin doctoring, Bush's movement from early nervousness to being in control, and Dukakis's ability to project an image of being steady, reliable, and competent.

Evaluations of the performance of the candidates during the debate varied somewhat, but almost all agreed that neither candidate had scored a decisive victory or suffered a major defeat. Other interpretations rated the debaters as near equals. Germond and Witcover (1989) suggested that Dukakis had won but "not by a knockout." A poll of 337 registered voters conducted just after the debate by *Newsweek* ("Playing hardball" 1988) indicated a virtual tie: 42% picked Dukakis as the winner, 41% picked Bush. A CBS poll of about 600 probable voters aired on September 26 saw it about the same: 39% thought Dukakis had won, compared with 42% who favored Bush. What was clear, at least by the interpretation of many in the audience and many members of the press, was that neither candidate had emerged as a clear winner.

However, as evaluated in network post-debate analyses, Dukakis came out on top. Lowry, Bridges, and Barefield (in press) content-analyzed post-debate commentary by ABC, CBS, and CNN. They found that ABC and CBS were favorable to Dukakis, while CNN gave the verdict to Bush. Our own analysis of post-debate commentary by ABC and CBS (see Chapter 4) showed that Michael Dukakis, with 70.1% positive verdicts, was seen as performing much better than George Bush, with only 42.1% verdicts rated positively; the percentage of negative verdicts for Dukakis was but 17.9%, while for Bush it reached 48.7%. In terms of possible post-debate analysis influence, the most important poll was the one done by ABC. Just before completing their post-debate analysis, they reported the results of a poll of 500 debate viewers. Dukakis was seen as the winner of the debate by 45% of this sample, Bush by 36%.

The lead news story at ABC and CBS on September 26, the night after the debate, was about the possible use of steroids by Canadian sprinter and 100 meter Olympic gold medal champion, Ben Johnson. Debate analysis followed. At ABC, the consensus was that the debate did not mark a turning point in the campaign for either candidate. At CBS, whether or not George Bush favored criminal penalties for women seeking abortions (brought up in response to a debate question) was the primary debate issue discussed. On September 27, ABC reported that poll results concerning the debates were inconclusive. The debate was not mentioned by CBS. On September 28, ABC presented the results of a debate winner poll, giving it to Bush by a 50 to 46 percent margin. Coverage of the debate, after September 26, was minimal. Like other daily campaign events, it had become a small story, something lost in the move to capture the next event, the vice-presidential debate.

POSSIBLE INFLUENCE OF THE DEBATE AND POST-DEBATE ANALYSIS

There are a number of possible ways the debate and post debate analysis might influence voters. Our content analysis indicated a strong pro-Dukakis bias in the immediate post-debate analysis aired on ABC and CBS. If audiences do, as many have suggested, rely on media interpretations to guide their own performance evaluations, then it should be expected that those who watched post-debate analysis on ABC or CBS would have evaluated Dukakis more favorably than Bush. Those not watching the debate or not watching post-debate analysis or both, should be comparatively less favorable to Dukakis and more favorable to Bush.

Another way of testing this assumption would be to compare people interviewed before the debate with those interviewed on debate night and later. If people were picking up media interpretations of the debate performance of the candidates, then those interviewed after the debate should differ from those interviewed before—that is, the "after group" should be more favorable toward Dukakis.

It is not quite that easy, however. Clearly, coverage of the debate on television fell to nearly zero after September 26, the night following the debate. By September 27 the debate had become just another old campaign story. If repetition of a story is necessary before the public comes to accept it, then perhaps candidate evaluations would begin to return to their pre-debate levels as the time since the debate increased. Certainly, no clear issue emerged from the debate that the press continued to carry. To attempt to make sense of some of this, we asked the following questions:

- What was the impact of the debate on voters' evaluations of the candidates, on who they think won the debate, and on which candidate would get their vote?
- What was the impact of post-debate analysis on voters' evaluations of the candidates, on who they think won the debate, and on which candidate would get their vote?

To test the influence of the debate on voters, comparisons between voters interviewed before the debate with those interviewed the night of the debate and afterward should illuminate any differences that exist. Also, since we are using a time-series design, day-by-day changes in voter evaluations should be apparent.

To test the influence of post-debate analysis on the voters, comparisons between subjects interviewed on debate night and later who had seen or had not seen post-debate analysis should provide evidence of differences, if any. Because of the immediacy of the interviews conducted on September 25, right after the debate, the differences here should be most visible, occurring as they did before other influences could take effect—influences such as news accounts and judgments and talks with family, friends, and co-workers.

METHOD

We conducted our first investigation of audience exposure to the debate and post-debate analysis using a time-series design starting on September 22, 1988, and continuing four days beyond the September 25 debate until September 29. Telephone interviews, with the numbers selected using random digit dialing techniques, were conducted in Philadelphia, Pennsylvania; Eugene-Springfield, Oregon; and Carbondale, Illinois. Interviewing normally began at about 7:00 P.M. and continued for approximately three hours. On the night of the debate, interviewing began immediately after the debate and continued as long as possible, until 11:00 P.M. in Philadelphia, 10:30 P.M. in Carbondale, and 10:00 P.M. in the Eugene area. A total of 798 interviews were completed in this time series, with a completion rate of 62.8%. The study design is diagramed in Figure 6.1.

Parallel questionnaires were administered at each location. Interviewers were instructed to interview the voting-age person available in the household whose birthday was closest to the time of the call. This procedure allowed us to balance male/female bias. Each interview lasted approximately 20 minutes.

VARIABLES AND ANALYSIS

Independent Variables

The independent variables of primary interest were those relating to debate exposure and the day of the interview. Beginning on September 25, immediately after the debate, each subject was also asked, "Did you watch or listen to Sunday night's debate between Michael Dukakis and George Bush?" If the respondents answered yes, their responses were coded to indicate whether they watched the debate only or both the debate and the post-debate analysis. We asked those who had indicated watching the debate which television network they had watched it on.

In addition to measures of time and debate exposure, we were interested in political affiliation and interest in the campaign. We measured the following variables based on responses to these questions:

• *Party Affiliation.* "Do you consider yourself a Republican, Democrat, Independent, or what?" Responses to this question allowed us to classify the subjects as Republicans, Democrats, and Independents/others.

• *Campaign Interest.* "At this stage in the 1988 campaign, how would you describe your interest in the presidential campaign? Would you say you are uninterested or interested in the campaign? If the subjects indicated "uninterested" or "interested," they were asked this follow-up question: "Would you say you are very uninterested (interested) or somewhat uninterested (interested)?" Those who indicated neither lack of interest nor interest were coded in the middle. Because of the high proportion of subjects indicating they were

Presidential Candidate Debate One
September 25, 1988

Debate - 3	Debate - 2	Debate - 1	Debate Night	Debate + 1	Debate + 2	Debate + 3	Debate + 4

Figure 6.1
First Presidential Candidate Debate Study Design

somewhat or very interested in the campaign, we combined the "very uninterested," "somewhat uninterested," and "neutral" responses into a single category for our analyses.

Demographic Measures. We also asked a number of demographic questions about sex, age, and education (measured in the number of total years), and we coded the location where the interview took place. Differences between the three locales on our demographic variables are presented in Table 6.1.

Differences in a number of the demographic variables and political variables did exist in the September 22–29 sample among our three communities. The proportion of women in the Eugene sample (58.1%) was higher than at either Carbondale (47.5%) or Philadelphia (52.7%). Reported family income was highest in Philadelphia, which also had the highest percentage of respondents indicating that they held full time jobs (61.8%). Carbondale was the best educated (average number of years of schooling at 14.8) as well as the youngest (average age 38.0). Politically, Republicans had the strongest representation in Carbondale (33.4%) while, at the other extreme, Democrats made up 59.3% of the Philadelphia sample. All three communities were similar in their levels of campaign interest.

Because of the differences between the communities, locale was used as a control variable in many of the analyses. In addition to locale, we also controlled for party affiliation, campaign interest, and sex.

Dependent Variables

Our dependent variables are classified into three groups: debate performance, candidate image, and voting intention. We used three measures of debate performance.

1. *Ratings as Debaters.* Each subject was asked to evaluate each of the two candidates using a "scale running from 0 to 10, where 0 means very weak and 10 very strong.[11] Specifically, respondents were asked, "How would you rate Michael Dukakis as a debater?" and "Last, as a debater, how would you rate George Bush?"

2. *Debate Winner.* Subjects interviewed before the September 25 debate were asked, "Who do you think will win Sunday night's presidential debate?" Follow-ups were used for subjects who indicated either Bush or Dukakis as the winner. Those who said "neither" were coded at the midpoint, 3. If they indicated a possible winner, they were asked, "Would you say that George Bush/Michael Dukakis will win by a lot or by a little?" Responses for George Bush winning by a lot were coded as "1," Michael Dukakis by a lot as a "5." Those subjects interviewed on September 25 and later were asked the same question, rephrased as, "Who do you think won Sunday's presidential debate?"

3. *Debate Performance Descriptions.* We also attempted to measure

Table 6.1
Demographic and Political Variables, by Location

Variables	Carbondale	Eugene	Philadelphia
Sex*			
Female	47.5%	58.1%	52.7%
Male	52.5%	41.9%	47.3%
N responding	297	315	169
Family Income**			
Less than $10,000	29.3%	20.6%	6.9%
$10,000 to $20,000	22.3%	21.1%	30.0%
$20,000 to $30,000	13.2%	22.1%	15.6%
$30,000 to $50,000	23.4%	21.6%	28.1%
More than $50,000	11.7%	14.6%	19.4%
N responding	273	199	160
Occupation**			
Full-Time Job	38.8%	46.0%	61.8%
Part-Time Job	8.6%	9.5%	4.6%
Student	31.6%	15.6%	9.8%
Retired	12.0%	14.3%	13.9%
Homemaker	5.2%	10.8%	6.9%
Unemployed	3.8%	3.8%	2.9%
N responding	291	315	173
Years Education (Mean)**	14.8	14.3	14.0
N responding	289	316	174
Age (Mean)**	38.0	42.6	41.0
N responding	289	316	174
Party Affiliation**			
Republican	33.4%	30.2%	24.0%
Democrat	29.6%	46.9%	59.3%
Independent/Other	37.0%	22.9%	16.8%
N responding	287	311	167
Campaign Interest			
Uninterested, Neutral	25.3%	24.9%	24.7%
Somewhat Interested	35.8%	39.1%	34.1%
Very Interested	38.9%	36.0%	41.2%
N responding	293	317	170
Total N	303	321	174

*   Difference between locales $p \leq .05$. Chi-square tests used for categorical variables, analysis of variance for ratio measures (age, education).
**   Difference between locales $p \leq .01$.

how the respondents described the candidates' debate performances using open-ended questions. On debate night and afterward, each respondent, whether she/he had seen the debate or not, was asked, "If you had to choose a word or two to describe the performance of George Bush during the debate, what would that word be?" A parallel question was asked about Michael Dukakis. We then categorized the answers of those who responded into negative (weak, cocky, questionable, a clown, boring, etc.); neutral (average, sincere, cautious, passable, satisfactory, etc.), and positive (good, excellent, likable, businesslike, informed, intelligent, trustworthy, mature, etc.). Thus, for each candidate, there was a score ranging from 1 (negative description) to 3 (positive).

Summed Candidate Image Scale. We looked at the influence of the debate on evaluations of each candidate's "image." To develop our measure of candidate image, we used each subject's evaluations of the candidates in terms of his knowledge of domestic issues, ability to lead the country, poise and self-confidence under pressure, and knowledge of foreign and defense policies. We used factor analysis to verify the existence of two dimensions on this variable (Bush, Dukakis) and checked the adequacy of summed scales developed using these measures. As a measure of the internal reliability of our summed scales, we computed Cronbach's alpha. Generally, alpha's in the range of .80 and higher are considered acceptable for the use of summated scales (Carmines and Zeller 1979). For the Michael Dukakis image variables, the standardized Cronbach's alpha was .86; for George Bush the rating was .82.

Each subject was asked to use a scale running from 0 (very weak) to 10 (very strong) to evaluate Bush and Dukakis separately with regard to (1) knowledge of domestic issues, (2) ability to lead the country, (3) poise and self-confidence under pressure, and (4) knowledge of foreign and defense policy.

Voting Intentions

Our final set of dependent variables was designed to evaluate the respondents' voting intentions.

1. *Candidate Voting Probability.* Again, we used the same type of 0 to 10 rating procedure, only this time 0 meant they definitely would not vote for the candidate and 10 that they definitely would.

2. *Today's Vote.* Immediately after the candidate voting probability question, the subjects were asked, "If you had to vote today for one of the candidates, who would you vote for?" Responses were coded for Bush, Dukakis, "other," and "don't know."

Analyses

We used several statistical techniques in analyzing our data. For many of the analyses, where the dependent variables represented interval level measures, we used "Multiple Classification Analysis." This technique, which is based on the linear regression model, allows the use of categorical and interval level variables as independent variables predicting interval-level-measure dependent variables. One of the primary benefits of Multiple Classification Analysis (MCA) is that it allows the calculation of mean scores for the dependent variable within each category of independent variable *after the influence of all other variables has been controlled.* This is the "adjusted mean score" for each group within the various MCA tables presented in this chapter.

When looking at a single categorical independent variable and an interval-measure-dependent variable, we used a one-way analysis of variance with tests for between group differences using the Scheffè test. This conservative test allowed us to investigate whether the differences between any of our groups could be attributed to chance or if the differences exceeded chance expectations. And finally, in those situations where both our independent and dependent variables were measured categorically, we relied on the analysis of cross-tabulations. In situations with small sample sizes, we used Fisher's Exact Test; otherwise, we used the Chi-square statistic.

RESULTS

Debate Performance

Ratings as Debaters and Debate Winner. Figure 6.2 presents the graphic representation of changes in subject evaluation of the candidates as debaters during the three days before the debate (September 22–24), through debate night (September 25), and for the four days following (September 26–29). The figure shows that Michael Dukakis's debater ratings remained fairly even over the time period, while George Bush's rose rapidly on debate night and then fell off afterward.

The relationships suggested in Figure 6.2 are borne out in Table 6.2. In this Multiple Classification Analysis, the column entries represent the adjusted mean scores for each of the variables being measured. George Bush's rating as a debater changed significantly over the interviewing period. The comparatively large Beta attached to the time of interview (.21) shows that the interview date was one of the two strongest predictors of George Bush's debater rating. His average pre-debate rating was 5.65 on a 10-point scale. That rating jumped to 6.64 on debate night (September 25), continued at a 6.29 level the next night, and then returned to approximately its pre-debate levels on September 27 through 29. No parallel pattern was observed for Michael Dukakis's debater rating. For our sample, Dukakis was consistently evaluated as a strong debater over the eight-day interviewing cycle.

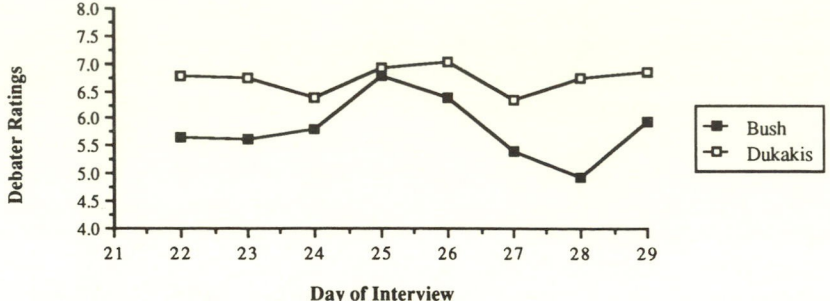

Figure 6.2
Presidential Candidate Ratings as Debaters, by Day

As we expected, party affiliation was significantly related to the debater ratings of both candidates. Republicans rated George Bush at 6.68, Democrats at 5.29, and Independents—in the middle—at 5.75. Republicans rated Michael Dukakis at 6.22, Democrats at 7.12, and Independents—again in the middle—at 6.67. As a debater, our sample seemed to prefer Dukakis. Republicans rated Dukakis much higher (6.22) than Democrats rated Bush (5.29). It appears that Bush might have been successful beforehand in lowering the public's expectations about his abilities as a debater. Unfortunately, from Bush's perspective, the comparatively low ratings seem to have returned just a couple of days after the debate. He seemingly gained little debating ground on Michael Dukakis.

Debater ratings were also significantly influenced by campaign interest. Campaign interest was related to candidate debater ratings. The uninterested in the campaign rated George Bush fairly low as a debater (5.49), while those indicating they were "somewhat interested" or "very interested" rated him higher (6.01 and 5.85, respectively). The pattern for Michael Dukakis appears linear, with increases in debater ratings rising with increases in interest. The uninterested gave him the lowest rating (6.37), with the middle rating for the "somewhat interested" (6.57) and the highest rating by the "very interested" (7.08). There was also a slight difference between men and women in the evaluation of George Bush as a debater. Women rated Bush higher (5.99) than did the men in our sample (5.67). No statistically significant difference between men and women was found for the ratings of Michael Dukakis.

We also present the debate winner measures in Table 6.2. On this 5-point scale, a "1" indicated that George Bush had "won by a lot," whereas a "5" indicated that Michael Dukakis had "won by a lot." In the middle, a 3 indicated that neither had won or that it had been a tie.

Table 6.2
Multiple Classification Analysis: Adjusted Mean Scores for Ratings as Debaters and Debate Winner, by Time of Interview, Party, Campaign Interest, Locale, and Sex (September 22 to September 29 Cycle)

Independent Measures	Ratings as Debaters		Debate Winner
	Bush	Dukakis	
Grand Mean	5.83	6.73	3.31
Time of Interview			
September 22-24 (Before Debate)	5.65	6.62	3.20
September 25 (Debate Night)	6.64	6.91	3.22
September 26	6.29	7.02	3.33
September 27	5.55	6.26	3.32
September 28	5.09	6.74	3.46
September 29	5.85	6.94	3.45
Beta	.21**	.12	.10
Party Affiliation			
Republican	6.68	6.22	2.67
Democrat	5.29	7.12	3.73
Independent/Other	5.75	6.67	3.34
Beta	.28**	.20**	.42**
Campaign Interest			
Uninterested, Neutral	5.49	6.37	3.18
Somewhat Interested	6.01	6.57	3.23
Very Interested	5.85	7.08	3.43
Beta	.09*	.15**	.11*
Locale			
Carbondale	5.92	6.87	3.30
Philadelphia	6.05	6.75	3.35
Eugene	5.62	6.58	3.30
Beta	.08	.07	.02
Sex			
Female	5.99	6.74	3.31
Male	5.67	6.72	3.31
Beta	.08*	.00	.00
Multiple R^2	14.7%**	7.9%**	20.2%**
Total N	659	640	503

* $p < .05$
** $p < .01$

(Subjects interviewed before debate night were asked who they thought would win.) In this case, the time of interview did not seem to influence perceptions of the debate winner.

Perceptions of the winner of the debate were influenced by party affiliation and campaign interest. Republicans leaned toward Bush (mean = 2.67), Democrats favored Dukakis (3.73), and Independents/others also tilted in Dukakis's direction (3.34). Again, the strength of partisan predispositions is evident. The higher the political interest, the greater the perception of Dukakis as the debate winner.

MCA results for the same dependent variables, this time excluding those subjects interviewed before debate night and looking at exposure to the debate and to post-debate analysis, are presented in Table 6.3. Here we were interested in the influence of debate viewing and post-debate analysis. These findings, which present the adjusted mean scores after controlling for party affiliation, campaign interest, locale, and sex, show that neither watching the debate nor watching the debate and post-debate analysis had a measurable impact on evaluations of George Bush as a debater, but that exposure to the debate and to post-debate analysis was an important factor for Michael Dukakis. Here Dukakis's highest debater rating was for those who watched the *debate plus analysis* (7.21), followed by debate-only viewers (6.56) and non-viewers (6.40). Dukakis apparently benefited from both coverage and analysis.

As in the analysis presented in Table 6.2, political party affiliation was related, as would be expected, to ratings of the candidates as debaters. Republicans rated George Bush at 6.77 on our 0-to-10-point debater rating scale, Democrats rated him at 5.44, and Independents gave him a 5.77. The parallel adjusted mean ratings for Michael Dukakis were 6.44, 7.03, and 6.83 respectively. Campaign interest remained an important factor for Michael Dukakis's ratings as a debater, with those least interested in the campaign rating him at 6.44, the "somewhat interested" at 6.66, and the "very interested" at 7.09. No statistically significant debater-rating differences were found for locale or sex. Party affiliation was the only one of our independent variables to be related to perceptions of the debate winner. As in Table 6.2, Republicans gave the nod to Bush (adjusted mean = 2.86), while Democrats (3.68) and Independents (3.44) picked Dukakis.

In Table 6.4 we look at the influence of exposure to debate and post-debate analysis on debater ratings and perceptions of the debate winner, this time for the night of the debate only. Exposure to the debate and post-debate analysis had an influence on only one of our dependent variables, the rating of Michael Dukakis as a debater. Interviewees who had watched both the debate and the post-debate analysis rated Michael Dukakis at 7.88 on our 0-to-10 rating scale. This rating compares with

Table 6.3
Multiple Classification Analysis: Adjusted Mean Scores for Candidate Ratings as Debaters and Debate Winner, by Debate and Post-Debate Analysis Exposure, Party, Campaign Interest, Locale, and Sex (Debate Night, September 25, to September 29 Cycle)

Independent Measures	Ratings as Debaters		Debate Winner
	Bush	Dukakis	
Grand Mean	5.93	6.80	3.38
Debate and Post-Debate Analysis			
Neither Debate nor Analysis	6.02	6.40	3.28
Debate Only	5.71	6.56	3.29
Debate Plus Analysis	6.00	7.21	3.48
Beta	.06	.19**	.10
Party Affiliation			
Republican	6.77	6.44	2.86
Democrat	5.44	7.03	3.68
Independent/Other	5.77	6.83	3.44
Beta	.28**	.13*	.35**
Campaign Interest			
Uninterested, Neutral	5.53	6.44	3.28
Somewhat Interested	6.03	6.66	3.32
Very Interested	6.02	7.09	3.46
Beta	.10	.13*	.08
Locale			
Carbondale	5.98	6.81	3.38
Philadelphia	6.10	7.00	3.44
Eugene	5.78	6.68	3.34
Beta	.06	.06	.04
Sex			
Female	6.07	6.89	3.44
Male	5.80	6.71	3.32
Beta	.07	.05	.06
Multiple R^2	9.2%**	10.3%**	15.6%**
Total N	428	427	336

* $p < .05$
** $p < .01$

Table 6.4
One-Way Analysis of Variance: Mean Scores for Ratings as Debaters and Debate
Winner, by Debate and Post-Debate Analysis Exposure (Debate Night Only)

	Ratings as Debaters		
Independent Measures	Bush	Dukakis[1]	Debate Winner
Grand Mean	6.75	6.88	3.12
Debate and Analysis			
Neither Debate nor Analysis	6.48	5.67	2.40
Debate Only	6.37	6.68	3.20
Debate Plus Analysis	7.11	7.88*	3.19
Total N	96	96	57

[1] Significant difference between groups, $F_{2,93} = 14.85$, p ,< .01.
* Differs from the "Neither Debate nor Analysis" and the "Debate Only" groups, p ≤ .10, Scheffé Test.

6.68 for those who watched only the debate, and with 5.67 for those watching neither the debate nor the post-debate analysis.

Debate Performance Descriptions. We analyzed the open-ended candidate descriptions of subjects who had watched the debate for debate night only and for the September 25–29 cycle. The responses, cross-tabulated by debate and post-debate analysis viewing, are presented in Table 6.5. Coverage by NBC-TV is excluded from this analysis because no post-debate analysis was provided by the network. (Instead, they returned to their coverage of the Olympic Games immediately after the conclusion of the debate.)

There were no statistically significant differences in the proportion of negative/neutral to positive open-ended descriptions of George Bush. However, the differences for Michael Dukakis were statistically significant. For those watching the debate only, about half (52.9%) evaluated Dukakis as negative or neutral, with the remaining half (47.1%) rating him as positive. For those watching the debate and the post-debate analysis, only 15.8% rated Dukakis as negative/neutral, while 84.2% gave him positive evaluations. The post-debate commentary which favored Dukakis (see Chapter 4) apparently was reflected in the way debate viewers described his performance.

A similar analysis is presented in Table 6.6, only this time the data cover debate viewers from debate night (September 25) through September 29. No statistically significant patterns are present in any of the cross-tabulations. In general, Bush received about the same descriptions

Table 6.5
Cross-Tabulations: Open-Ended Debate Performance Descriptions, by Exposure to the Debate and Post-Debate Analysis (Debate Night Only)

Independent Measures	Bush Descriptions		Dukakis Descriptions	
	Negative/ Neutral	Positive	Negative/ Neutral	Positive
Debate Only	50.0%	50.0%	52.9%	47.1%[1]
(N)	(9)	(9)	(9)	(8)
Debate Plus Analysis	61.1%	38.9%	15.8%	84.2%
(N)	(22)	(14)	(6)	(32)

[1] Using Fisher's Exact Test, p = .0056

Table 6.6
Cross-Tabulations: Open-Ended Debate Performance Descriptions, by Debate and Post-Debate Analysis Exposure (September 25 to September 29 Cycle—Debate Viewers Only)

Independent Measures	Bush Descriptions			Dukakis Descriptions		
	Negative	Neutral	Positive	Negative	Neutral	Positive
Debate Only	46.2%	16.0%	37.7%	34.6%	9.3%	56.1%
(N)	(49)	(17)	(40)	(37)	(10)	(60)
Debate Plus Analysis	52.3%	10.9%	36.8%	25.4%	11.0%	63.5%
(N)	(91)	(19)	(64)	(46)	(20)	(115)

whether or not just the debate or the debate and post-debate analysis had been watched—evaluations that were predominantly negative. For those watching the debate only, 37.7% evaluated him positively, compared with 36.8% positive evaluations by those who watched the debate and post-debate analysis. In terms of negative evaluations, 46.2% of those watching the debate only and 52.3% of those watching the debate plus the post-debate analysis evaluated Bush's performance in negative terms.

The pattern was parallel, but in the reverse direction, for Dukakis. Of those watching only the debate, 56.1% described him positively, compared with 63.5% of those who watched the debate and post-debate analysis. He was described unfavorably by 34.6% of those watching the debate only and by 25.4% of those who watched both the debate and the post-debate analysis.

Summary. We feel that a relationship has been established between the time of the debates, exposure to the debates, and exposure to post-debate analysis, on the one hand, and candidate ratings as debaters, perceptions of the winner of the debate, and debate performance descriptions, on the other hand. Evaluations of George Bush as a debater improved noticeably on debate night and the night following, then returned to their previous level. Michael Dukakis's ratings as a debater were influenced significantly by whether or not individuals watched post-debate analyses. This was particularly apparent when looking at the results from the debate night only. Here, the debater ratings for Michael Dukakis given by those watching the debate and post-debate analysis (7.88 out of 10) were significantly more favorable than the ratings of those who watched the debate but not the post-debate analysis (6.68) and those who watched neither the debate nor the analysis (5.67). In terms of our open-ended descriptions of the performance of the two candidates collected on debate night, there was a statistically significant influence of exposure to post-debate analysis for the descriptions of Michael Dukakis. Those who watched the debate and post-debate analysis used positive descriptions more often (84.2%) than those who saw the debate only (47.1%).

What can we say, then, in summary, about the influence of the debate and post-debate analysis on perceptions of debate performance?

- Debate exposure can be related to changes in the evaluation of candidates as debaters. It may be, as it seems in this case, that the candidate who is seen as the poorer debater going into the debates benefits most in the short run from the debate, a confirmation of Bush's attempt to downplay his debating skills. This benefit, however, may be temporary. For Bush, it had evaporated within two days of the debate.

- Post-debate analysis also seems to have had an influence on debater ratings, this time for the lesser known of the two candidates, Michael Dukakis. Those who watched the debate and post-debate analyses gave Dukakis higher debater ratings than either those who did not watch the debate or those who watched the debate but no analysis. No parallel pattern was observed for George Bush.

- The influence of post-debate analysis appears to be strong, particularly on debate night, with those watching the debate *and* post-debate analysis rating Michael Dukakis significantly higher than either non-viewers of the debate or those who watched the debate only. This held also for open-ended descriptions of the two candidates. Dukakis was described significantly more positively by viewers of both debate and post-debate analysis than by viewers of the debate only.

- The impact of post-debate analysis on viewer evaluations appears to be relatively short-lived. Over the entire September 25 (debate night) to September 29 cycle, differences in candidate evaluations were reduced. By September 29, not only had counter-findings about the debate winner been made public, but other campaign events and issues were taking more of the news time and, likely, more of the attention of the voters.

Candidate Image

The changes over the interviewing period for evaluations of each candidate's image are shown in Figure 6.3. Candidate image was measured by summing respondents' scores on a 0-to-10-point scale across four variables measuring each candidate in terms of knowledge of domestic issues, knowledge of foreign affairs and defense, poise and self-confidence, and leadership. The images of the candidates show parallel paths over the interviewing period, with each showing improvement around debate night and some deterioration after that. The evaluations for Bush and Dukakis rise considerably on debate night (September 25) and then return to their original positions. For Bush, however, the improvement continues through September 26, while for Dukakis there is a decrease on the 26th and 27th, followed by an increase and leveling off.

The MCA of the candidate image ratings is presented in Table 6.7. The adjusted mean scores for the image ratings of both George Bush and Michael Dukakis show significant changes across the interviewing period. In Bush's case, the highest adjusted mean image evaluation[1] (26.45) occurred on debate night, September 25. The second highest rating (26.39) occurred the night after the debate, September 26, and his lowest image rating (24.15) was on September 27, two days after the debate. For Dukakis, the highest image rating (26.05) was on debate night, followed by a decrease in his rating and then an increase in evaluations.

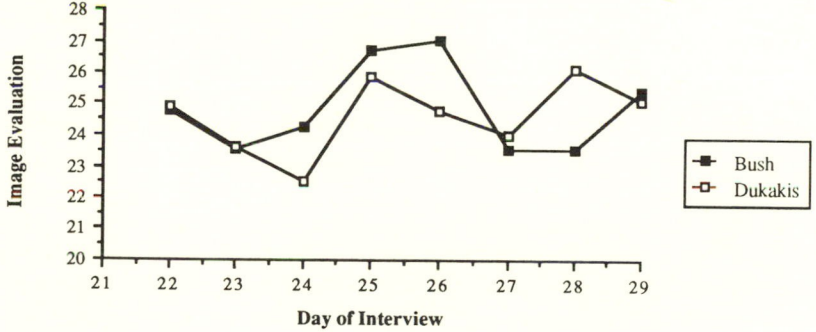

Figure 6.3
Presidential Candidate Composite Image Evaluations, by Day

Table 6.7
Multiple Classification Analysis: Adjusted Mean Scores for Candidate Image, by Time of Interview, Party, Campaign Interest, Locale, and Sex (September 22 to September 29 Cycle)

	Image Rating	
Independent Measures	Bush	Dukakis
Grand Mean	24.94	24.50
Time of Interview		
September 22-24 (Before Debate)	24.18	23.42
September 25 (Debate Night)	26.45	26.05
September 26	26.39	24.70
September 27	24.15	23.48
September 28	24.20	25.82
September 29	25.10	25.35
Beta	.13*	.16**
Party Affiliation		
Republican	29.41	20.78
Democrat	21.80	27.49
Independent/Other	24.70	24.02
Beta	.43**	.41**
Campaign Interest		
Uninterested, Neutral	23.70	22.02
Somewhat Interested	25.32	24.26
Very Interested	25.25	25.96
Beta	.09*	.22**
Locale		
Carbondale	25.16	25.08
Philadelphia	26.18	24.14
Eugene	24.04	24.12
Beta	.11**	.07
Sex		
Female	25.01	24.64
Male	24.87	24.35
Beta	.01	.02
Multiple R^2	22.7%**	23.9%**
Total N	656	639

* $p < .05$
** $p < .01$

Party affiliation strongly predicted image ratings. Republicans gave George Bush a 29.41 image evaluation, whereas Democrats gave him a 21.80 and Independent/other a 24.70. It was approximately the mirror image for Dukakis, although his average rating was somewhat lower than Bush's (24.50 vs. 24.94, respectively). Republicans rated Dukakis at 20.78, while Democrats rated him at 27.49 and Independents at 24.02.

Campaign interest was also related to the image ratings of both candidates. For George Bush, the uninterested/neutral subjects gave him a relatively low image rating of 23.70, while the somewhat and very interested subjects rated him more favorably at adjusted mean scores of 25.32 and 25.25, respectively. The influence of campaign interest was stronger for Michael Dukakis's image rating (Beta = .22). The pattern was quite linear. The uninterested subjects rated him at 22.02, followed by the somewhat interested at 24.26 and the very interested at 25.96. Taken together, these findings suggest that those most interested in a campaign are also the individuals most likely to evaluate the candidates favorably.

There were image differences by locale, but only for George Bush. His rating in Eugene was lowest (24.04), while in the other two sites it was about the same (25.16 in Carbondale and 26.18 in Philadelphia).

In Table 6.8 we present the Multiple Classification Analysis for only the subjects interviewed debate night and later. Here, we are attempting to determine the influence of exposure to the debate and to post-debate analysis on the images of both candidates.

Debate exposure seemingly had little to do with George Bush's composite image. Likely, most people had a pretty well-developed idea of who Vice President Bush was long before the debate, while Michael Dukakis's image was less solidified and still developing. Our findings certainly indicate that is the case. Those who saw neither the debate nor any post-debate analysis rated Dukakis at 23.03. If they watched only the debate, his rating improved to 25.54; watching both the debate and post-debate analysis increased it to 26.33. The Beta for debate and analysis exposure for Dukakis was a substantial .22. As indicated in the earlier analysis of the influence of post-debate analysis exposure on candidate ratings as debaters, the lesser-known candidate—in this case Michael Dukakis—benefited considerably. For George Bush, the well-defined candidate, the relationship between debate and post-debate analysis exposure seems minimal.

Campaign interest as a significant factor for George Bush falls out in this analysis but remains a strong predictor for Michael Dukakis's image, with the least interested rating his image at 22.88, the somewhat interested at 25.07, and the very interested at 26.15. In our sample, any advantage Michael Dukakis might have had clearly was among the most interested subjects. When comparing candidate ratings, Dukakis is evaluated lower than George Bush among the least interested and among the

Table 6.8
Multiple Classification Analysis: Adjusted Mean Scores for Candidate Image Ratings, by Debate and Post-Debate Analysis, Party, Campaign Interest, Locale, and Sex (Debate Night, September 25, to September 29 Cycle)

Independent Measures	Image Rating	
	Bush	Dukakis
Grand Mean	25.39	25.09
Debate and Analysis		
Neither Debate nor Analysis	24.93	23.03
Debate Only	25.42	25.54
Debate Plus Analysis	25.71	26.33
Beta	.05	.22**
Party Affiliation		
Republican	29.67	22.13
Democrat	22.46	27.35
Independent/Other	24.97	24.82
Beta	.43**	.34**
Campaign Interest		
Uninterested, Neutral	24.28	22.88
Somewhat Interested	25.82	25.07
Very Interested	25.54	26.15
Beta	.08	.19**
Locale		
Carbondale	25.55	24.95
Philadelphia	26.31	25.48
Eugene	24.71	25.01
Beta	.09	.03
Sex		
Female	25.39	25.62
Male	25.39	24.58
Beta	.00	.08
Multiple R^2	19.9%**	26.5%**
Total N	429	421

* $p < .05$
** $p < .01$

somewhat interested. Neither Locale nor Sex was a significant predictor in this analysis.

The results of a one-way analysis of variance for the candidate image ratings by debate and analysis exposure immediately after the debate are shown in Table 6.9. While the mean scores for the image ratings of George Bush appear to be independent of exposure to the debate or to post-debate analysis, the mean image rating scores for Michael Dukakis vary in a linear manner. The lowest image rating for Dukakis (21.79) occurred among those who did not watch the debate or the post-debate analysis. For those watching the debate only, the image rating was 24.56. Those who watched the debate and post-debate analysis rated Dukakis at 29.38, statistically higher than either of the other groups.

Either the people who watched the post-debate analysis did so to confirm their favorable evaluation of Dukakis or the post-debate analysis, which was favorable toward Dukakis, influenced their evaluations. We tend to favor the second interpretation, in part because the first explanation would also imply something that did not happen. Bush's image evaluations did not plunge as Dukakis's rose. In other words, had self-selective tendencies been at play, then the people who chose to watch the analysis should have both downgraded Bush and elevated Dukakis. But only the latter happened.

Summary. Candidate image, like evaluations of debate performance, was influenced by the time of the interview, debate exposure, and exposure to post-debate analysis. Exposure to the debate and to post-

Table 6.9
One-Way Analysis of Variance: Mean Scores for Candidate Image Ratings, by Debate and Post-Debate Analysis (Debate Night Only)

	Image Rating	
Independent Measures	Bush	Dukakis[1]
Grand Mean	26.69	25.74
Debate and Analysis		
Neither Debate nor Analysis	26.61	21.79
Debate Only	26.59	24.56
Debate Plus Analysis	26.79	29.38*
Total N	96	92

[1] Significant difference between groups, $F_{2,89} = 17.04$, $p < .01$.
* Differs from the "Neither Debate nor Analysis" and the "Debate Only" group, $p \leq .10$, Scheffé Test.

debate analysis of that debate seemed to have a stronger impact on the composite image of Michael Dukakis than on that of George Bush. The lesser-known candidate, Dukakis, gained most. Whether the gain was because he did well during the debate or simply because he was becoming better known is unclear. Whatever the reason, exposure to the debate and post-debate analysis, at least in the short run, helped Michael Dukakis. Several tentative generalizations seem warranted:

- Debate exposure appears to be related to the image evaluations of the candidates. The impact of exposure for this debate, however, appears to be limited to roughly the time of the debate, either debate night (as it appeared to be for Dukakis) or debate night and one night afterward (as it appeared to be for Bush).
- Post-debate analysis appears to influence also candidate image ratings, but here the influence seems to be limited to the lesser-known candidate. For Michael Dukakis, post-debate analysis was strongly linked to his highest candidate ratings. For George Bush, neither post-debate analysis nor debate exposure was strongly linked to differences in his image ratings.

Voting Intentions

Figure 6.4 graphically displays the probabilities, on a 0-to-10 scale, of voting for either candidate. The probability measure was based on separate responses to a 0-to-10-point index indicating the likelihood of voting for each candidate. With this index, a subject strongly favoring George Bush could indicate the probability of voting for Bush at 10, the probability of voting for Dukakis at 0. A strong Dukakis supporter might rate the probability of voting for Bush at a 1, the probability of voting for Dukakis at a 9. Someone who had not made up his or her mind might give the

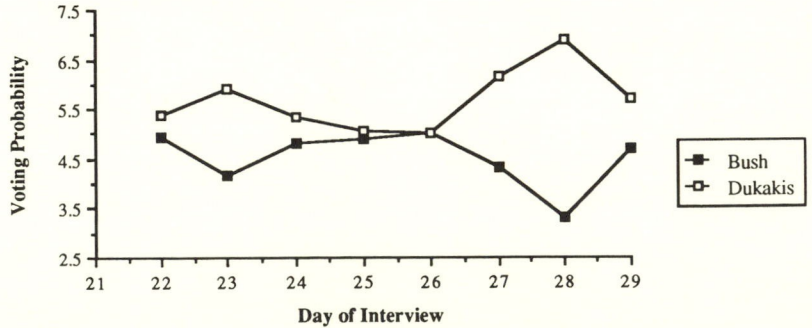

Figure 6.4
Voting Probability for Presidential Candidates, by Day

probability of voting for either candidate at 5. The pattern displayed in Figure 6.4 shows a converging of probabilities of voting for each of the candidates on September 25th and 26th and a divergence afterward, with the probability of voting for Bush decreasing as the probability of voting for Dukakis increased.

The analysis of the probabilities of voting for the candidates over the interviewing time frame is presented in Table 6.10. The time of the interview was not statistically related to voting probabilities for either George Bush or Michael Dukakis. As would be expected, the strongest predictor of voting intention was party affiliation. Republicans were strongly in favor of George Bush, with an adjusted mean score of 8.15 out of 10.00. Democrats placed their probability of voting for Bush at only 2.08, while the Independent/other voters listing a pro-Bush probability of 4.37. Michael Dukakis was rated at only a 2.05 probability among the Republicans, at a 8.21 probability among the Democrats, and at a 5.63 among the Independent/others.

Campaign interest was related to the probability of voting for Michael Dukakis but not to the probability of voting for George Bush. The uninterested/neutral subjects gave Dukakis a 4.99 probability, compared with a 5.53 from the somewhat interested and a 6.09 from the very interested. No parallel pattern existed for George Bush. Locale was related to the probability of voting for George Bush but not for Michael Dukakis. Bush encountered the lowest probabilities in Eugene, with a probability of only 4.01. The highest probability of voting for him occurred in Philadelphia, where his 5.47 probability was greater than the adjusted probability for Michael Dukakis of 5.27. Carbondale was between the two, with an adjusted mean probability of 4.68. Sex was not significantly related to voting probability for either candidate.

The MCA for the influence of exposure to the debate and post-debate analysis is presented in Table 6.11. This analysis is restricted to subjects interviewed from September 25, when the debate was held, to September 29, the end of the interviewing period. Although the influence is not particularly large (Beta = .09), exposure to the debate and to post-debate analysis was significantly related to the probability of voting for Michael Dukakis but not for George Bush. The lowest adjusted mean probability of voting for Michael Dukakis, (5.32), was for the subjects who had watched neither debate nor analysis, while those watching the debate only had an adjusted mean of 5.57. The highest mean probability score (6.16) was for those subjects who had watched both the debate and the post-debate analysis.

While exposure to post-debate analysis was significantly—though not powerfully—related to an increased probability of voting for Michael Dukakis, the apparent impact of viewing post-debate analysis seems greater when we look only at the results from September 25, the night of

Table 6.10
**Multiple Classification Analysis: Adjusted Mean Scores for Candidate Voting
Probabilities, by Time of Interview, Party, Campaign Interest, Locale, and Sex
(September 22 to September 29 Cycle)**

| | Voting Probability For | |
Independent Measures	Bush	Dukakis
Grand Mean	4.57	5.63
Time of Interview		
September 22-24 (Before Debate)	4.68	5.43
September 25 (Debate Night)	4.78	5.45
September 26	4.53	5.42
September 27	4.73	5.68
September 28	4.09	6.08
September 29	4.39	6.14
Beta	.05	.07
Party Affiliation		
Republican	8.15	2.05
Democrat	2.08	8.21
Independent/Other	4.37	5.63
Beta	.63**	.65**
Campaign Interest		
Uninterested, Neutral	4.22	4.99
Somewhat Interested	4.91	5.53
Very Interested	4.45	6.09
Beta	.07	.11**
Locale		
Carbondale	4.68	5.76
Philadelphia	5.47	5.27
Eugene	4.01	5.70
Beta	.13**	.05
Sex		
Female	4.52	5.79
Male	4.63	5.45
Beta	.01	.04
Multiple R^2	42.0%**	45.4%**
Total N	693	694

* $p < .05$
** $p < .01$

Table 6.11
Multiple Classification Analysis: Adjusted Mean Scores for Candidate Voting Probabilities, by Debate and Post-Debate Analysis Exposure, Party, Campaign Interest, Locale, and Sex (Debate Night, September 25, to September 29 Cycle)

Independent Measures	Voting Probability For	
	Bush	Dukakis
Grand Mean	4.52	5.72
Debate and Analysis		
Neither Debate nor Analysis	4.86	5.32
Debate Only	4.70	5.57
Debate Plus Analysis	4.12	6.16
Beta	.08	.09*
Party Affiliation		
Republican	7.94	2.34
Democrat	2.10	8.11
Independent/Other	4.36	5.87
Beta	.61**	.62**
Campaign Interest		
Uninterested, Neutral	4.23	5.04
Somewhat Interested	4.69	5.72
Very Interested	4.52	6.08
Beta	.04	.10*
Locale		
Carbondale	4.82	5.60
Philadelphia	5.26	5.39
Eugene	3.90	5.99
Beta	.14**	.06
Sex		
Female	4.42	5.98
Male	4.62	5.45
Beta	.03	.07
Multiple R^2	41.2%**	44.6%**
Total N	450	450

* $p < .05$
** $p < .01$

the debate. These are shown in the results of a one-way analysis of variance presented in Table 6.12. Interestingly, the apparent effects were not limited to Dukakis. The probability of voting for George Bush appears to have been negatively influenced by viewing the post-debate analysis (p < .10). Those who watched neither the debate nor the analysis and those who watched the debate only had similar mean probabilities of voting for George Bush—5.53 and 5.85, respectively. But those who watched the debate and the post-debate analysis had an average probability of voting for Bush of only 3.75. For Dukakis, the differences were just reversed. Those who watched both the debate and the analysis rated their probability at 6.63, substantially higher than the complete non-viewers and the debate-only watchers.

Our final set of findings deals with how the people we interviewed responded to the question, "If you had to vote today for one of the candidates, who would you vote for?" We analyzed those responding either Bush or Dukakis. The results for those interviewed from debate night (September 25) through the end of the interviewing cycle on September 29 are presented in Table 6.13. Here the results are analyzed in terms of exposure to the debate and post-debate analysis.

In terms of their voting preferences, the percentages were evenly split for those who did not watch the debate or the analysis. The pattern was similar for those watching the debate only. Dukakis, however, came out clearly ahead among those who watched both debate and post-debate

Table 6.12

One-Way Analysis of Variance: Mean Scores for Candidate Voting Probabilities, by Debate and Post-Debate Analysis (Debate Night Only)

	Voting Probability For	
Independent Measures	Bush[1]	Dukakis[2]
Grand Mean	4.87	5.00
Debate and Analysis		
Neither Debate nor Analysis	5.53	3.84
Debate Only	5.85	3.95
Debate Plus Analysis	3.75	6.63*
Total N	98	98

[1] Significant difference between groups, $F_{2,95} = 2.49$, p < .10.
[2] Significant difference between groups, $F_{2,95} = 5.74$, p < .01.
* Differs from the "Neither Debate nor Analysis" and the "Debate Only" group, p ≤ .10, Scheffé Test.

Table 6.13
Voting Choice, by Debate and Post-Debate Analysis Exposure (Debate Night, September 25, to September 29 Cycle)

	Voting for	
Independent Measures	Bush	Dukakis
Debate and Post-Debate Analysis*		
Neither Debate nor Analysis	51.3%	48.7%
(N)	(80)	(76)
Debate Only	47.3%	52.7%
(N)	(53)	(59)
Debate Plus Analysis	34.3%	65.7%
(N)	(61)	(117)

* $p < .01$, Chi-square test.

analysis, receiving a 65.7% preference, compared with Bush's 34.3%, in this group of respondents.

The final voting analysis table, this time for debate night only, is presented in Table 6.14. There was a difference ($p < .10$) for exposure to the debate and post-debate analysis. Those individuals who watched neither the debate nor the analysis would have voted for George Bush by a 61.8% to 38.2% margin. Those who watched the debate still preferred Bush, but by a smaller 55.6% to 44.4% margin. Those who watched both the debate and the post-debate analysis were leaning heavily toward Dukakis, 65.8% to 34.2% for Bush. Again, post-debate analysis seemed to heavily favor Michael Dukakis, this time where it really counts in politics—in voting preference.

Summary. Our findings are important regarding the relationships between voting intentions and exposure to the first presidential debate and post-debate analysis. While the time of the interview was not significantly related to the probability of voting for either candidate, exposure to both debate and post-debate analysis was significantly related to the probability of voting for Michael Dukakis. This finding was particularly true for the subjects interviewed on debate night only, the time when other influences had not had the opportunity to alter the immediate audience response to the post-debate verdicts.

Equally as important and interesting are the findings concerning a voting choice between Bush and Dukakis at the time of the interview.

Table 6.14
Voting Choice, by Debate and Post-Debate Analysis Exposure (Debate Night, September 25, Only)

	Voting for	
Independent Measures	Bush	Dukakis
Debate and Post-Debate Analysis*		
Neither Debate nor Analysis	61.8%	38.2%
(N)	(21)	(13)
Debate Only	55.6%	44.4%
(N)	(10)	(8)
Debate Plus Analysis	34.2%	65.8%
(N)	(13)	(25)

* p < .10, Chi-square test.

Here Dukakis apparently again benefited from exposure to post-debate analysis. When looking at debate night only, again those who watched both the debate and post-debate analysis favored Michael Dukakis, while the others preferred George Bush.

In summary, our findings regarding voting probabilities and voting preferences suggest that the content of post-debate analysis, which was favorable to Michael Dukakis (see Chapter 4), had a decided impact on voting probabilities and voting preference. Here Michael Dukakis benefited significantly as a result of post-debate analysis.

CONCLUSION

We began this study of the first presidential debate attempting to answer two general questions. First, did exposure to the debate have an influence on the public's evaluation of the candidates as debaters, on their evaluation of the images of the candidates, and on their voting probabilities and preferences? Second, did viewing of the post-debate analyses influence the same set of variables?

The answer to both questions was "yes." Analysis of the day-by-day changes in our respondents' evaluations of the candidates shows that George Bush's image as a debater improved on debate night (September 25) and the night following, although it returned to its pre-debate levels beginning September 27. Bush, seen as the weaker debater before the debate, benefited in the short run from it. Both candidates' images showed momentary improvements on the night of the debate, and the improvement for Bush continued at least for one day after the debate before returning to the lower levels associated with the pre-debate period. Voting probabilities for the candidates, however, were relatively uninfluenced by the day of the interview.

The strongest influence appears to be associated with exposure to post-debate analysis, usually to the benefit of Michael Dukakis. In some cases, post-debate analysis was harmful to George Bush. Michael Dukakis, the lesser-known of the two candidates, was evaluated most favorably as a debater by those who watched post-debate analysis. The same pattern was shown for image ratings. On debate night, George Bush's image was apparently harmed by exposure to the post-debate analysis, while Dukakis's image was most positive among those watching post-debate analysis. Such a finding matches well with our content analysis presented in Chapter 4 (see Table 4.5). During the post-debate analysis, 70.1% of the Dukakis verdicts were positive, and only 17.9% were negative. For Bush, only 42.1% were positive, while 48.7% were negative.

Finally, those who watched both the debate and post-debate analysis showed the highest probability of voting for Michael Dukakis and the lowest probability of voting for George Bush, especially on debate night. That pattern held when respondents were asked who they would vote for "today." Those who had watched both the debate and the post-debate analysis were more likely to select Michael Dukakis as their voting choice than were the other two groups.

While the evidence does support the influence of post-debate analysis, there are some necessary qualifications. The most important is that the debates make up a small portion of a total campaign. Stovall and Solomon (1984) found that news coverage of the debates in 1980 made up only 2.8% of all election campaign stories and that polls on the debates added another 1.5% of the total campaign stories, summing to a pretty skimpy 4.3% total of all campaign stories. Major and Atwood (1990) reported similar percentages for the 1988 election campaign. In their analysis, the debates ranked second, behind general social issues, as a campaign issue, with 6.76% of all issue references. Still, neither the 4.3% reported by Stovall and Solomon nor the 6.76% reported by Major and Atwood suggests that the debates are likely to dominate campaign coverage.

Whatever influence debates might have, the Bush camp moved skillfully to control them in number and in time. By making sure that the debates took place far enough before the general election, any negative impact would probably have diminished by the time of the actual vote. Even within the nine days covered in our survey, the influences of the September 25 debate can be seen to decay quickly. The pattern suggested is that even though post-debate analysis can influence something as important as voting choice, that influence may be short-lived and can be offset by other events.

In the campaign of 1988, the debates represented the only way the majority of the voters could get a glimpse of the candidates in an open environment. Many of the public must have felt overwhelmed and confused by commercial messages, pictures from flag factories, and "Joe Isuzu" sound bites. The debate was the first alternative to the information control exercised by each candidate over the campaign and it did have an impact, as it should have. It was, in a very real sense, the first opportunity for the electronic media, in the form of post-debate analysis, to comment directly on the substance of the campaign. It was the voters' first opportunity to participate in open political dialogue, and they did this through watching the debate and watching the post-debate analysis. It was the candidates' first opportunity to go before the voters to make a personal appeal for people's votes.

People responded to the debate, and particularly to post-debate analysis, in ways that were rational and appropriate. Unfortunately, within just a few days of the debate, media coverage returned to the ad, the image, the photo opportunity, and the sound bite. The brief moment of relative freedom from professional control of the campaign passed as the media began gearing up for the next major campaign event, the debate between Lloyd Bentsen and Dan Quayle on October 5.

NOTES

1. The adjusted mean scores differ slightly from the scores presented in Figure 6.3. In the figure, the scores on image evaluation are the raw scores, before adjustments. For George Bush, the mean on debate night (September 25) was 26.72, and on the next night was 27.01. For Michael Dukakis, the corresponding mean scores were 25.87 and 24.79.

REFERENCES

Carmines, E. G., and R. A. Zeller. 1979. *Reliability and validity assessment.* Beverly Hills, Calif.: Sage.

Germond, J. W., and J. Witcover. 1989. *Whose broad stripes and bright stars? The trivial pursuit of the presidency 1988.* New York: Warner.

Hershey, M. R. 1989. The campaign and the media. In *The election of 1988: Reports and interpretations,* ed. G. M. Pomper, R. K. Baker, W. D. Burnham, B. G. Farah, M. R. Hershey, E. Klein, and W. C. McWilliams, 73–102. Chatham, N.J.: Chatham House.

Lowry, D. T., J. A. Bridges, and P. A. Barefield. In press. The effects of network TV "instant analysis and querulous criticism" following the first Bush-Dukakis debate. *Journalism Quarterly.*

Major, A. M., and L. E. Atwood. 1990. *The U.S. press covers two presidential elections*. Paper presented at the International Communication Association, Dublin, Ireland, June.

Playing hardball. 1988. *Newsweek*, October 3, 22–26.

Shapiro, W. 1988. The phantom race: Call it politics Lite, with lots of froth and little annoying substance. *Time*, September 19, 18–19.

Stovall, J. G., and J. H. Solomon. 1984. The poll as a news event in the 1980 presidential campaign. *Public Opinion Quarterly* 48:615–623.

7

THE QUAYLE-BENTSEN DEBATE: A VERDICT EFFECT?

At first, we did not plan to survey audience reaction to the October 5 Quayle-Bentsen debate. We had two principal reasons for that decision: (1) a bare-bones budget that could not be stretched further, and (2) an expectation, based on previous research, that the vice-presidential choice would not be very important when people made up their minds about each party's ticket.

However, we reconsidered that decision when three things happened. First, it seemed to us that there was no lasting and clear-cut verdict in the news about the first Bush-Dukakis debate on September 25. (It was a considerable time later that we were able to combine our surveys after the first debate and discern a short-lived verdict effect.) The absence of a clear news verdict meant that, unless we added the vice-presidential debate, we would be betting all our marbles on getting a clear media verdict about the second Bush-Dukakis debate. Second, a drumfire of media stories were continuing about questions of Quayle's competence, long after the Republican convention and into late September. Third, Dukakis had raised Quayle as an issue, with some effect, in the September 25 debate itself. Taking these last two points together, it seemed to us that if Quayle faltered in the October 5 debate, the news media would be especially ready to reach a clear negative verdict about his performance.

Logistical problems forced us, however, to a very constricted time series, one that had only one evening of interviewing before the debate, plus three additional evenings afterwards. Fortunately, we were going to be interviewing on October 11 and 12 anyway, as part of the October 13 time series,[1] so we knew we could extend our vice-presidential series by tacking on the 11th and 12th. The interviewing dates we *added* specifically for the Wednesday, October 5, Quayle-Bentsen debate are shown in Figure 7.1. As in our other two short time series, we started interviewing immediately after the debate ended—and before any post-debate analysis began.

Events—and the media—showed that we had made the right decision. A CBS News poll, taken within 24 hours of the Quayle-Bentsen debate, showed an apparent increase (to 43%) in the number of people who felt the vice-presidential choice was "very important" to their choice between the Democratic and Republican tickets.[2] Not only did the Quayle-Bentsen choice seem to have become more important, but the media verdicts themselves were, to say the least, very clear—and negative toward Quayle. Quayle's comparison of himself with John F. Kennedy was endlessly replayed on videotape in the aftermath, as was Bentsen's climactic, "Senator, you're no Jack Kennedy!" In the days following the debate, network corespondents covering Bush made much of the fact that Bush was trying to distance himself even further from Quayle. Meanwhile, correspondents covering Dukakis prominently mentioned that Dukakis and Bentsen were jubilantly inseparable in the debate aftermath.

This debate therefore seems to be a prime candidate for a media verdict effect. But what kind of verdict effect? An effect on *voting intentions* was less likely than an effect on *"winner" perceptions*, it seemed to us, given the greater importance of the presidential candidates on the ticket. How could we separate the two vice-presidential candidates from their running mates, and thus give the verdict a fighting chance to show up as an effect on voting? We tried to do this by asking people to rate the odds, from 0 to 10, that they would vote for Quayle as well as the odds they would vote for Bentsen *if each were running alone against the other*. In this chapter, we present our survey results from October 4, 5, 6, 9, 11, and 12.

METHODOLOGICAL CONSIDERATIONS

Chapter 2 provides most of the necessary information about the survey methodology we used. As always, a common questionnaire was used at

Added Interview Days
Vice Presidential Candidate Debate
October 5, 1988

| Debate - 1 | Debate Night | Debate + 1 | | Debate + 4 |

Figure 7.1
Vice-Presidential Candidate Debate Study Design

the three research sites. The October 4, 5, 6, and 9 questionnaires were tailored specifically to the vice-presidential debate, although they had many questions common to the series surrounding the other two fall debates. The October 11 and 12 questionnaires did double duty, serving as "before" measures for the October 13 Bush-Dukakis debate and also extending the vice-presidential time series.

At each location, a crew of four to seven experienced and trained telephone interviewers began calling during or just after the network evening news broadcast, with the exception of the night of the October 5 Bentsen-Quayle debate. On that date, Oregon and Illinois interviewers began calling immediately after the debate itself, in an effort to interview as many people as possible before they had been exposed to post-debate analysis. Because the vice-presidential debate ended at 10:30 P.M., Eastern time, no attempts were made in Philadelphia to contact respondents immediately after the debate. Table 7.1 presents the total numbers of interviews by day and by location.

Overall, the mean October 4–12 completion rate was 70.9% for the Eugene-Springfield interviewers, 50.1% for the Philadelphia interviewers, and 57.1% for the Carbondale interviewers. In each case, the completion rate is calculated by dividing the number of interviews done by the total

Table 7.1
Number of Interviews for Each Location, by Date

Date	Oregon	Philadelphia	Carbondale	Total
October 4	35	23	34	92
October 5*	49	--**	27	76
October 6	30	25	27	82
October 9	40	26	43	109
October 11	45	20	34	99
October 12	38	24	26	88
Total	237	118	191	546

* Interviewing began immediately after the end of the Quayle-Bentsen debate. On the other nights it began after, or during, the early evening network news.

** Since the debate ended at 10:30 p.m. in Philadelphia, no interviewing was attempted there.

number of refusals and completions. Before we lay out our predictions, let us recap what was being said after the debate on early evening network news.

THE NETWORK NEWS ENVIRONMENT

October 5 (Wednesday) Post-Debate Analyses. ABC and CBS lead with the sound bites from the exchange in which Quayle compares his experience with John F. Kennedy's; NBC's Brokaw calls it a memorable exchange, but the bites themselves are buried in middle of program. NBC seems slower to call the exchange a major turning point in debate than ABC and CBS are. ABC reports poll showing 51% said Bentsen won, 27% said Quayle, and 22% called it even. CBS's Bob Schieffer says Bentsen "zinged" Quayle with the "you're no Jack Kennedy" exchange; ABC's Jeff Greenfield says the exchange made Quayle look "a little rattled." NBC's Andrea Mitchell stresses repetitive, rehearsed-sounding Quayle answers to repeated questions asked about his qualifications; Mitchell terms this "the big question."

October 6 (Thursday). The entire "Jack Kennedy" sequence plays on all three newscasts. CBS, ABC (first nine minutes each), and NBC (first six minutes) all open with Wednesday's debate. CBS uses a poll to declare Bentsen as "far and away" the winner. ABC stresses jubilation in the Dukakis camp and efforts by Bush camp to downplay the debate. NBC reports Dukakis's campaign will introduce the anti-Quayle "empty [president's] chair" ad in gleeful attempt to take advantage of Quayle debate performance.

October 7 (Friday). ABC's lead story examines Quayle's qualifications for about two and a half minutes. As part of story on the Bush campaign, CBS's Bob Schieffer says, "Quayle is seen as Bush's main liability." In NBC's campaign coverage, Dukakis and Bentsen each single out Quayle for criticism. NBC cites newspaper editorials and stories criticizing Quayle's debate performance.

October 8 (Saturday). NBC describes Dukakis's hope to gain from Quayle debate performance, but there is more emphasis on criticism of the Willie Horton ad by Dukakis's mother: "Can anybody get as low as that?"

October 9 (Sunday). CBS, looking ahead to the October 13 Bush-Dukakis debate, says Bush can offset the damage from Quayle's performance in the next debate; Dukakis questions Bush's judgment in selecting Quayle as running mate.

October 10 (Monday). ABC poll implies Bush-Dukakis race is still close. CBS more explicitly refers to Quayle debate by giving heavy emphasis to Quayle's complaint about the "inappropriate" question he was asked during debate about what he would do if he suddenly became president. Sixth (and last) item in NBC's election news package gives Quayle's newly revised answer about what he would do if suddenly he were president.

October 11 (Tuesday). CBS includes 17 seconds of sound bites from Quayle-Bentsen, but pays very little attention to debate otherwise. ABC quotes Quayle in Ohio saying that he is tired of being controlled, wants to campaign his own way. Same Quayle story embedded in midst of other campaign news in NBC newscast.

October 12 (Wednesday). CBS poll shows Bush lead grows, but Quayle's presence on the ballot hurts. Quayle's "declaration of independence" to run his own campaign follows. On ABC, buried in the middle of an examination of Dukakis campaign problems, is a statement that he benefits from his own and Bentsen's debates. First item in NBC package, buried in middle of newscast, is Quayle's claim that he is now taking charge of his own campaign; second item is advance story on tomorrow night's final debate.

This brief synopsis suggests that, with some differences between the networks and a decline over time in amount of emphasis, the news verdicts about Quayle and Bentsen were being repeated throughout the October 5 to 12 study period. However, the verdicts may have become more condensed, abstract, and implicit over the weekend—that is, *before* Monday the 10th.

IF A VERDICT EFFECT, WHAT SHOULD HAPPEN?

Open-Ended Responses

Earlier we pointed out a great advantage of our time-series design as being that we had also embedded a number of open-ended questions in our interview. Among other things, what these free-response questions can do is to allow respondents to say, in their own words, what is on their minds. When we match these free-response answers with what is going on in the news, we have a very powerful research design. We need to stress here that, other than asking the question itself, our interviewers did *not* "put words in the mouth" of respondents.

What should happen, then, with open-ended questions *if* a verdict effect happens? We foresee two consequences. First, at least through the interviews on October 9, respondents will spontaneously mention news stories at an increasing rate about Quayle's poor performance as time goes by and the verdict diffuses. In other words, respondents will mention such stories more often on October 6 and 9 than will those interviewed just after the debate. This pattern will hold regardless of the respondent's party identification. (Party identification—Republican, Democrat or Independent—is a good way, in this study, of indexing the dominant wishful thinking phenomenon found so often in previous studies of winner perceptions. With each of the open-ended questions, we shall try to control partisanship by holding party identification constant, then looking at whether interview day still makes a difference.) And second, when asked, later in the interview, to describe Quayle's performance in the debate, respondents will be much more likely to use critical descriptions a day or more after the debate than immediately after it. We can specify the nature of those critical descriptions as well: *The verdicts will concentrate on Quayle's competence, not on his trustworthiness.*

News verdicts concerned matters of Quayle's competence claims in the debate much more than his trustworthiness. Perhaps provoked by news coverage prior to the debate, Quayle himself gave overwhelming attention to questions of his competence during the debate: According to Hershey (1989, p. 92), Quayle himself used the words *qualifications* or *experience* in the debate some 27 times. Given the frequent use of the "you're no Jack Kennedy" sound bite, it was inevitable that the verdicts would focus on questions of competence and experience.

Since we know that both news media verdicts and Quayle himself stressed his competence much more than his trustworthiness, a news verdict effect would find incompetence descriptions given by respondents more often a day or more after the debate than immediately afterward. This delayed pattern, too, should hold regardless of our respondents' party identification and despite the fact that Quayle's competence had been the subject of many stories for months before the debate. Thus, we foresee, first, that when respondents are asked whether any issue had emerged from the October 5 debate that might influence the election, "Quayle himself," or words to that effect, will be mentioned more often as we move away from immediately after the debate. This delayed-reaction pattern also will occur regardless of party identification and despite a lot of media attention to the "Quayle problem" long before the debate itself. Second, when we then ask which side had benefited the most from whatever debate issue respondents had just cited, a verdict effect predicts that respondents will more often cite the Bentsen-Dukakis ticket as benefiting later rather than immediately after the debate. Once again, we expect this pattern will hold for both Democrats and for Republicans.

We turn from our open-ended questions to the ratings measures, which ask respondents to choose among the response categories we offer them. At their best, ratings allow great gains in precision and analytical power. A major advantage of our study design is that we do not have to choose between using the two kinds of questions—and we can gain considerable confidence in our results if both open-ended and ratings questions produce similar results. So we turn now to our predictions concerning the ratings of the candidates.

Ratings

- Ratings of who won the debate—and by how much—will tilt increasingly toward Bentsen over time, even after party affiliation is controlled. (Party identification as an index of wishful thinking will be used as well in these analyses, but this time we can directly control partisanship by extracting its apparent influence on the ratings before we look at the influence of verdict-related variables.)
- Among debate viewers, those who watched a post-debate analysis program will be more likely to pick Bentsen as the debate winner than will other debate viewers who did not watch a post-debate analysis, even after party identification is controlled.
- Ratings of Quayle's prowess as a debater will decline over time and Bentsen's will rise over time, even after party identification is controlled.
- Viewers of both the debate and the analysis will be much more likely than debate-only viewers to downgrade Quayle's prowess and upgrade Bentsen's, even after party identification is controlled.
- When respondents are asked to rate the chances that they would vote for Bentsen or for Quayle if the two candidates were on the ballot alone, party identification will remain the strongest predictor, regardless of day of interview or exposure to post-debate analysis. However, either/both day or exposure to analysis may play an important secondary role.

RESULTS

Open-Ended Items

One of the first questions we asked in the interview was whether people had watched any television news in the past week and, if so, whether they could recall any television news stories about *either* the September 25 or the October 5 debate. As expected most persons' responses clearly referred to the more recent Quayle-Bentsen debate. Table 7.2 presents the overall results in the section at the top, then breaks results down separately for people who identified themselves as Republicans or Democrats. The same presentation format was used for all the open-ended measures (Tables 7.2 through 7.6), plus the table on presidential voting preference (Table 7.7).

Overall, Table 7.2 shows a big increase from October 5 to October 6 and 9 in the number of spontaneous references to Quayle's having been beaten. By October 11 and 12, such story references had fallen even below the percentage given just after the debate. The peak was reached on October 9, when just under 30% of all the answers given to this question concerned Quayle's poor performance. As we can see by looking below at the separate figures for Republicans and Democrats, both groups showed the same October 9 peak, but the surge upwards for the Republi-

Table 7.2
Television News Story About Debate* Mentioned by Respondent, by Day of Interview

	Night of Interview: October					
Debate Story	5	6	9	11	12	N
Quayle loses/Bentsen wins/ "JFK comparison"	7.9%	20.2%	29.7%	3.0%	3.4%	62
Other (Includes Don't Know, pre-debate stories, non-directional generics such as "Highlights," Who Won," etc.)	92.1%	79.8%	70.3%	97.0%	96.6%	396
(N)	(76)	(84)	(111)	(99)	(88)	(458)

Chi-square = 42.221, df = 4, p <.001

RESULTS ANALYZED SEPARATELY BY PARTY:

Party	Oct 5	Oct 6	Oct 9	N	Oct 11	Oct 12
Republicans						
Quayle loses/Bentsen wins/"JFK" comparison	10.0%	19.0%	45.5%	23	5.3%	--
Other	90.0%	81.0%	54.5%	66	94.7%	100.0%
(N)	(30)	(26)	(33)	(89)		
Democrats						
Quayle loses/Bentsen wins/"JFK" comparison	6.7%	29.0%	32.7%	27	--	7.9%
Other	93.3%	71.0%	67.3%	83	100.0%	92.1%
(N)	(30)	(31)	(49)	(110)		

Republicans: Chi-square = 11.118, df = 2, p < .01, for October 5, 6, 9 dates
Democrats: Chi-square = 8.628, df = 2, p < .05, for October 5, 6, 9 dates

*   The question was an open-ended one, asked only of those who reported viewing TV news at least once a week: "Of all the television news stories you have seen, do you remember any... about the Sept. 25 presidential debate or the Oct. 5 vice-presidential debate? (IF YES) Which debate story do you remember best?"

cans seemed dramatically greater than for the Democrats. Most of the Democrats' big surge seemed to have happened by the night after the debate, but perhaps it took the Republicans longer to test, and then accept, the reality of the verdict.

Once again, however, while it is important to see whether Republicans accept a verdict as fast as Democrats do, the main reason for looking at party subgroups is to control for party by holding it constant. Since party affiliation is constant, it cannot explain whatever differences are going on in the two sub-tables. Both of those sub-tables show a delayed spurt upwards corresponding to the time needed for a delayed news verdict effect to occur. For the Republicans, it took until October 9 for Quayle's poor performance to be mentioned often, while most of the surge upward for Democrats happened on October 6. In each case, though, there was a delayed reaction.

Perhaps, however, the debate-night interview gave respondents little chance to mention a television news story about Quayle, since some of these respondents might not have had much of a chance to encounter such a story by the time the interviewer called. We need, therefore, to see whether the same delayed-reaction pattern occurs for the other open-ended items.

Table 7.3 presents the findings when we asked for one or two words to describe the impression Quayle made in the debate. (We asked the same question about Bentsen, of course.) This question was asked of those who said they had watched at least part of the debate or had learned about it later.

We expected the negative media verdict about Quayle to show up in the form of descriptions implying incompetence, inexperience, et cetera, and we expected such words to peak on a delayed basis—that is, some time after October 5. As in the table about stories, we find a surge upwards after October 5 in respondents' use of incompetence-type descriptions.[3] Once again, the delayed reaction seems to hold for Republicans as well as Democrats, though there are some differences between them in the precise pattern. For the Republicans, the delayed spurt in incompetence descriptions is from October 5 to 6 only, while the spurt for Democrats generally lasts through October 12. While the spurt upward in incompetence descriptions does not last long for the Republicans, a downward plunge in favorable words did, and that plunge among Republicans continued from October 9 through October 12.

Our next open-ended item again was asked of respondents with at least some exposure to the Quayle-Bentsen debate: Was there an issue raised in the debate that might influence the election? Entered into Table 7.4 is the proportion of people who said, in effect, Quayle himself (his competence, his character, his ability to function) was an issue that might influence the election itself. As Table 7.4 shows, once again there is a

Table 7.3
"One or Two Words" Describing Quayle's Debate Performance*, by All Respondents and by Party

| Description | Night of Interview: October | | | | | |
	5	6	9	11	12	N
All Respondents						
"Positive" Words**	25.0%	30.8%	19.2%	11.5%	13.5%	52
Words Connoting Incompetence***	11.0%	20.5%	22.0%	22.8%	23.6%	127
Other	17.7%	15.4%	26.8%	22.4%	17.7%	254
(N)	(72)	(81)	(106)	(92)	(82)	(433)
Republicans						
"Positive" Words	39.1%	34.8%	13.1%	4.3%	8.7%	23
Words Connoting Incompetence	18.5%	29.7%	18.5%	14.8%	18.5%	27
Other	20.5%	13.7%	31.5%	19.2%	15.1%	73
(N)	29	26	31	19	18	123
Democrats						
"Positive" Words	16.7%	27.8%	22.2%	11.1%	22.2%	18
Words Connoting Incompetence	6.0%	17.9%	26.9%	26.9%	22.3%	67
Other	22.0%	14.3%	26.4%	20.9%	16.5%	91
(N)	(27)	(30)	(46)	(39)	(34)	(176)

All Respondents: Chi-square = 21.75, df = 8, p < .01
Republicans: Chi-square = 12.789, df = 4, p < .02, because of low Ns for the "positive" row, October 9-12 columns were combined
Democrats: Chi-square = 9.267, df = 4, p < .10, because of low Ns for the "positive" row, October 9-12 columns were combined

*   Asked of those who saw/heard debate or learned about it later: "If you had to choose a word or two to describe the performance of Dan Quayle during the debate, what would those one or two words be?"
**   "Positive" words were words such as "good," "likable," "well-prepared," "sincere," "intelligent,""confident," etc.
*** Words connoting "incompetence" included "inexperienced," "immature," "stiff," "pre-programmed," "erratic," "uptight," "scared," "childish," "unprepared," etc.

Table 7.4
Proportion of Respondents Who Said "Quayle Himself" When Asked Whether Any Issue Raised in the Debate Might Influence the Election*

	Night of Interview: October					
Debate Issue Named	5	6	9	11	12	N
All Respondents						
"Quayle" himself	6.6%	23.8%	13.5%	17.2%	22.7%	77
All others	93.4%	76.2%	86.5%	82.8%	77.3%	381
(N)	(76)	(84)	(111)	(99)	(88)	(458)
Republicans						
"Quayle" himself	3.3%	23.1%	6.1%	5.3%	22.2%	14
All others	96.7%	76.9%	93.9%	94.7%	77.8%	112
(N)	(30)	(26)	(33)	(19)	(18)	(126)
Democrats						
"Quayle" himself	6.7%	35.5%	24.5%	25.0%	23.7%	45
All others	93.3%	64.5%	75.5%	75.0%	76.3%	147
(N)	(30)	(31)	(49)	(44)	(38)	(192)

All Respondents: Chi-square = 11.776, df = 4, p < .02
Republicans: Fisher's Exact Probability Test, 5th vs. 6th, p=.065, two-tailed test. Low
 expecteds prevented Chi-square calculation.
Democrats: Chi-square = 7.92, df = 4, NS. For Oct. 5 vs. 6 and 9 vs. 11 and 12,
 Chi-square=6.57, df = 2, p <.05.

* Respondents were asked first whether they thought there was an issue (arising from the debate) that could influence the election. Tabled responses are for issues named by respondents who had been exposed, directly or indirectly, to the debate and answered yes to the first question.

spurt upwards *after* October 5 in the proportions of people giving this response. Once again, the general pattern seems to hold for both Republicans and Democrats, though the Quayle issue was not mentioned often enough by Republicans for us to get very stable day-by-day estimates. As one would probably expect, a higher proportion of Democrats than Republicans mentioned the Quayle issue.

As a follow-up to the debate-issue question, we asked respondents to tell us which party's debater benefited more from the debate issue they had just mentioned. Given the way the question was phrased, we can now include responses for October 4, the day *before* the Quayle-Bentsen debate. In the case of interviews on October 4, what we were asking about was which side benefited from any issue raised in the first Dukakis-Bush debate, so it is possible to use these responses as one kind of comparative baseline for the Quayle-Bentsen responses (Table 7.5). Clearly, there was a major drop, from October 4 and 5 to later, in the proportions of people saying that the Republican debater had gained from the issue. In other words, Bush on October 4 did better than Quayle, especially on October 6, 9, 11, and 12.

However, our major interest remains in any delayed effects of post-debate verdicts on Quayle. In the overall table, even though the majority

Table 7.5
Which Debater Benefited from the Issue Raised* in the Debate, by Date

	Night of Interview: October						
Who Gained?	4	5	6	9	11	12	N
All Respondents							
The Republican**	53%	42%	25%	4%	19%	23%	36
The Democrat**	47%	58%	75%	96%	81%	77%	104
(N)	(19)	(19)	(24)	(24)	(32)	(22)	(136)
Republicans							
The Republican	100%	80%	63%	20%	50%	33%	18
The Democrat	0%	20%	37%	75%	50%	67%	12
(N)	(5)	(5)	(8)	(5)	(4)	(3)	(30)
Democrats							
The Republican	22%	30%	0%	0%	0%	25%	8
The Democrat	78%	70%	100%	100%	100%	75%	68
(N)	(9)	(10)	(11)	(17)	(17)	(12)	(76)

All Respondents: Chi-square = 16.59, df = 5, p < .01 for all days. When Oct. 4 deleted and Oct. 11-12 combined, Chi-square = 9.16, df = 3, p < .05
Republicans: Fisher's p=.053 (two tailed) for 4&5 vs. 6-12 combined. Fisher's p=.225 (two tailed) for 5 vs. 6-12 combined. Too few cases to calculate Chi-square value.
Democrats: Fisher's p= .028 (two tailed) for 5 vs. 6&9 combined. Low expecteds (N too small) prevent Chi-square calculation.

* This question asked only of those who said that the debate had raised an issue that could affect the election: "Which of the two candidates do you think came out best on that issue?"

** On October 4, Bush was the Republican; on Oct. 5 through 12, Quayle was. Same for Dukakis (Oct. 4) and Bentsen (5-12).

percentage (for Bush on October 4) had already slipped to a minority (for Quayle) just after the debate, much more slippage was to come, Quayle's percentage falling to a low of only 4% on October 9. The same two patterns (Bush better than Quayle and Quayle's delayed slippage) occurred for Republicans, but only the slippage occurred for Democrats. Interestingly, Democrats showed a very slight surge upward for Quayle (over Bush the day before) on October 5, but Quayle quickly hit bottom after that. So Democrats showed the delayed slippage, but not the October 4 vs. 5 reaction that Bush had done better than Quayle. Both patterns held for the Republicans, but not always significantly so. The very small number of cases available with these open-ended responses meant that we could not use Chi-square tests in the sub-tables.

In summary, we think that results for the four open-ended items are rather clear:

- Overall, Quayle's performance always looked worse 24 hours or more after the debate than it did immediately afterward.

- The same "delayed verdict" pattern generally held up for Republicans as well as Democrats, although sometimes the length of the delay—or how long the effect lasted—was not the same for both groups.

- Although none of the four questions was very directive in terms of the desired answers, the most non-directive one (name a story about the September 25 or October 5 debates) also was the one with the shortest life span in terms of casting Quayle in a bad light. Overall, mentions of this story peaked on October 9 and plunged on October 11 and 12. This life span more or less corresponded to the period of greatest network emphasis. Meanwhile, those questions eliciting responses about more enduring traits—such as Quayle's competence, or whether he would remain an issue in the campaign—hung in there over the entire time. This may mean that relatively enduring impressions of Quayle were created during this time period, when Quayle had his brief moment at center stage.

- These open-ended questions make a strong circumstantial case for a verdict effect, especially when combined with the time series survey design. The basis for saying this is not only that the mentioning of "Quayle loses" stories dropped at roughly the same time as media emphasis did but also that the delayed surge in "incompetence" descriptions corresponded in time to the frequency of post-debate media replays of Quayle's "I'm as experienced as John F. Kennedy" claim, followed by Bentsen's deft riposte. That the news media may have already laid the groundwork before the debate for Quayle's competence to be questioned only allowed the competence issue to reverberate, after the debate, when the media emphasized it even more. Recall that Quayle himself emphasized his competence repeatedly during the debate, but viewers we interviewed immediately after the debate did not pick up on that theme as often as viewers interviewed days later.

Bush vs. Dukakis—A Surprise?

Earlier, we said that we did not expect news verdicts about the Quayle-Bentsen debate to have much impact on presidential preferences. On the other hand, there was that October 6 CBS News poll story showing an increase to 43% in the percentage of Americans saying that the vice-presidential candidates were a "very important" consideration in their voting preferences (Stahl 1988).

Somewhat to our surprise, when we did an analysis similar to those applied to the open-ended questions, we found some evidence of a delayed effect on presidential choice (Table 7.6). In this short time series, support for Bush peaked immediately after the Quayle-Bentsen debate, falling considerably after that. In the section of the table at the top, which covers all cases, the only day Michael Dukakis failed to receive a majority in our three locations was, in fact, immediately after the debate.

Recall, however, that no interviews were done in Philadelphia on October 5. During this time series, interviews in urban Philadelphia produced 59.4% Democrats, compared with 44.9% in Eugene-Springfield and 41.5% in southern Illinois. Could this result, then, be an artifact of not interviewing in Philadelphia on October 5? We can eliminate this possibility by doing what we did before—that is, by holding party constant.

Looking first at the Republicans, we find somewhat stronger evidence of another verdict-delayed effect among them than we do among all respondents. Nearly all Republicans interviewed on October 4 and 5 said they would vote for Bush, but (especially on October 9) Dukakis's support grows after that. In addition, even when we delete October 4 and compare only October 5 against later days, we find less (p <.10) support for Bush later than immediately after the Quayle-Bentsen debate. Since we have removed party as an explanation in this sub-table, it appears that having more Republicans on October 5 does not explain all the day-to-day variations in Table 7.6.

For the Democrats, the day-by-day results are in the same direction as for the Republicans, but not significantly so. Unlike the Republicans, who showed 34% preferring Dukakis on one of their days, no day produced more than 12% support for Bush.

These results are intriguing, to say the least, but we must remind ourselves that many campaign events, including the October 13 debate and media interpretations of it, could offset any apparent effect on voting preferences. Leaving many weeks for recovery from the debates and post-debate verdicts was, after all, one of the purposes the Bush campaign had in mind when it insisted on a final debate no later than October 15.

Table 7.6
Voting Choice, Bush vs. Dukakis, by Day of Quayle-Bentsen Cycle

| Choice* | Night of Interview: October | | | | | | |
	4	5	6	9	11	12	N
All Respondents							
Bush	42%	52%	35%	33%	37%	35%	177
Dukakis	58%	48%	65%	67%	63%	65%	283
(N)	(76)	(66)	(71)	(97)	(82)	(68)	(460)
Republicans							
Bush	100%	93%	90%	66%	100%	82%	117
Dukakis	0%	7%	10%	34%	0%	18%	17
(N)	(21)	(28)	(21)	(29)	(18)	(17)	(134)
Democrats							
Bush	12%	12%	4%	8%	7%	10%	18
Dukakis	88%	88%	96%	92%	93%	90%	189
(N)	(33)	(26)	(27)	(48)	(42)	(31)	(207)

All Respondents: Chi-square = 7.39, df = 5, NS for all days. However, for 4 & 5 combined vs. 6 & 9 vs. 11 & 12 combined, Chi-square=7.34, df = 2, p < .05. Similarly, for Oct 5 vs. 6 & 9 vs. 11 & 12, Chi-square=6.58, 2 df, p <.05.
Republicans: Low expecteds prevent Chi-square calculation, but when 4 & 5 combined compared vs. 6 & 9 combined vs. 11 & 12, Chi-square=13.21, 2 df, p <.01. Comparing Oct. 5 only vs. 6 & 9 vs. 11 & 12, Chi-square=5.54, 2 df, p <.10.
Democrats: Low expecteds prevent Chi-square calculation, but when 4 & 5 combined compared vs. 6 & 9 vs. 11 & 12, Chi-square = 1.48, df = 2, NS. Similarly, Oct. 5 vs. 6 & 9 vs. 11 & 12 Chi-square is not significant.

* Tables contain only those who expressed a choice. Here's the way we asked the question: "If you had to vote today for one of the presidential candidates, who would you vote for?"

Ratings

We have been using Chi-square tests and, where needed because of low numbers of cases, Fisher's Exact Probability tests. These tests are most appropriate for so-called nominal-level variables—that is, when we are comparing day-by-day rates for open-ended variables. Another way of putting this is that, in the case of the open-ended variables, the values taken by the variable are *categorical*. That is, when describing Quayle's

debate performance, did the respondent use adjectives that would fall
into the category of "incompetence," or did the respondent use words
falling into some other category? As we have seen, it has not been
possible, with data of this sort, to control for more variables than the
most important one, party affiliation, because we quickly run out of
cases.

Unlike categories, ratings provide scores where it is appropriate to
compute means and variances, then subject those scores to more powerful
analytic tests, such as those explained in Chapter 2. Here we will use the
technique called Multiple Classification Analysis (MCA). What MCA
allows us to do is statistically eliminate the apparent impact of multiple
extraneous variables and then—and only then, to look at whether media
variables can explain any of the rest of what is going on with the ratings.
Using MCA, we can simultaneously control for party and several other
variables, something we could not do when dealing with the open-ended
questions. We turn now briefly to consideration of these potentially
powerful "extraneous" or "control" variables—and a rationale for their
selection.

Control Variables. In order to make the strongest possible case for a
news verdict effect, we need to bend over backward in the direction of
the extraneous variables. Then, if we find that media verdict variables
still account for much of what is happening with the ratings, we can make
a very strong case for the importance of these media variables. So, first
we need to identify those variables whose influence may *precede* in time
those short-term media messages that interest us the most. We know
already one of these extraneous variables: political party identification.
Presumably, whatever led respondents to identify themselves as a Democrat, a Republican or an Independent preceded any debate verdicts they
may have encountered in the Bush-Dukakis campaign. Social scientists
customarily assume a causal order here, where "long-term" habits, life
styles, and ways of relating to politics are causally more important than
"short-term" factors such as media messages. Thus, the word *extraneous*
does not imply irrelevance or unimportance; it implies that we feel it
necessary to control or extract this variable before we can look at what
really interests us. Here is our list of extraneous/control variables and the
rationale for selecting each.

- *Party Identification.* This may be the most important control variable, since we
  know it is powerfully related to perceptions of debate performance and to
  presidential preferences. We therefore need to extract its apparent influence
  before we look for media influences.

- *Gender.* There is some evidence (e.g., Rosenberg and Elliott, 1987, Engstrom,
  et al., 1989) that viewers' sex may affect how they react to a debate. The
  Engstrom re-analysis of University of Florida student responses to the Quayle-

Bentsen debate is especially pertinent here, since we are, of course, examining the same debate. What they found was that when their student respondents were women, exposure to the Gergen-Shields analysis apparently dampened their reactions against Quayle.

• *Locale.* One of the great advantages of our sample design is that each locale differs from the others in several respects, ranging from a very large eastern urban center to a middle-size western city, to a small city perched on the edges of the rural midwest and the south. These obvious discrepancies also are associated with large differences in the makeups of the three populations sampled. Those differences (along lines of age, income, race, employment, and education) showed up as well in our samples for this time period. If we find that, despite these differences in demographic characteristics, people responded the same ways in all three locations, we have powerful evidence for the universality of our findings. Therefore, we are entering "locale" as our final control variable.

Media Variables. After first introducing party, gender, and locale as controls, we then will introduce three media-related predictors, each in the order listed:

• *Day of the Time Series.* We have already seen that day makes a big difference with open-ended responses, so we are entering it first among the media-related predictors. Essentially, day may reflect the day-to-day changes in media emphasis on the Quayle verdict, but it does not directly represent specific media content, since it merely reflects the *availability* of that content, not its consumption by audience members.

• *Exposure to Analysis.* This is the first direct measure of exposure to media messages. Asked only of people who watched at least part of the debate, it compares people who saw a post-debate analysis with those other debate viewers who did not stay tuned for a post-debate analysis program. This is a very clear test of whether news verdicts deliver something that the debates themselves do not, since everyone in this comparison watched at least part of the debate. This measure, and the next one, depend on the accuracy of respondents' reports about what they did. One of the advantages of our time-series design is, of course, that there is a relatively short time lag between the behavior of viewing and the report of that behavior, thus minimizing the problem of forgetting.

• *Portion of Debate Viewed.* Persons who watched or heard the entire debate might feel more confident about their own impressions than people who watched only part of it. Having seen or heard only parts of the debate might predispose people to want a quick "fill-in" from news verdicts.

Let us begin with an overview of day-by-day fluctuations in the means for each of the five ratings. Table 7.7 presents a descriptive summary of the day-by-day means. These means have already been adjusted for the apparent influence of party, gender, locale, and the other variables.

Table 7.7
Day-by-Day Adjusted* Means for Five Dependent Variables

	Night of Interview: October				
Variable	5	6	9	11	12
Who won Oct. 5 Quayle-Bentsen Debate? (1=Quayle by a lot . . . to 5=Bentsen by a lot)	3.88	3.99	4.30	4.10	4.17
Rating of Quayle as a debater (0 to 10, with 10 being the "good" end)	5.24**	5.20**	4.39**	4.44**	4.31**
Rating of Bentsen as a debater (0 to 10)	7.10	7.38	7.43	7.63	7.04
Rating of chance respondent would vote for Bentsen if Bentsen were on ballot alone vs. Quayle (0=no chance; 10=certainty)	6.88	6.87	7.44	6.74	7.11
Rating of chance respondent would vote for Quayle if Quayle were on ballot alone vs. Bentsen (0 to 10)	3.62	2.64	2.11	3.09	2.25

*   "Adjusted" means are mean scores after adjusting for influence of variables *other than* "Day of Time Series" on them. Further explanation in footnote to Table 7.8.

**   This is the only time that means for day, after adjustment for other variables, differ at $p < .10$ or better. For details of this result, see Table 7.9.

Generally, these adjustments make the day-to-day fluctuations in means smaller than they would otherwise be.

Perhaps the first thing one sees in Table 7.7 is that the day-to-day fluctuations generally are headed in the direction of the verdict hypothesis. In particular, compare the mean for any set of ratings for October 5 against the mean for October 6 or 9. The second thing to notice is that the means for October 11 and 12 are more erratically placed, sometimes extending trends shown on October 6 and 9, sometimes wobbling toward a slight reversal. Only one set of adjusted daily means even approaches a statistically significant difference—ratings of Quayle's prowess as a debater. Clearly, in this case, the downward slide in Quayle's rating is delayed until October 9, but then it takes a big fall and stays there, with minor variations, on October 11 and 12.

Stronger support for the news verdict hypothesis comes when we look at exposure to post-debate analysis. In every case, people who said they watched a network analysis after the debate were more favorable toward Bentsen or less favorable toward Quayle. For every one of the five ratings, the differences reached at least the p <.10 level.

Readers who are not statisticians may find the next five tables a bit intimidating, so we will spend a little extra time explaining the first of them in the hope that this will help with the remaining ones. Table 7.8 presents the results for ratings of who won the Quayle-Bentsen debate. Scores could range from 1 (Quayle won by a lot) to 5 (Bentsen won by a lot). In the table are listed only the predictors whose relationships to "winner" ratings were strong enough to reach at least the p <.10 level of statistical significance.

Party identification is always the first variable to be tested as a predictor in these tables. The mean "winner" ratings for each party identification group are listed under the heading of "Party: Means" on the upper left side of the table. These means show that even Republicans rated Bentsen a slight winner (at 3.53 on the 5-point scale) but Independents (3.96) and Democrats, on average, gave Bentsen even higher ratings. The headings across the top of the table—"Source," "df," "Sum Squares," "MS," "F," and "Probability"—tell the statistical sophisticate that the data are being presented in the format of an analysis of variance table. From the point of view of readers who are not adept at statistics, the two main points of interest in this table should be the means for each value of the three important predictors and the probability figure given in the extreme right margin of the table. The figure .000, for example, refers to the party variable and means that the odds that these differences are merely an accident are so slim that they do not even make 1 in 1,000. In other words, it is no accident that means for Republicans, Independents, and Democrats differ by that much; these three means differ significantly.

The second variable to be significantly related to winner ratings was exposure to post-debate analysis. People who heard or saw an analysis after the debate rated Bentsen as a bigger (4.26) winner than did those who did not see or hear an analysis (3.87). Remember, all of the respondents being compared had seen/heard the debate, so we have a rather clear sign here that the analysis did something that the debate itself did not.

The third and final variable to predict winner ratings was the portion of the debate viewed or heard. People who attended to most, but not all, of the debate gave the highest rating to Bentsen as the winner, followed by those who saw the whole debate. In other words, the people who

Table 7.8
Multiple Classification Analysis: Ratings of Who Won Quayle-Bentsen Debate
(Scale: 1, Quayle by a lot; to 5, Bentsen by a lot)

Source*		df	Sum of Squares	MS	F-Ratio	Prob.
Party: Means**		2	45.012	22.506	23.225	.000
Republican	3.53					
Independent	3.96					
Democrat	4.45					
Exposure to post-debate analysis		1	9.450	9.450	9.752	.002
Yes	4.26					
No	3.87					
Section of debate seen or heard		3	8.733	2.911	3.004	.031
All	4.06					
Most	4.35					
Some	3.82					
Little	3.90					
Error***		208	201.560	.969		

Multiple R = .474 (N = 222)

---

* Only independent variables listed in tables are those which reach at least p <.10. Six independent variables, Party, Sex, Locale (the three survey sites), Day (Oct. 5-12), exposure to post-debate analysis, and portion of the debate watched, are tested in this and following tables. Multiple R in this and following tables will be for the six independent variables.

** Means are the "adjusted" means for each value of a variable. Multiple Classification Analysis adjusts the means for the influence of every other factor, then uses ANOVA to test whether the adjusted means differ. The process is conceptually identical to what happens in multiple regression when "partial" regressions are calculated.

*** Interactions between variables were folded into the error term. While Multiple Classification Analysis gives the researcher the option of doing this, it will do it automatically when some combinations of predictor variables produce too many cells with no cases in them. Largely because we didn't interview in Philadelphia on October 5, this is what happened. Folding the interactions into the error term is a conservative thing to do, and may underestimate the significant regularities in these data.

presumably had more information from the debate itself to work with also went farther in the direction of the post-debate news verdicts, while the people who spent the least time with the debate seemed to be the least inclined to go along with the verdict. At first glance, one would think that those who attended least to the debate itself would be most vulnerable to post-debate verdicts, since they might feel it necessary to use the news verdicts to help them "fill in the blanks," but this did not happen.

A verdict effect on winner perceptions seems clear in Table 7.8. Will this verdict also show up primarily in terms of Quayle—more often the object of the verdict, after all—or will it show up on the "positive" side, that is, in terms of Bentsen? The remaining possibilities, of course, are two: The verdict effect appears in ratings of both rivals, or it does not show up in either set of ratings. Let us look first at ratings of Quayle as a debater, then at ratings of Bentsen's debating prowess.

Table 7.9 presents the results for ratings of Quayle as a debater. Predictably, Republicans gave Quayle higher ratings than did Democrats and Independents. As mentioned earlier, this is the only one of the five ratings tables where day predicts a rating strongly enough ($p < .10$) to be included. Finally, those exposed to post-debate analysis gave Quayle lower ratings (4.51) than did those not exposed (4.94). In other words, the negative verdict on Quayle reached in post-debate analysis shows up, as predicted, in Quayle's ratings as a debater.

What about Bentsen's ratings as a debater? Did the verdict have an impact only on Quayle? These results are presented in Table 7.10. As we would expect, Bentsen's ratings were far higher than Quayle's, even when Republicans did the ratings. Once again, party identification powerfully predicts ratings of Bentsen, with Independents giving Bentsen the lowest ratings (the same thing they did to Quayle) and Democrats the highest. For the only time in these ratings tables, the locale control variable ($p < .10$) merits inclusion. Even after the apparent influences of party and locale are extracted, exposure to analysis remains a significant factor: Those exposed to post-debate analysis gave Bentsen higher ratings than those not, so it appears that the verdict's effects were not limited to only one of the rivals.

You will recall that a major reason for including gender as a control variable was the finding by the Florida researchers that exposure to analysis led women to moderate, or "dampen," their reactions to the debaters. So far, there is no evidence of a gender-related effect in any of the first three ratings tables. However, some support for the importance of gender is found in Table 7.11. Not only does party remain a powerful predictor, but for the first and only time gender is significantly related to one of the ratings: respondents' self-described odds that they would vote for Bentsen if he were running alone against Quayle. In this case, women's mean rating was more than a point lower than the men's.

Table 7.9
Multiple Classification Analysis: Ratings of Quayle as a Debater (Ratings from 0 [poor] to 10 [tops])

Source*		df	Sum of Squares	MS	F-Ratio	Prob.
Party: Means**		2	90.218	45.109	10.519	.000
Republican	5.51					
Independent	4.14					
Democrat	4.42					
Day of interview: October		4	37.131	9.283	2.165	.074
5	5.24					
6	5.20					
9	4.39					
11	4.41					
12	4.31					
Exposure to post-debate analysis?		1	13.278	13.278	3.096	.080
Yes	4.51					
No	4.94					
Error		217	930.585	4.288		

Multiple R = .395 (N = 231)

---

* Only independent variables listed in the table are those which reach at least p < .10. See first note in Table 7.8 for further information.

** Means are "adjusted" means. See second footnote for Table 7.8.

However, exposure to post-debate analysis continues to show an influence, independent of party and gender. Once again, those who saw a post-debate analysis made higher ratings of the chances that they would vote for Bentsen than those who were not exposed to post-debate analysis (p = .057).

In fairness to the Florida researchers, however, we should point out that what their findings would lead us to expect is that women *exposed to post-debate analysis* might have given less enthusiastic ratings to Bentsen than those who were not. This is what would be called an *interaction* hypothesis: Gender interacts with exposure to post-debate analysis. Instead, what we have been testing through these tables is a "main effect" hypothesis—that is, *regardless of exposure to analysis*, gender

Table 7.10
**Multiple Classification Analysis: Ratings of Bentsen as a Debater (Ratings from 0
[poor] to 10 [tops])**

Source*		df	Sum of Squares	MS	F-Ratio	Prob.
Party: Means**		2	51.333	25.667	9.449	.000
Republican	7.02					
Independent	6.73					
Democrat	7.69					
Locale		2	13.866	6.933	2.552	.080
Southern Illinois	7.00					
Philadelphia	7.43					
Oregon	7.51					
Exposure to post-debate analysis?		1	17.347	17.347	6.386	.012
Yes	7.63					
No	7.11					
Error		217	589.472	2.716		

Multiple R = .395 (N = 231)

* Only independent variables listed above are those which reached at least p<.10. See first note to Table 7.8.

** These are "adjusted" means. See second note to Table 7.8.

makes a difference in the ratings. Largely because of the absence of interviews in Philadelphia immediately after the October 5 debate, the analytic program did not allow a test of any interactions.

Interestingly, both party and exposure to analysis remain as important factors when we turn to voting for Quayle, but gender disappears as a factor (Table 7.12). Women were slightly more favorable than men toward Quayle as a candidate, but not significantly so. Earlier we saw that Independents had been even more negative toward Quayle as a debater than were Democrats. However, the Independents also had rated Bentsen lower as a debater than even the Republicans had, so perhaps it is no surprise to find Independents midway between the Democrats and Republicans when the question of voting for Bentsen or for Quayle arises. Even the Republicans' mean of 5.44 for Quayle hardly represented enthusiastic commitment, but it was substantially above the Democrats' rock-bottom

Table 7.11
Multiple Classification Analysis: Ratings of Chance That They Would Vote for Bentsen If He Were Running Alone vs. Quayle (Ratings from 0 [poor] to 10 [tops])

Source*		df	Sum of Squares	MS	F-Ratio	Prob.
Party: Means**		2	745.308	392.654	40.083	.000
Republican	4.50					
Independent	6.79					
Democrat	8.56					
Gender		1	49.060	49.060	5.277	.023
Females	6.60					
Males	7.63					
Exposure to post-debate analysis?		1	34.079	34.079	3.666	.057
Yes	7.27					
No	6.67					
Error		224	2082.562	9.297		

Multiple R = .545 (N = 239)

*   Only independent variables listed above are those which reached at least p < .10. See first note to Table 7.8.

**   These are "adjusted" means. See second note to Table 7.8.

1.23 and the Independents' 2.28. Once again, exposure to analysis was related to Quayle votes—in the usual direction. Those exposed to an analysis rated the odds they would vote for Quayle lower than those not exposed to post-debate media analysis.

Summary of Results for Ratings. Of the six predictors we entered, only two consistently appeared in these Multiple Classification Analysis tables: party (a control variable) and exposure to post-debate analysis. In every case, party identification, entered early and given analytic priority, powerfully predicted each of the five ratings variables. Exposure to post-debate analysis, given only the fifth-best chance to predict the ratings, emerged in every MCA table, suggesting that an important verdict effect operates independent of partisanship and of the debates themselves, and that it seems to extend beyond perceptions to voting intentions.

Finally, we should not forget the earlier results for the open-ended questions, which seemed very sensitive to the surge of newscast verdicts

Table 7.12
Multiple Classification Analysis: Ratings of Chance That They Would Vote for
Quayle If He Were Running Alone vs. Bentsen (Ratings from 0 [poor] to 10 [tops])

Source*		df	Sum of Squares	MS	F-Ratio	Prob.
Party: Means**		2	885.115	442.558	56.480	.000
Republican	5.44					
Independent	2.28					
Democrat	1.23					
Exposure to post-debate analysis?		1	24.135	24.135	3.080	.081
Yes	2.48					
No	2.99					
Error		226	1770.850	7.836		

Multiple R = .545 (N = 241)

---

* Only independent variables listed above are those which reached at least p < .10. See first note to Table 7.8.

** These are "adjusted" means. See second note to Table 7.8.

about Quayle in the first few days after the debate. Nor should we forget the surprising hint that even the Bush-Dukakis choice might have been at least temporarily influenced by the delayed effects of the Quayle-Bentsen media verdict.

It is worth repeating here that day of the interview is an indirect measure of what was in the news environment (as well as what might have been slowly diffusing from the media via discussions at work, at home, at leisure). Thus, day-to-day changes in the open-ended responses may reflect reactions to any media content (post-debate analysis, the next night's newscast, the newspaper two days after the debate, etc.) but the tie to media is greatly strengthened by the similarity between day-to-day shifts in media content and in the open-ended responses themselves.

Clearly, we have a strong and relatively long-lasting delayed verdict effect in the aftermath of the Quayle-Bentsen debate. In the next chapter, we turn to results for the October 13 Bush-Dukakis debate.

NOTES

1. Because of the World Series, at the time that the research team had committed to interview dates of October 11 and 12 it still was not clear whether

the second Bush-Dukakis debate would be October 13 or 14. However, we knew that if we interviewed on October 11 and 12, we would have at least two interview days before that debate. Because the debate was October 13, we were then able to use the money saved to pay for interviews on November 6, just two days before the election. The November 6 interviews provided a valuable late-campaign baseline that allows us to fill in many otherwise-missing observations about respondents' views very late in the campaign.

2. Reported by Leslie Stahl on the CBS Evening News with Dan Rather, October 6, 1988. Stahl's report did not make clear whether the interviews were done immediately after the debate, early the next day, or both. However, she did report that the 43% who said the vice-presidential choice was a very important consideration represented a gain of 9% over poll findings prior to the debate. Probably we can infer that what she meant was that 34% had given this response some time before the Quayle-Bentsen debate.

3. Because of low expecteds, another category of negative descriptions ("arrogant," "evasive," "abrasive," "dishonest") was not tabled. Results were not changed by eliminating these cases from the tables, since the most defensible place to have put them would have been with incompetence descriptions, and the daily changes in these "untrustworthy" descriptions closely matched the ups and downs for incompetence. Overall, 29 respondents used such untrustworthy synonyms over the six-day interview cycle, among them 4 self-described Republicans and 18 Democrats.

REFERENCES

Engstrom, E., J. Gentry, and G. Melwani. 1989. *Evidence for differential effects on males and females in the wake of the post-debate analyses.* Paper presented to annual meeting of Committee on the Status of Women, Association for Education in Journalism and Mass Communication, Washington, D.C.

Hershey, M. R. 1989. The campaign and the media. In *The election of 1988: Reports and interpretations,* ed. G. R. Pomper, R. K. Baker, W. D. Burnham, B. G. Farah, M. R. Hershey, E. Klein, and W. C. McWilliams, 73–102. Chatham, N.J.: Chatham House.

Rosenberg, W. L., and W. R. Elliott. 1987. Effect of debate exposure on evaluation of 1984 vice-presidential candidates. *Journalism Quarterly* 64: 55–64.

Stahl, L. 1988. CBS poll report. "CBS Evening News with Dan Rather," October 6.

8

THE FINAL PRESIDENTIAL DEBATE

The campaign pattern was pretty well established as we prepared for the October 13 presidential debate. While Dukakis had not caught up with Bush, the performance of Lloyd Bentsen in the vice-presidential debate seemed to have helped. For us, this second presidential debate provided an opportunity to determine whether or not the flow of the campaign and of public sentiment was switching to Michael Dukakis and whether the strong attack made by Lloyd Bentsen on the Republican vice-presidential candidate, Dan Quayle, would hurt George Bush's chances for the presidency. We followed the same design and logic in this study that we used in the previous presidential debate. The time-series design for the second debate is shown in Figure 8.1.

On October 11 and 12, the two interview nights before the second presidential debate, we asked a series of questions dealing with both the vice-presidential and presidential candidates. For instance, we asked the subjects to evaluate the performance of the Republican or Democratic

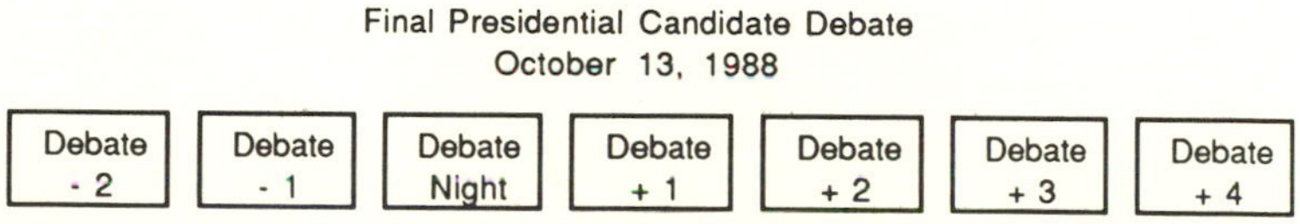

Final Presidential Candidate Debate
October 13, 1988

Debate - 2	Debate - 1	Debate Night	Debate + 1	Debate + 2	Debate + 3	Debate + 4

Figure 8.1
Final Presidential Candidate Debate Study Design

candidates during the last debate. On October 11 and 12, we were referring to Dan Quayle and Lloyd Bentsen; from October 13 through 17, it was George Bush and Michael Dukakis. Results obtained on the debate night and the nights following also allowed us to follow any continuing changes in the way our subjects responded after debate exposure and media coverage of the debate.

The sample for this portion of the study was made up of subjects selected by random digit dialing in our three test communities (Carbondale, Illinois; Eugene, Oregon; and Philadelphia, Pennsylvania). Telephone interviews were conducted in each community on the nights of October 11 through October 17. Interviewing began at approximately 7:00 P.M. and continued until approximately 10:00 P.M., except on October 13 (the night of the debate), when it started immediately after the debate and continued until approximately 10:30 P.M. A total of 758 interviews were completed: 235 in Carbondale, 273 in Eugene, and 250 in Philadelphia. The completion rate over the three sites was 55.3 percent.

As always, a parallel questionnaire was used at each data collection point. Respondents were selected from each telephone location by requesting an interview with the voting-age person whose birthday was closest to the day of the call. This procedure was followed to better balance male/female biases in telephone responses, since there is little reason to assume that birthday is gender-biased. Interviews lasted approximately 20 minutes.

NEWS COVERAGE OF THE DEBATE

The second presidential debate presented a must-win situation for Michael Dukakis. Trailing in the polls, with time rapidly running out, he needed not only to beat George Bush in the debate but to do so decisively. Dukakis did feel helped, however, by the performance of his vice-presidential running mate, Lloyd Bentsen. CBS's Bruce Morton (1988a) reported on October 10, the night before our interviewing began, that spirits in the Dukakis camp were up after the vice-presidential debate.

On October 12, the night before the final debate, Dan Rather (1988) reported on CBS News that Dukakis, behind 50 to 45 percent in the preference polls, was facing his "last big chance" to catch George Bush. Rather suggested that Dukakis's biggest problem was Dukakis himself—that the voters judged him less likable than Bush by a margin of 47 to 37 percent.

The situation for George Bush was better. He needed only to put up a good show; a tie would be seen as the equivalent of a win. Bush's major problem seemed to be Dan Quayle. CBS had reported that only one-third of the voters considered him a qualified vice-presidential candidate. If Bush could just get around the Quayle issue, the forecast looked good.

Sam Donaldson and Brit Hume of ABC, in their analysis of the upcoming October 13 debate, summarized both positions. Donaldson (1988a), reporting on the Dukakis campaign, said, ". . . he knows he must win this debate, must win the hearts and minds of a lot of voters, . . . particularly their hearts." Hume (1988) compared the campaign to a baseball game, stating, "What the Bush camp wants tonight is like what the Dodger dugout wanted at the end, last night. They're ahead, and while they'd like some more runs and hits, what they want most is no errors . . . and no late rallies."

The debate produced no major slips by either candidate, although the first question of the debate, asked by Bernard Shaw and directed to Michael Dukakis, caught many in the audience and probably Dukakis himself off-guard. Dukakis was asked, "If Kitty Dukakis (Dukakis's wife) were raped and murdered, would you favor an irrevocable death penalty for the killer?" Dukakis's response to the question, at least as later interpreted by Ken Bode (1988) of NBC, was too abstract, too unemotional.

As everyone expected, Bush had to answer questions about his vice-presidential candidate. Bush defended his running mate and attacked Quayle's critics for an "unfair pounding" of a young senator. Surprisingly, Michael Dukakis made little of the Quayle issue, spending little time attacking Bush on what many felt was a particularly weak spot in Bush's campaign. Michael Dukakis closed by asking for the "hands and hearts" of the American voters; George Bush stressed a "kinder and gentler nation."

The candidates emphasized different themes during the debate (Hershey 1989). Bush focused on symbolic themes: liberalism, Democrats, the next generation. Dukakis tried to raise domestic issues, hitting on the national debt, the budget deficit, and drug problems. Both emphasized defense issues, with Dukakis hitting hard on weapons and weapons systems.

As with the vice-presidential debate (see Chapter 7), the second presidential debate had a clear media winner, George Bush. On October 14, 1989, ABC's "World News Tonight" gave the results of instant polls indicating that Bush had won the debate. NBC "Nightly News" reported an audience of 62 million, with poll results favoring George Bush in the debate. Tom Brokaw (1988a) of NBC gave the media summary at the start of the October 14 newscast: "The consensus tonight is that Vice President George Bush won last night's debate and made it all the harder for Governor Michael Dukakis to catch and pass him in the 25 days remaining. In all of the Friday morning quarterbacking, there was common agreement that Dukakis failed to seize the debate and make it his night."

At CBS, Leslie Stahl (1988) reported the results of a CBS News poll of 440 debate viewers indicating that Bush had won by a two-to-one margin.

Sam Donaldson of ABC later described Michael Dukakis on the night of the debate as "unfocused, unaggressive, unimpressive . . ." (1988b, 104). The general feeling among many in the print media was summed up by Bob Adams of the St. Louis *Post-Dispatch* (1988): "But both Bush and Dukakis, with their painstaking preparation and coaching, appeared to avoid a fatal misstep. If a tie made Bush, in effect, the winner, then Bush had reason to be happy about the outcome."

Our own study of post-debate analysis, presented in Table 4.5 in Chapter 4, showed an important shift in the performance verdicts from the first to the second presidential debates. Where Bush had received a 42.1% favorable rating in post-debate analysis after the first presidential debate, his positives had increased to 76.1% after the second debate. Dukakis did the opposite. His 70.1% positive rating after the first debate fell to 36.1% after the second.

By Monday, October 17, the networks had pretty much given the election to George Bush. Tom Brokaw (1988b) reported the results of an NBC/*Wall Street Journal* poll that put Bush ahead of Dukakis by a 17-point margin, 55 percent to 38 percent. CBS's Bruce Morton (1988b) commented on the Dukakis campaign, stating "When you're losing, everything is a symbol . . . ." To still show that the country was not sure of Dan Quayle, CBS reported that the Teamsters had endorsed George Bush but not Dan Quayle. But, no longer did the Bush-Dukakis issue seem to boil down to Dan Quayle.

RESEARCH QUESTIONS

We looked at one general research question in our study of the second presidential debate. Did the debate itself or post-debate analysis seem to have an influence on the ways the voters evaluated and viewed the presidential candidates? What about the post-debate analysis? Did the comments of the media "experts" change or solidify the perceptions of the viewers? Specifically, we attempted to answer the following question: What was the impact of the debate on voters' evaluations of the candidates, on their perceptions of debate winners and losers, on the issues they saw as important in the campaign, and on their voting preferences, as well as on who they saw as most likely to win the election?

A debate influence here would be indicated by differences between subjects depending on the day of the interview and whether or not they had watched the debate. Change would be apparent, if the debate had had an effect, in comparisons between interviews conducted on October 11 and 12 (before the debate) and on October 13 through 17 (debate night and after). Differences would also be noted between those who watched the debate and those who did not.

The second question we asked was, what was the impact of post-debate analysis on subjects' evaluations of the candidates, on their perceptions of debate winners and losers, on the issues they saw as important in the campaign, on their voting preferences, and on who they considered most likely to win the election? The primary comparison to be used here would be between people who saw neither the debate nor post-debate analysis, people who saw the debate only, and people who saw the debate and post-debate analysis. If the commentary of those conducting the post-debate analysis had an influence on their viewers, then those attending to post-debate analysis should differ from the other two groups.

VARIABLES AND ANALYSIS

Independent Variables

Interview Date. The primary independent variable was the day of the interview. A number of our analyses were conducted by breaking down the time of interview to before the debate night, debate night, and after the debate. In addition, we were interested in the subjects' exposure to the debate and whether or not they had watched the post-debate analysis. Exposure to the debate was measured beginning on October 13 and continuing through October 17. Subjects were also asked about their exposure to post-debate analyses if they indicated they had watched the debate. Subjects interviewed on October 13, the night of the debate, were divided into three groups: (1) those who had seen the post-debate analysis, (2) those who had seen the debate but not the post-debate analysis, and (3) those who had seen neither the debate nor the post-debate analysis.

While our primary concern was the date of the interview, we also recognized the need to control for other potential influences on debate evaluations. In addition to the measures of debate exposure, we used the following independent variables as control measures in the Multiple Classification Analysis.

1. *Party Affiliation.* "Do you consider yourself Republican (1), Democrat (2), Independent (3), or what (4)?"

2. *Campaign interest.* "At this stage in the 1988 campaign, how would you describe your interest in the presidential campaign? Would you say that you are uninterested or interested in the campaign? If uninterested or interested, "Would you say you are very uninterested (interested) or somewhat uninterested (interested)?" Responses ranged from 1 (very uninterested) to 5 (very interested), with 3 indicating neither uninterested nor interested. The original responses were recoded as 1 (very uninterested, somewhat uninterested, neither), 2 (somewhat interested), and 3 (very interested) because of the very small percentage of subjects indicat-

ing they were very uninterested (7.9 percent), uninterested (13.1 percent), and neither interested nor uninterested (4.1 percent).

3. *Demographic Measures*. While we had used a number of demographic measures as independent control variables in Chapter 6, for this analysis we limited the demographic measures to locale. Subjects were coded according to their place of interview (Eugene-Springfield, Oregon; Philadelphia, Pennsylvania; or Carbondale, Illinois). The differences on these variables are presented in Table 8.1

In this time series we found differences between the three locales in family income, occupation, education, age, party affiliation, and campaign interest. For instance, Carbondale had the highest percentage of people making $10,000 or less (36.7%), the highest percentage of students (31.8%, reflecting the city's role as a university community), the highest average education level (14.9 years), and the lowest average age (37.2 years). Eugene had the highest percentage of respondents indicating membership in the Republican party (33.0%), as well as the highest percentage indicating that they were very interested in the campaign (43.8%). These differences reinforced our decision to use locale as a surrogate for these demographic measures (income, occupation, education, and age) in the Multiple Classification Analyses. Using locale allowed us to preserve the maximum number of cases, many more than had we entered each demographic variable individually, as can be seen by examining fluctuations in the numbers of cases in Table 8.1.

Dependent Variables

Again, as in Chapter 6, our dependent measures were classified into three groups: debate performance, candidate image, and voting intention. Our debate performance variables were made up of the following measures.

1. *Ratings as Debaters*. Each respondent was asked to "Use a scale running from 0 to 10 where 0 means that they are very weak debaters and ten that they are very strong debaters." They were then asked, "How would you rate Michael Dukakis as a debater?" and ". . . as a debater, how would you rate George Bush?" Information on the ratings for George Bush and Michael Dukakis for the two nights before the debate, October 11 and 12, was available only for the Carbondale and Eugene samples.

2. *Debate Winner*. "Who do you think won Thursday's presidential debate?" Subjects interviewed before the debate on October 11 or 12 were asked, "Who do you think will win Thursday night's presidential debate?" Responses were coded: "George Bush by a lot (1), George Bush by a little (2), Neither (3), Michael Dukakis by a little (4), Michael Dukakis by a lot (5)."

3. *Debate Performance Descriptions*. To get a general feeling of how

Table 8.1
Demographic and Political Variables, by Location

Variables	Carbondale	Eugene	Philadelphia
Sex			
Female	54.8%	57.2%	64.1%
Male	45.2%	42.8%	35.9%
N responding	221	271	231
Family Income**			
Less than $10,000	36.7%	18.2%	17.4%
$10,000 to $20,000	21.1%	26.7%	20.2%
$20,000 to $30,000	14.1%	19.0%	25.8%
$30,000 to $50,000	20.1%	24.8%	19.7%
More than $50,000	8.0%	11.2%	16.9%
N responding	199	258	213
Occupation**			
Full-Time Job	34.6%	50.8%	56.1%
Part-Time Job	13.4%	6.8%	6.1%
Student	31.8%	11.4%	7.8%
Retired	11.1%	18.9%	14.8%
Homemaker	6.5%	9.5%	11.9%
Unemployed	2.8%	2.7%	3.3%
N responding	217	264	244
Years Education (Mean)**	14.9	14.2	13.4
N responding	214	263	240
Age (Mean)**	37.2	43.5	42.6
N responding	213	265	243
Party Affiliation**			
Republican	29.8%	33.0%	22.9%
Democrat	34.9%	49.8%	55.8%
Independent/Other	35.3%	17.6%	21.2%
N responding	215	261	231
Campaign Interest**			
Uninterested, Neutral	22.6%	23.4%	33.5%
Somewhat Interested	38.2%	32.8%	25.0%
Very Interested	39.2%	43.8%	41.5%
N responding	217	265	236
Total N	235	273	250

*   Difference between locales $p \leq .05$. Chi-square tests used for categorical variables, analysis of variance for ratio measures (age, education).
**   Difference between locales $p \leq .01$.

the subjects would describe the performance of the Republican debaters, each one was asked, "If you had to choose a word or two to describe the performance of Dan Quayle (asked October 11, October 12)/George Bush (asked October 13 to October 17), what would those one or two words be? Parallel questions were asked about Democrats Lloyd Bentsen (asked October 11, October 12) and Michael Dukakis (asked October 13 to October 17). Responses like the following were coded as positive: excellent, good, informed, well-prepared, skillful, mature, confident, trustworthy, sophisticated and strong. Typical negative responses included bland, boring, evasive, stiff, weak, timid, wishy-washy, arrogant, inexperienced, insincere and immature. Neutral responses included average, adequate, and the like.

4. *Summed Candidate Image Scale.* Again, following the pattern used in Chapter 6, we asked each respondent to evaluate Dukakis and Bush on a scale from 0 to 10 with regard to ability to lead the country, poise and self-confidence under pressure, knowledge of foreign and defense policy, and knowledge of domestic policy. Each subject's responses to each scale were summed separately for Bush and Dukakis, forming a composite image for each candidate.

5. *Campaign Issues.* To find out the issues people were concerned about, each of our respondents was asked, "As far as you are personally concerned, what are the one or two most important issues in this presidential campaign? Begin with the issue you think is most important." The open-ended responses were coded and later content-analyzed. For our purposes, we were concerned about the public's response to the issues identified by Hershey (1989) as the domestic and foreign policy/defense issues: drugs and drug programs, the national debt and budget deficit, and military weapons and weapons systems. In our coding, these translated to responses related to the budget deficit, drugs and crime control, defense, and the arms race and disarmament.

Finally, we asked our subjects a number of questions about their voting intentions and who they thought would win the election.

6. *Candidate Voting Probability.* "Based on a scale from 0 to 10, where 0 means that you definitely would not vote for the candidate and 10 that you definitely would vote for that candidate, what would you say, from 0 to 10, describes your likelihood of voting for Michael Dukakis? For George Bush?"

7. *Today's Vote.* "If you had to vote today for one of the presidential candidates, who would you vote for?"

8. *Expected Election Winner.* We added another question for this analysis, one tapping who the respondents thought would win the election rather than who they were voting for: "Who do you personally think will win the election for president on November 8, Michael Dukakis or George Bush?"

Analysis

We analyzed the data and addressed the research questions using Chi-square, Multiple Classification Analysis, and one-way analysis of variance techniques. For the Multiple Classification Analyses, all independent variables were entered simultaneously into the regression equations. To test the influence of exposure to post-debate analyses, comparisons were made between those subjects who had watched the post-debate analysis, those who had watched the debate but not the analysis, and those who had watched neither the debate nor the analysis.

RESULTS

Debate Performance

Ratings as Debaters and Debate Winner. In Figure 8.2 the mean ratings of the candidates as debaters are presented from October 11 through October 17. What the figure shows is that George Bush's rating as a debater was above Michael Dukakis's on October 11 and 12, despite Dukakis's apparent win in the first debate and the very strong showing of his running mate, Lloyd Bentsen, in the vice-presidential debate. Dukakis apparently did pull much closer on debate night (October 13) and the nights following.

These observations are supported in the MCA results presented in Table 8.2. For both candidates, there is an improvement in their mean ratings as debaters from before the debate (October 11 and 12) through the night of the debate and after. George Bush improved from a 6.72

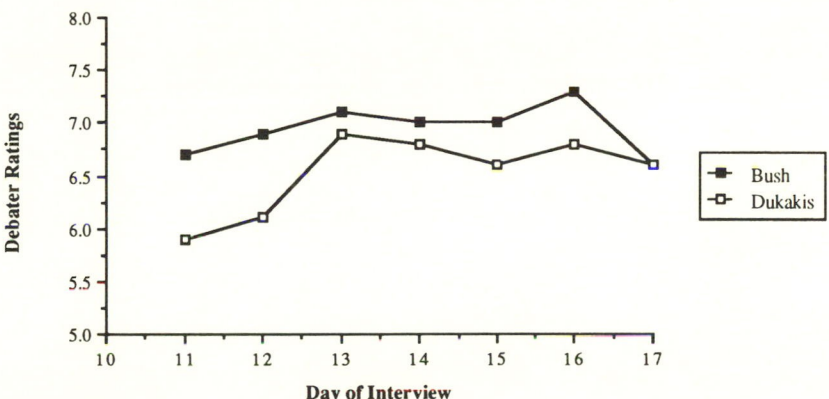

Figure 8.2
Presidential Candidate Ratings as Debaters, by Day

Table 8.2
Multiple Classification Analysis: Adjusted Mean Scores for Ratings as Debaters and Debate Winner, by Time of Interview, Party, Campaign Interest, Locale, and Sex (October 11 to October 17 Cycle)

Independent Measures	Ratings as Debaters		Debate Winner
	Bush	Dukakis	
Grand Mean	7.01	6.62	2.58
Time of Interview			
October 11-12 (Before Debate)	6.72	6.08	2.50
October 13 (Debate Night)	7.18	6.89	2.94
October 14	7.08	6.85	2.49
October 15	7.30	6.64	2.68
October 16	7.16	6.77	2.47
October 17	6.61	6.45	2.60
Beta	.13*	.13*	.12
Party Affiliation			
Republican	6.96	7.12	1.91
Democrat	7.30	6.48	3.02
Independent/Other	6.43	6.26	2.57
Beta	.18***	.17***	.41***
Campaign Interest			
Uninterested, Neutral	6.45	6.05	2.61
Somewhat Interested	7.11	6.94	2.53
Very Interested	7.23	6.68	2.60
Beta	.16***	.17***	.03
Locale			
Carbondale	7.05	6.59	2.80
Philadelphia	7.40	6.63	2.69
Eugene	6.52	6.64	2.28
Beta	.18***	.01	.20***
Sex			
Female	7.09	6.65	2.65
Male	6.90	6.58	2.49
Beta	.05	.02	.07
Multiple R^2	11.2%***	7.6%***	22.9%***
Total N	536	537	488

* $p < .10$
** $p < .05$
*** $p < .01$

mean score before the debate to 7.18 the night of the debate. He remained at about this level except for the last interviewing night, when his average fell to 6.61. Michael Dukakis also improved from a 6.08 average debater rating prior to the debate to 6.89 the night of the debate, his highest rating of the interviewing period, but still below the 7.18 average rating for George Bush.

Party affiliation was also related to the ratings of the candidates as debaters. Surprisingly, Democrats rated George Bush as a better debater than did the Republicans (7.30 vs. 6.96), while Republicans returned the compliment by rating Dukakis higher as a debater than did the Democrats (7.12 vs. 6.48). Apparently, both candidates were more impressive to people in the opposing parties, although, when asked about who had won rather than simply rating the candidates as debaters, subjects clearly indicated that Bush came out ahead.

The perceptions of who won or would win the debate show little difference on any of the variables except party affiliation, where the usual pattern after the debates holds. Republicans saw Bush as the winner (mean = 1.91 on a 5-point scale where 5 indicated a definite win for Dukakis, 3 that neither candidate had won, and 1 a definite win for Bush), Democrats placed it about even (mean = 2.97), and Independents and others slightly favored Bush with a mean of 2.58. Locale also showed differences: Eugene picked Bush most strongly (mean = 2.28), although Carbondale and Philadelphia also selected Bush as the winner (means of 2.80 and 2.69, respectively).

Campaign interest was also related to debater ratings. For George Bush, the most interested in the campaign rated his debating skills highest, with an average rating of 7.23. For Michael Dukakis, the middle interest group (those indicating they were somewhat interested) rated him highest at 6.94. People in Eugene rated George Bush quite low (6.52) in comparison with Carbondale (7.05) and Philadelphia (7.40).

Table 8.3 presents the results for the analysis from debate night (October 13) through October 17, this time broken down by debate exposure. Our primary interest was in the comparison between those who watched neither the debate nor post-debate analysis, those who watched the debate but not the post-debate analysis, and those who watched both the debate and the analysis. In this table, debate exposure was related to George Bush's rating as a debater. Here the pattern followed what would be expected if both the debate and the post-debate analysis influenced the viewers. Bush's lowest ratings came from those who watched neither the debate nor the analysis (mean = 6.40). Those who watched the debate only rated him at 7.08 on the 10-point scale. Viewers of both the debate and the analysis rated him highest, 7.25. No parallel influence was seen for Michael Dukakis. The suggestion here is that the debate and post-debate analysis might have influenced the audience. The benefit

Table 8.3
Multiple Classification Analysis: Adjusted Mean Scores of Candidate Ratings as Debaters and Debate Winner, by Debate and Post-Debate Analysis Exposure, Party, Campaign Interest, Locale, and Sex (Debate Night, October 13, to October 17 Cycle)

Independent Measures	Ratings as Debaters		Debate Winner
	Bush	Dukakis	
Grand Mean	6.89	6.71	2.52
Debate and Post-Debate Analysis			
Neither Debate nor Analysis	6.40	6.59	2.52
Debate Only	7.08	6.59	2.64
Debate Plus Analysis	7.25	6.93	2.44
Beta	.20***	.09	.07
Party Affiliation			
Republican	6.99	6.92	1.90
Democrat	7.10	6.70	2.97
Independent/Other	6.33	6.43	2.58
Beta	.16**	.09	.42***
Campaign Interest			
Uninterested, Neutral	6.58	6.30	2.52
Somewhat Interested	7.04	7.00	2.40
Very Interested	6.92	6.67	2.62
Beta	.09	.14**	.09
Locale			
Carbondale	6.98	6.70	2.60
Philadelphia	7.93	6.62	2.26
Eugene	6.48	6.74	2.49
Beta	.26***	.02	.09
Sex			
Female	7.05	6.79	2.61
Male	6.68	6.61	2.41
Beta	.10*	.05	.09*
Multiple R^2	11.5%***	4.5%*	20.6%***
Total N	346	348	290

* $p < .10$
* $p < .05$
*** $p < .01$

seems to go to the candidate favored in post-debate analysis, in this case George Bush. In the first presidential debate, the pattern for candidates had been reversed (see Table 6.3), with the ratings for Michael Dukakis then apparently reflecting the favorable post-debate commentary directed at him.

While political party affiliation and locale remained significant predictors in this table, campaign interest no longer was tied to ratings for George Bush, although it still remained a significant predictor for Michael Dukakis, with those indicating that they were somewhat interested (mean = 7.00) rating Dukakis higher than the uninterested (mean = 6.30) and very interested (6.67). There was also a slight tendency for women to rate Bush higher (mean = 7.05) than men (mean = 6.68).

The possible influence of post-debate analysis as measured on debate night only is presented in Table 8.4. Unlike Table 8.3, which covers the period from October 13 through October 17, looking at debate night only allows an investigation of possible debate and post-debate analysis influence before other factors (press influence, interpersonal discussion, etc.) could play much of a role in candidate interpretations.

For those subjects interviewed just after the debate on October 13, there was a significant influence of exposure to the debate and post-debate analysis for the ratings of Michael Dukakis. Viewers of the debate only rated Dukakis (mean = 6.15) well below viewers of both the debate and post-debate analysis (7.68). For our relatively small sample on debate

Table 8.4

One-Way Analysis of Variance: Mean Scores for Ratings as Debaters and Debate Winner, by Debate and Post-Debate Analysis Exposure (Debate Night, October 13, Only)

	Ratings as Debaters	
Independent Measures	Bush	Dukakis[1]
Grand Mean	6.92	7.01
Debate and Analysis		
Neither Debate nor Analysis	6.82	6.82
Debate Only	6.53	6.15
Debate Plus Analysis	7.22	7.68*

[1] Significant difference between groups, $F_{2,49} = 2.90$, $p < .10$.
* Differs from the "Debate Only" group, $p < .10$, Scheffe´ Test

night only (N = 52), the analysis still seemed to help Dukakis, even though the content of that analysis was more favorable to George Bush (see Chapter 4). No significant differences were observed for Bush's ratings, although the analysis group also gave Bush a marginally higher rating.

Debate Performance Descriptions. Subjects were asked to describe the debate performance of each candidate "in a word or two." Responses were then classified into negative (weak, cocky, boring, etc.), neutral (average, sincere, cautious, etc.), and positive (good, excellent, powerful, etc.) categories. The responses recorded from debate night through October 17 are presented in Table 8.5. The influence of exposure to the debate and to post-debate analysis is most clearly displayed in the descriptions of George Bush. Only 38.3% of our respondents who watched neither the debate nor the analysis described Bush in positive terms. That figure increased to 55.4% for those who saw the debate only and to 64.4% for those watching both the debate and the analysis. There is less difference in the pattern shown for Michael Dukakis. Here, viewers of the debate (those watching the debate only and those going on to watch the post-debate analysis) seemed more likely to describe Dukakis positively and less likely to use neutral terms than non-debate viewers.

Summary. The findings on debate performance during the second presidential debate suggest, once again, an influence of both exposure to the debate and exposure to post-debate analysis. For this debate, the influence of debate exposure, and especially of exposure to post-debate analysis, seemed to favor George Bush's rating and description as a

Table 8.5
Cross-Tabulations: Open-Ended Debate Performance Descriptions, by Debate and Post-Debate Analysis Exposure (October 13 to October 17 Cycle)

Independent Measures	Bush Descriptions**			Dukakis Descriptions*		
	Neg	Neu	Pos	Neg	Neu	Pos
Neither Debate nor Analysis	40.0%	21.6%	38.3%	41.8%	25.5%	32.7%
(N)	(24)	(13)	(23)	(23)	(14)	(18)
Debate Only	31.3%	13.3%	55.4%	45.6%	11.4%	43.0%
(N)	(26)	(11)	(46)	(36)	(9)	(34)
Debate and Analysis	29.7%	5.9%	64.4%	44.2%	10.0%	45.8%
(N)	(35)	(7)	(76)	(53)	(12)	(55)

*   p < .10, Chi-square test.
**   p < .01

debater. The highest debater ratings for Bush were among those watching both the debate and the analysis. The same pattern occurred for open-ended descriptions of George Bush as a debater. Michael Dukakis did seem to fare slightly better among debate only and post-debate analysis viewers.

The following observations regarding our respondents' ratings and descriptions of the candidates as debaters seem warranted:

- Watching the October 13 debate contributes to positive performance descriptions of the candidates. This result was true for both George Bush and Michael Dukakis.

- Post-debate analysis has a consistent impact on the way viewers rate the candidates as debaters. This result showed up very strongly in the analysis of the debater ratings gathered on debate night only, where Michael Dukakis's ratings among those watching the analysis were significantly higher than those watching the debate only.

We now turn our attention to the images of the candidates held by our respondents.

Candidate Image

We present our analyses of the influence of the debate and post-debate analysis on our composite candidate image measure in Tables 8.6 and 8.7. The changes in the candidates' image measures are shown graphically in Figure 8.3. Examination of Figure 8.3 shows that both candidates experienced a strong increase in their composite image evaluations beginning on October 13. But, after that, things were different. Michael Dukakis's improvement declined by the next day, before rising and again falling. For George Bush, the image improvement held for three days before falling. The figure indicates that Bush showed the most improvement in his image over the time period.

The Multiple Classification Analysis for the composite candidate image measures is first presented in Table 8.6 for the entire second presidential debate interviewing period. At this level, the time of the interview had no statistically significant impact on candidate image. George Bush's composite image was influenced by party affiliation where Republicans, not surprisingly, scored Bush at an average 30.57 out of a possible 40, compared with the Democrats' average score of 22.59. Democrats saw Dukakis as having the strongest image, with an adjusted mean of 27.53, while Republicans at 21.56 saw Dukakis less positively. Independents fell between the other two groups for both candidates.

Campaign interest also was related to candidate image. For George Bush, those expressing moderate interest levels (somewhat interested)

Table 8.6
Multiple Classification Analysis: Adjusted Mean Scores for Candidate Image, by Time of Interview, Party, Campaign Interest, Locale, and Sex (October 11 to October 17 Cycle)

Independent Measures	Image Rating	
	Bush	Dukakis
Grand Mean	25.38	25.01
Time of Interview		
October 11-12 (Before Debate)	24.58	24.58
October 13 (Debate Night)	25.41	25.71
October 14	26.97	24.73
October 15	25.74	26.16
October 16	25.12	25.06
October 17	24.70	24.32
Beta	.11	.09
Party Affiliation		
Republican	30.57	21.56
Democrat	22.59	27.53
Independent/Other	24.26	24.25
Beta	.45***	.36***
Campaign Interest		
Uninterested, Neutral	22.98	22.71
Somewhat Interested	26.25	24.29
Very Interested	25.95	26.69
Beta	.17***	.22***
Locale		
Carbondale	25.22	24.50
Philadelphia	25.37	25.68
Eugene	25.52	24.86
Beta	.02	.07
Sex		
Female	25.03	25.61
Male	25.82	24.27
Beta	.05	.09**
Multiple R^2	25.6%***	23.0%***
Total N	583	561

*   p < .10
**   p < .05
*** p < .01

Table 8.7
Multiple Classification Analysis: Adjusted Mean Scores for Candidate Image Ratings, by Debate and Post-Debate Analysis, Party, Campaign Interest, Locale, and Sex (Debate Night, October 13, to October 17 Cycle)

Independent Measures	Image Rating	
	Bush	Dukakis
Grand Mean	25.75	24.60
Debate and Analysis		
Neither Debate nor Analysis	24.66	23.57
Debate Only	25.63	24.83
Debate Plus Analysis	27.03	25.51
Beta	.14*	.12
Party Affiliation		
Republican	30.54	20.84
Democrat	22.46	27.55
Independent/Other	24.78	24.23
Beta	.47***	.41***
Campaign Interest		
Uninterested, Neutral	23.98	23.68
Somewhat Interested	27.02	23.80
Very Interested	25.55	25.75
Beta	.15***	.14**
Locale		
Carbondale	25.47	24.15
Philadelphia	26.91	26.29
Eugene	25.58	24.44
Beta	.07	.10
Sex		
Female	25.57	25.44
Male	25.97	23.61
Beta	.03	.13**
Multiple R^2	26.4%***	25.9%***
Total N	334	322

* $p < .10$
** $p < .05$
*** $p < .01$

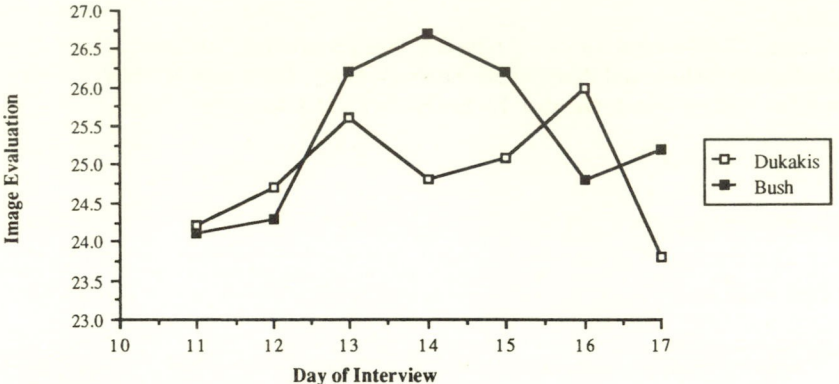

Figure 8.3
Presidential Candidate Composite Image Evaluations, by Day

gave him the highest adjusted mean image score, 26.25. For Michael Dukakis, the very interested saw his image most positively, with an adjusted mean of 26.69. Women were more favorable to Dukakis's image than men.

In Table 8.7 we look at the same composite image ratings, but this time only for the October 13 (debate night) to October 17 cycle. Our primary analysis focused on whether or not the respondents had watched neither the debate nor analysis, watched the debate only, or watched both debate and post-debate analysis. The image data suggest that George Bush benefited from the debate and post-debate analysis, much as his rating as a debater benefited from exposure to the debate and post-debate analysis. Those who watched neither the debate nor the analysis and those who watched only the debate saw Bush's image similarly. Those who saw both debate and analysis gave him the highest adjusted mean image score. That image score reflects the direction one would expect, based on the judgments expressed in post-debate commentary, where Bush was evaluated more favorably than Michael Dukakis. No significant differences were found among the debate exposure groups for Michael Dukakis's image ratings. As was the case in Table 8.6, party affiliation and campaign interest remain significant predictors for the image ratings of George Bush and Michael Dukakis, and women continue to evaluate Dukakis's image more favorably than men.

Summary. What can we say about the candidates' composite image ratings? First, the influence of the debate and post-debate analysis on candidate images appears to have decreased since the first presidential debate, when Michael Dukakis apparently benefited the most from post-debate analysis (see Tables 6.8 and 6.9). Although weaker, the pattern was similar for this debate, this time with Bush benefiting most from post-debate analysis. Post-debate analysis has an apparent influence on the audience's image of the candidates. This influence results in that audience adopting the most favorable image toward the candidate favored in the post-debate analysis. In this case, George Bush, considered the winner of the final presidential debate, benefited most among the viewers of the post-debate analysis. For the candidate seen in the analysis as the debate loser in this case, Michael Dukakis, there seems to be little impact.

Our final analyses turn to the outcomes of most concern to the politicians: the way people evaluate the likelihood they will vote for either candidate, the way they would vote if the election were held at the time of their interviews, and who they think is going to win the election.

Voting Intentions and Expected Election Winner

Voting Intentions. People's voting probabilities for the two presidential candidates, as measured on a 0 to 10 scale, where 0 indicated that people definitely would not vote for the candidate and 10 that they definitely would, are graphically displayed in Figure 8.4. As shown, there was a shift in the probabilities of voting for George Bush at the time of the debate and a very slight decrease in the probabilities of voting for Michael Dukakis on debate night (October 13).

The Multiple Classification Analysis of these findings is presented in Table 8.8. No statistically significant influences were detected based on the time of the interviews. Further multiple classification analyses of exposure to the debate and to post-debate analysis also failed to show

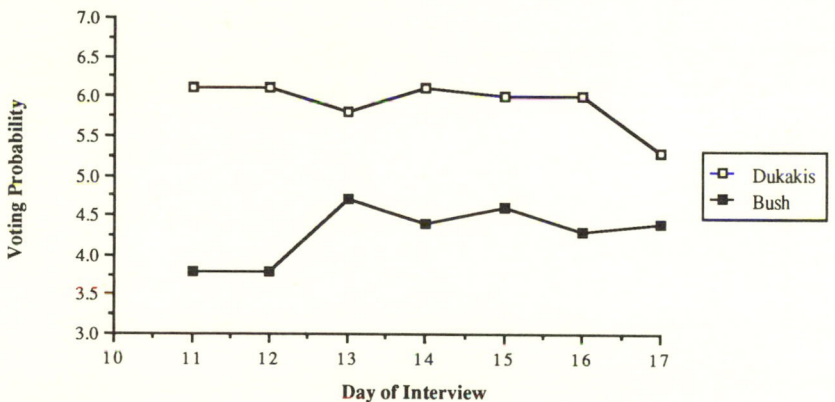

Figure 8.4
Voting Probability for Presidential Candidates, by Day

Table 8.8
Multiple Classification Analysis: Adjusted Mean Scores for Candidate Voting Probabilities, by Time of Interview, Party, Campaign Interest, Locale, and Sex (October 11 to October 17 Cycle)

Independent Measures	Voting Probability For	
	Bush	Dukakis
Grand Mean	4.24	5.94
Time of Interview		
October 11-12 (Before Debate)	4.01	6.08
October 13 (Debate Night)	4.43	5.97
October 14	4.69	5.88
October 15	3.84	6.53
October 16	4.58	5.48
October 17	3.99	5.67
Beta	.08	.08
Party Affiliation		
Republican	8.32	1.93
Democrat	2.06	8.39
Independent/Other	3.39	6.04
Beta	.67***	.68***
Campaign Interest		
Uninterested, Neutral	3.78	5.56
Somewhat Interested	4.77	5.81
Very Interested	4.09	6.25
Beta	.10***	.07*
Locale		
Carbondale	4.15	5.79
Philadelphia	4.52	6.19
Eugene	4.37	5.86
Beta	.05	.04
Sex		
Female	3.96	6.03
Male	4.63	5.82
Beta	.08**	.03
Multiple R^2	47.2%***	47.9%***
Total N	610	609

* $p < .10$
** $p < .05$
*** $p < .01$

statistically significant influences (data not tabled). The expected influences, particularly party affiliation, played the major role in determining candidate voting probability. This result does represent a slight shift from the first presidential debate, where Michael Dukakis seemingly benefited from the debate and post-debate analysis. Perhaps voting preferences were more fixed late in the campaign.

In addition to asking about voting probabilities, we also asked subjects to choose whom they would vote for if they had to vote today. These findings, which compare levels of debate and post-debate analysis exposure, are presented in Table 8.9. No statistically significant differences were found between subjects who had watched neither, the debate only, or the debate plus post-debate analysis. A follow-up analysis of October 13 respondents also failed to show any statistically significant differences among the three exposure groups.

Expected Election Winner. The final set of findings regarding the election is presented in Table 8.10. Here we were looking at who people think will actually win the election, broken down by debate and analysis exposure. While there were no statistically significant differences based on debate and post-debate analysis exposure, one thing is very clear from the table. By the time of the second presidential debate, the public had conceded the election to George Bush. The overwhelming percentage of our respondents thought Bush would win. Clearly, the majority, regardless of who they were intending to vote for, expected George Bush to win.

Summary. By mid-October, at the time of the final presidential debate,

Table 8.9
Voting Choice, by Debate and Post-Debate Analysis Exposure (Debate Night, October 13, to October 17 Cycle)

	Voting Probability For	
Independent Measures	Bush	Dukakis
Debate and Post-Debate Analysis		
Neither Debate nor Analysis	51.1%	48.9%
(N)	(72)	(69)
Debate Only	42.9%	57.1%
(N)	(39)	(52)
Debate Plus Analysis	41.1%	58.9%
(N)	(46)	(66)

Table 8.10
Expected Winner, by Debate and Post-Debate Analysis Exposure (Debate Night, October 13, to October 17 Cycle)

Independent Measures	Who Will Win the Election?	
	Bush	Dukakis
Debate and Post-Debate Analysis		
Neither Debate nor Analysis	75.7%	24.3%
(N)	(109)	(35)
Debate Only	80.2%	19.8%
(N)	(65)	(16)
Debate Plus Analysis	82.5%	17.5%
(N)	(85)	(18)

support for each candidate appears to have solidified, at least to the point where watching the debate or viewing the post-debate analysis had little or no influence on the way people were going to vote. Not only that, by this time our subjects had pretty much conceded the election to George Bush, regardless of who they personally were going to vote for.

CONCLUSION

In general, the findings we have presented covering the second presidential debate parallel those of the first debate (see Chapter 6). Exposure to the debate and to post-debate analysis influenced audience ratings of the candidates as debaters, particularly for the candidate receiving the most favorable treatment in televised post-debate analysis. In this case, the beneficiary was George Bush. Similarly, when asked to describe the debate performance of the candidates, subjects who had watched the debate and post-debate analysis were more likely to describe George Bush favorably, reflecting the interpretation given his performance in post-debate commentary. In this case, 76.1% of the verdicts regarding George Bush by post-debate commentators were favorable, compared with only 36.1% for Michael Dukakis (see Table 5, Chapter 4). In our study, 64.4% of the people who watched both the debate and post-debate analysis described George Bush favorably, in comparison with 45.8% using similar positive descriptions to describe Michael Dukakis.

The image of the candidate, at least as measured by us with the composite image scale, indicated that post-debate analysis influenced evaluations in the direction suggested by the post-debate commentators. That is, given that the post-debate commentary regarding George Bush's performance was positive, the image of George Bush seemingly benefited, with his highest ratings taking place among those watching both the debate and the analysis. By the time the final presidential debate had been completed, neither the debate nor analysis seemingly had much of an influence on voting intentions for either candidate. In fact, most of our sample had pretty much given the election to Bush.

Overall, the influence of the third debate and post-debate analysis continued to play an important role in the way people were responding to the campaign and to the candidates. Even though their influence at this time appears to be less than it was for the first presidential debate, it is still noticeable. In a closer race, the issues discussed during the debate and the comments made during televised analysis could play a politically significant role. In this campaign, the final presidential debate virtually assured Bush's victory in November.

REFERENCES

Adams, B. 1988. Bush probably gained more than Dukakis from match. St. Louis *Post-Dispatch,* October 14, A8.

Bode, K. 1988. "NBC Nightly News with Tom Brokaw," October 14.

Brokaw, T. 1988a. "NBC Nightly News with Tom Brokaw," October 14.

Brokaw, T. 1988b. "NBC Nightly News with Tom Brokaw," October 17.

Donaldson, S. 1988a. "ABC World News Tonight with Peter Jennings," October 13.

Donaldson, S. 1988b. On the Dukakis campaign trail. *Gannett Center Journal* 2 (4):87–118.

Hershey, M. R. 1989. The campaign and the media. In *The election of 1988: Reports and interpretations,* ed. G. M. Pomper, R. K. Baker, W. D. Burnham, B. G. Farah, M. R. Hershey, E. Klein, and W. C. McWilliams, 73–102. Chatham, N.J.: Chatham House.

Hume, B. 1988. "ABC World News Tonight with Peter Jennings," October 13.

Morton, B. 1988a. "CBS Evening News with Dan Rather," October 10.

Morton, B. 1988b. "CBS Evening News with Dan Rather," October 17.

Rather, D. 1988. "CBS Evening News with Dan Rather," October 12.

Stahl, L. 1988. "CBS Evening News with Dan Rather," October 14.

9

DEBATES IN THE EYES OF THE AUDIENCE

Political campaign debates serve an institutional role in promoting democracy in the United States. Political debates, like elections, provide a ritual for citizens to evaluate current and potential political leaders. Campaign debates give the public the opportunity to evaluate candidates in terms of how they present both themselves and their issue positions.

While debates have been a predominant feature in the last few presidential campaigns, there is no guarantee that they will be held. The delicate balance of having or not having presidential debates is integrally related to the concepts of democracy and risk. The participants in the debate—the candidates, the media, the debate sponsors, and the audience—all have certain goals. It would be safe to assume that, at least at some level, they are united in a goal to promote the notion of public discourse, which ultimately fosters a democratic society. The linkage of a common goal is moderated by potentially divisive self-interests that exist among and between all four sets of participants.

THE PARTICIPANTS

Candidates

The candidate leading in popular support generally wishes to avoid the debates, if at all possible, since there is much to lose and little to gain. The challenger seeks debates because they provide a chance to force the opponent into a mistake which will enhance the challenger's opportunity for a victory. Challengers also sense that their presence itself in the debate may serve to legitimize their own candidacy. In terms of format and staging, presidential debates present the participants as authoritative and powerful individuals who command respect and legitimacy.

Presidential candidates themselves view the debates as a source of legitimization. In the 1980 presidential race, the League of Women Voters originally extended debate invitations to Jimmy Carter, Ronald Reagan, and John Anderson. Anderson, while a third-party candidate, was invited because he had exceeded a 15% minimum in the poll ratings, the League's standard for an invitation. However, when the invitation was made, Carter refused to participate because he felt that Anderson's candidacy would be legitimized by Anderson's presence in the debate—a candidacy that Carter felt was largely a creation of the media. The result was the eventual single two-candidate match-up between Carter and Reagan, since Anderson's poll ratings fell below the 15-point mark a week before the election. Anderson was, however, able to present himself in a presidential debate format earlier by squaring off with Reagan in a two-candidate debate. Surely, the presence of Anderson with Carter in a three-candidate debate would have increased Anderson's support, assuming that he did not blunder in his performance.

Candidates seek to create positive images of themselves and legitimize their role in debates. As much as a candidate may be reluctant to debate the rival party's nominee, he or she is even more reluctant to allow third-party or fringe candidates to participate.

Media

The media also have a primary goal associated with the debates: transmitting the debate to the public. Often active participants in the negotiations surrounding the development, promotion, and format of a debate, the media appear to believe, as an industry, that the promotion of debates is a means to ensure the continuance of democracy in the United States and that debates, like elections, provide the public with an opportunity for assessment of our leaders prior to casting a ballot.

Sponsors

The sponsors also have goals to promote. Both the League of Women Voters (LWV) and the Commission on Presidential Debates (CPD) want to ensure the image of an open and free exchange of ideas—although only within a narrow context. In return for the chance to present the "production" to the public, sponsors are at the very least amenable to the demands of the candidates to restrict participants, including candidates and questioners, as well as to limit alternative debate formats.

The Audience

Finally, the audience has a series of goals which must be addressed in terms of presidential debates. First, the public may seek to address certain motives or gratifications related to political activity. Among others, McLeod and Becker (1974) have suggested a number of motives related to one's uses of communication, including surveillance, vote guidance, anticipated communication with others, excitement, reinforcement, partisanship, relaxation, alienation, and entertainment. These gratifications may cause the individual differentially to seek or avoid political communications such as political debates. The degree to which people monitor presidential debates is moderated by their life situation (i.e., work, family, health, etc.) and the degree of utility they feel they will achieve with each of the above motives or gratifications.

The presidential campaign debates are promoted in a concerted manner by all of the actors associated with the debates—candidates, media, sponsors, and the public—moderated by each group's perceived or actual risks, constraints, or desires.

HISTORY OF PRESIDENTIAL DEBATES

Prior to 1960, presidential campaign debates had a longstanding but limited role in our political history. Not until the candidacy of Stephen Douglas in 1860 did candidates for the presidency begin to campaign publicly and actively for the office. Many still simply remained near their homes or in the political offices they currently held and fostered the image of a reluctant draftee for the presidency. To appear eager to obtain the office was presumed to be the kiss of death for a presidential candidate; it was not until the advent of modern media that much of this aura began to disappear. In the earlier presidential campaigns candidates simply allowed their campaign managers to create specific, market-segmented, issue positions to various portions of the country that would appeal to the specific localized desires. In this way support could be garnered even if inconsistent positions were being presented to various electorates. With the advent of a more sophisticated and nationally distributed media coverage, this practice became increasingly more difficult to carry on. However, even when the candidates did begin to campaign actively, they still did not participate in face-to-face presidential debates for quite some time.

The 1960 Kennedy-Nixon debates are generally considered groundbreaking events marking the entrance of presidential election campaign debates into the television age. Modern televised political debates give us the opportunity to evaluate the presidential and vice-presidential debates in terms of their influence on and consequences for the political system.

One important component of this investigation is how both the audience and the non-audience view the institution of political debates. Modern debates also give us the chance to examine the acceptance of political system legitimacy through the power relationships that develop between the public, the media, and the political leadership of our society.

Although they began on an irregular basis, debates—since 1976—are generally presumed to be a standard part of each fall presidential election campaign. Debates now take place during both the primary and general election periods. In the primary period, the debates may serve to narrow the scope of candidates within each party. The general election debates may serve to further crystallize voting choices after each party's standard bearers have been selected at the conventions.

POSITIVE AND NEGATIVE ASSESSMENTS OF DEBATES

A number of arguments have been proposed regarding the positive and negative aspects of political debates as an institution. These arguments relate to the way audiences interact with debates. Dye and Ziegler (1989), in *American Politics in the Media Age*, present a very cogent list of points to consider. They argue affirmatively for debates as an institution, because debates attract more viewers than any other political event and provide an audience which includes not only a candidate's supporters but undecided and opposition voters as well. In addition, we would add that media coverage of the debates may well enlarge the sphere of the influence even more through a secondary, mediated audience who watch or read coverage about the event. The importance of presidential debates to the public is highlighted by the ABC News and John F. Kennedy School of Government study (Kraus 1988, 128) in which 58% indicated that the actual debates were more helpful in deciding who to vote for than either television news reports or the candidate's own political advertisements. According to Watson (1984), in *The Presidential Contest*, the estimated audience size of the 1980 debates was 100 million viewers.

Dye and Ziegler also suggest that debates provide the public with the opportunity to witness a "drama of confrontation" in which the viewers may directly compare the responses of the candidates side by side, rather than being dependent on controlled spot advertisements or small sound bites on news programs. Finally, they propose that the televised debates allow viewers to make judgments about candidates in terms of how they react as human beings under pressure.

Dye and Ziegler also posit a series of negative assessments regarding political debates. For example, the emphasis on the showmanship of the candidates may unjustly penalize candidates who make verbal and non-verbal mistakes, gaffes, or inappropriate gestures which have little relevance to their ability to govern. In the 1976 presidential debate, Ford's comment about Poland not being under Soviet domination—presumably a blunder rather than an error made as a result of a lack of understanding—served as a devastating blow to his image as an informed leader in foreign affairs. A second negative argument is Dye and Ziegler's assessment that the debates are really not debates over issues but, rather, joint press conferences into which candidates can weave carefully crafted stump speeches and rehearsed responses. Candidates may recognize that the large size of the audience for a debate may actually be a threat rather than a benefit because the stakes are so high. We would argue that the public presentation of candidates in a debate format in which there is a potential of risk may not necessarily be a bad feature of debates, since ultimately the candidate who is elected must face difficult and highly stressful situations. Fortunately or not, part of contemporary political leadership is handling the media and presenting one's image to the public. However, because of the possibility of making a mistake, the candidates may well try to avoid spontaneous debates. When they find themselves in such a situation, they choose to seek safe positions for themselves, while trying to undermine or embarrass their opposition rather than explaining and debating substantive policy positions and differences.

RITUALIZATION OF POLITICAL EVENTS AND LEGITIMIZATION

Presidential debates provide the public with a ritual that reinforces political system legitimacy. In *Public Opinion and American Politics,* Bennett (1980, 381) states that "all institutions have rituals to display the procedures, deliberations, or decisions to the public." He recognizes that sometimes the public may be an active participant in the ritual or a member of the passive audience whose approval is necessary for the legitimate operations of the institution. Regardless of its role, the ritual according to Bennett is "designed to capture the public's attention, promote understanding, limit conflict, and structure the public's responses." He goes on to say that rituals use symbolic references to themes, images, and values of enduring political myths to accomplish this task. Political scientists have recently begun to recognize the role of elections as rituals, but this recognition must extend further to televised political debates which have as their cornerstone a ritualized procedure.

Similarly, Murray Edelman (1964) suggests that elections serve as a vehicle for symbolic reassurance, helping tie the masses to the established order by giving them a sense that they have a role in the political process. Symbolic reassurance tends to reinforce system legitimacy. We would argue that, like elections, political debates have a legitimizing influence on the electorate. While Edelman argues that the public has little influence on eventual policy decisions, he suggests (1964, 17) that elections serve to "quiet resentments and doubts about particular political acts, reaffirm belief in the fundamental rationality and democratic character of the system, and thus fix conforming habits of future behavior." Edelman also suggests that politics plays a role in the formulation of a resolution or law which may in no way specifically solve a substantive problem but somehow relieves the tension associated with the situation and directs the public's attention elsewhere. Candidate debates, like policy-making debates in non-electoral settings such as legislative or public meeting forums, utilize the political process of ritualization. The ritualization provides the opportunity for individuals to discuss the issues and relieve tension, even if the attempt is not to resolve them.

According to Paletz and Entman (1981), legitimacy is closely tied to the concept of political socialization. They define legitimacy as "the widely shared belief that the political system is right for society and their governing institutions, and officials rightly hold and exercise power. Political socialization is the process by which members of the society acquire political norms, attitudes, values, and beliefs" (Paletz and Entman, 1981, 150). How the media present candidates and develop debate verdicts influences the public's beliefs about their political system's legitimacy. With manifestly open and free public debates, the central beliefs about the way our political system should operate are reinforced.

SPONSORSHIP OF THE DEBATES: THE LEAGUE OF WOMEN VOTERS VS. THE COMMISSION ON PRESIDENTIAL DEBATES

In order to have presidential debates, some organization must organize and or sponsor them. For a number of years the League of Women Voters, a non-partisan good-government group, has been actively involved in the promotion and hosting of a number of debates. In order for the debates to enhance system legitimacy, the public must perceive the sponsor as neutral and unbiased, seeking to promote free and open political discourse. In 1988 the League found it difficult to ensure participation of the candidates in the presidential debates. Another group, the Commission on Presidential Debates, which was organized by the political parties themselves and created with the hope that it would be able to insure candidate participation, wished to sponsor a presidential debate. While both groups may be considered by many to be neutral, they are in fact not out of the realm of partisan politics. Specifically, one may well question the strength of these organizations in handling the access of third-party candidates. However, even given the fact that these organizations might have problems presenting third-party candidates because of their orientations, the question remained: Who should sponsor the debates? The League, which was given only the option to present the third debate, eventually withdrew its sponsorship, primarily as a protest of the candidates' rather autocratic control of the debate. Then the Commission stepped forward as the sponsor of all the debates in 1988. Many would argue, however, that the CPD is actually under the control of the candidates, an arrangement which prevents a free and open exchange. All in all, the issue has been raised as to whether either organization can actually provide legitimate debates between the candidates.

In order at least partially to address the question of sponsorship, we asked our respondents whether there should be a single sponsor of the presidential debates. Just after the spring primaries in Pennsylvania, Illinois, and Oregon and on November 6, we posed specific questions for our respondents regarding sponsorship of the debates. First, they were informed about the CPD and the LWV as rival sponsors of separate fall debates. They were asked whether in future elections there should be a single sponsor of the fall debates.

Table 9.1 presents the results of this analysis. Of those who felt that there should only be one sponsor, 23.4% preferred the CPD and 76.6% preferred the LWV. Of those who said there should not be a single sponsor, 46.2% preferred the CPD and 53.8% preferred the LWV. The LWV may be advantaged in terms of recognition, even though the CPD played such an important role in the 1988 presidential debates, because the LWV has historically been so involved in presenting debates not only at the presidential level but also in other races, such as gubernatorial, senatorial, and mayoral elections.

Table 9.2 presents the results of our analysis of whether people think the campaigns should have more control of the debate format than the preferred debate sponsor. Respondents who indicated that they preferred LWV sponsorship were, not surprisingly, of the opinion that the campaigns should have less control over the debate format than were people who favored the CPD as sponsor. Based on the experience with the CPD's sponsorship of the 1988 fall debates, there is little reason to believe that the campaigns have *less* control of debate format and ground rules than when the LWV was sponsor (see Chapter 5). Whether the CPD can ever exert appropriate control over the campaign organizations is presently doubtful, at best.

HISTORICAL BACKDROP OF POLITICAL DEBATES IN THE UNITED STATES

It is important to review the historical backdrop of American debates. The ideal held by Americans regarding presidential campaign debates is, unfortunately, mythic. Opinion leaders such as scholars and journalists, when thinking about debates, often reflect on the classic confrontations between Abraham Lincoln and Stephen Douglas. Those debates actually

Table 9.1
Preferred Sponsor of Presidential Debates, by Whether There Should Be Only One Sponsor*

	Sponsor Preference	
Single Sponsor? (N)	Commission	League
Yes (N=128**)	23.4 %	76.6 %
No (n=156**)	46.2 %	53.8 %

Chi-square = 14.792, df = 1, p < .001.

* The questions were worded as follows:

Post-Primary Survey question item:

"As you may know, for the first time, both a special commission from the two major parties and the League of Women Voters are sponsoring two separate sets of debates this fall, one set for each of the rival sponsors. Some say the League should be the sponsor of the debates since it has long experience in doing so. Others say that the parties should be the sponsors, since the parties have the clout to make sure their own nominees will agree to debate. In future elections, do you think there should be a single sponsor of the fall debates?"

November 6th survey question item:

"As you may know, for the first time both a special commission from the two major parties and the League of Women Voters were to sponsor separate debates this fall. The League of Women Voters turned down the invitation to sponsor the October 13th debate. Some say the League should be the sponsor of the debates since it has long experience in doing so. Others say that the parties should be the sponsors, since the parties have the clout to make sure their own nominees will agree to debate. In future elections, do you think there should be a single sponsor of the fall debates?"

Post-Primary and November 6th survey question item:

"If there is only to be one sponsor holding fall debates in the future, which organization do you think it should be? The Commission representing the two parties or the League of Women Voters?"

** Cases in the table combine Post-Primary and November 6 interviews with registered voters.

occurred during the Illinois senatorial elections of 1858; there were no formal presidential-level debates until 1860. The televised debates beginning in 1960 bear little resemblance to the "real" debates of that earlier period.

In the original Lincoln-Douglas debates, the first speaker was given an hour to present his case; then the opponent was given an hour and a half

Table 9.2
Comparison of Mean Scores on Whether the Campaigns Should Have Less Control Over Format of Debates, by Preferred Sponsor (1 = strongly disagree; 5 = strongly agree)

Preferred Sponsor	N	Mean	t-value	d.f.	prob.
Commission on Presidential Debates	20	3.2500	1.92	56	.06
League of Women Voters	38	3.7895			

Note: Interviews with registered voters collected on November 6, 1988.

to present a counterargument, which was followed by a half hour rebuttal by the first speaker. The process involved rotating which speaker was first each time they debated. In the 1858 senatorial race the candidates debated seven times, allowing each congressional district the opportunity to witness a debate whose duration and structure provided a totally different format from the candidate-controlled press conference debates of the modern age. These early debates allowed the public to compare issue positions in great detail.

The Lincoln-Douglas debates were extensively covered by the partisan newspapers of the era. The early spin doctors, the journalists for the two partisan papers in Illinois, sought to create positive images of their respective candidates. With the newspapers taking such partisan positions, one would assume that the readers may have been selectively reading and perceiving information regarding candidates. This would presumably allow the coverage to reinforce voters' existing opinions or at least to create an information base for the individual's interpretation. Coverage by the rival presses of the time differed substantially in terms of both factual information and how different audiences responded to it. The material presented in the debates actually became the text for a political document used in the 1860 presidential contest. Ironically, this debate document is an example of early American "dirty tricks."

The political leaders of 1860 felt that the material presented in the 1858 senatorial debates was, indeed, a valuable information source for the voters. Since much of the material dealt with national rather than local issues and thus provided voters with a rather extensive presentation of the candidates' respective positions on the issues of the day, political leaders decided to publish the text of those debates. The text of the debate speeches was published in such a way as to allow Lincoln to edit his materials, resulting in a more impressive image of himself, while Douglas was not given the same opportunity.

In the mid 1900s the debates began to be covered to a limited extent by other than simply print media, as enabled by new technologies. The debate between Dewey and Stassen in 1948 was broadcast over the radio, as was the 1952 debate between Harriman, Hoffman, Kefauver, Kerr, Stassen, and Warren. In 1956 Kefauver and Stevenson debated, and coverage was provided by both television and radio. In 1960 Kennedy and Humphrey debated on television, as did Johnson and Kennedy. All of the debates—except the last, which was a convention debate—were primary election debates.

Televised Debates and the FCC

General election televised debates between the standard bearers of their respective parties began with the Kennedy-Nixon debates of 1960, providing the audience with the opportunity to evaluate the two candidates side-by-side. Many would argue that these debates played a pivotal role in the election of 1960. After this election, however, the public was denied this opportunity for 16 years due to questions raised about the equal-time provisions and the fairness doctrine. There was no ban on debates but, rather, restrictions on how they operated, resulting in reluctance by the candidates, the parties, and the networks to provide debates.

Incumbent presidents leading in the polls had many incentives to use the FCC provisions to avoid debating. In fact, many actors could use the FCC regulations to minimize political risk. The candidates—particularly front runners—did not have to risk enhancing the candidacy of third-party candidates or their major party rival if they chose not to debate. The networks were protected in that if the debates were not held, the responsibility did not lay just at their doorsteps. They could still provide coverage of the campaign and conventions as well as the elections, but they did not have to allow alternative candidates the same degree of access that they might have received had there been presidential debates. When these restrictions were relaxed, the media maintained debates between only the two major party candidates, with only a single exception in 1980.

The "equal time rule," a provision of Section 315 of the Federal Communications Act of 1934, requires broadcasters who permit one candidate for public office to campaign on their stations to give equal opportunity to every other candidate for that office. The "fairness doctrine," also listed in the same section of the act, requires radio and television broadcasters who air material on a controversial issue to provide reasonable time for the expression of opposing points of view. Hence, for many years the public was denied the opportunity to evaluate presidential candidates through a televised debate format because of unwillingness by the broadcasters and some mainstream candidates to grant equal air time or participation to all.

It was not until 1976 that televised presidential debates again were presented to the American electorate. The 1976 election produced the matchup of Gerald Ford, the incumbent who was trailing in the polls, and Jimmy Carter. In 1980 the incumbent Carter, trailing in the polls, was anxious to debate challenger Reagan. In 1984, confident in his abilities, Reagan agreed to debate Mondale. Finally, in 1988 presidential and vice-presidential debates were held between Bush and Dukakis and Quayle and Bentsen. While the emphasis of this book is on presidential and vice-presidential debates during the general election periods, presidential candidates have on a number of occasions participated in debate formats both within and between political parties during non-general election periods—for example, those held during primaries or (in 1960) between Johnson and Kennedy at the Democratic National Convention.

Audience Size for Debates

The size of the televised presidential debate audiences is staggering. Table 9.3 presents the televised general election debates since 1960 with their respective audiences. The 1960 debates between Kennedy and Nixon received the largest relative audience size of any of the presidential debates examined, ranging in average household rating percentage from 57.8% to 61.0%. The ratings for the debates between Carter and Ford, as well as their respective running mates, declined from the 1960 levels. The 1976 debate ratings ranged from a low of 47.8% for the last debate between Carter and Ford to a high of 53.5%. The debate between the vice-presidential candidates was substantially lower, 35.5%.

An increase in ratings to approximately 1960 levels occurred in the lone 1980 major party debate between Carter and Reagan, with 58.9% of the households viewing it. In 1984 the debates began to slide again in the ratings, with the Mondale-Reagan debates receiving 45.3% for the first and 46.0% for the second debate. The vice-presidential debate between Ferraro and Bush had a slightly smaller rating of 43.6% of the households viewing.

The pattern of decline continued with the 1988 debates. These debates recorded the lowest ratings of any televised general election debates except for the vice-presidential debate of 1976, with 36.8% for the first and 35.9% for the second. The vice-presidential debate received an audience of only 33.6%. This debate was critical to Dukakis's ultimate chances for victory, since he was trailing in the polls at the time. Even the clearly decisive victory attributed to Bentsen, however, was not enough to recover the lead for the Dukakis-Bentsen tandem.

The decline in audience sizes for the 1988 presidential and vice-

Table 9.3
Presidential and Vice-Presidential Debates Television Audience Ratings (1960–1988)*

Year/Date	Candidates	Average Household Rating %	Average # Household (Millions)	Average # Persons (Millions)
1960				
Sept. 26	Kennedy-Nixon	59.1	27.9	NA
Oct. 7	Kennedy-Nixon	59.1	27.9	NA
Oct. 13	Kennedy-Nixon	61.0	28.8	NA
Oct. 21	Kennedy-Nixon	57.8	27.3	NA
1976				
Sept. 23	Carter-Ford	53.5	38.0	69.7
Oct. 6	Carter-Ford	52.4	37.3	63.9
Oct. 13	Mondale-Dole	35.5	25.3	43.2
Oct. 22	Carter-Ford	47.8	34.0	62.7
1980				
Sept. 21	Anderson-Reagan	NA	NA	NA
Oct. 28	Carter-Reagan	58.9	47.1	NA
1984				
Oct. 7	Mondale-Reagan	45.3	38.5	65.1
Oct. 11	Ferraro-Bush	43.6	37.0	56.7
Oct. 21	Mondale-Reagan	46.0	39.1	67.3
1988				
Sept. 25	Dukakis-Bush	36.8	33.3	55.6
Oct. 5	Bentsen-Quayle	33.6	30.4	46.9
Oct. 13	Dukakis-Bush	35.9	32.5	52.0

*   Data provided by the Nielsen Media Research News organization, 1989.

presidential debates may be attributed to at least two factors. First, there has been a proliferation of public affairs programming in general dealing with presidential campaigns. This includes the increasing number of primary presidential debates and the increasing amount of primary and general election coverage, convention coverage, and debate coverage on television and in the press. A second reason is the increasing role of political surveys during the presidential campaign. These surveys indirectly influence public perceptions about the utility of debates, since the surveys are continually providing the electorate with an evaluative measure of how the public generally, as well as certain specific groups, view the candidates, their images, and the issues. This continual evaluation mechanism provides individuals with a means to compare their own personal perceptions with those of others. Therefore the surveys may in some ways replace the individual's dependency on watching the debates, because the survey results will give them an "electorate-wide" assessment of the candidates.

Audience Images of Debates

Even though the televised presidential debates have a decreasing audience share, the candidates still reach a large and diverse audience. Schramm and Carter (1959) discovered that the public tends to expose themselves selectively to political messages. Nevertheless, Chaffee and Dennis (1979) suggest that the debates are not subject to the selective attention barrier but reach partisans on both sides, because, in order to watch one candidate, viewers must also watch the other.

During the 1988 spring post-primary interviews, respondents were asked whether they saw live broadcasts or excerpts of the primary debates. Table 9.4 presents the results of that investigation. Overall, most (56.9%) registered voters indicated that they had either seen at least one of the primary debates or news excerpts. Interestingly, when the question item was examined by political party, the same overall pattern was found for both parties, with most watching either the live debate or the excerpts. However, a difference did appear between Democrats and Republicans with regard to watching the opposition party's debates. Democrats were less likely to have watched the live Republican debates (19.3%) than were the Republicans to have watched the Democratic ones (32.0%). An explanation for this difference may be that Republicans wanted to find out more about the larger, less well-known and more diverse field of Democratic contenders while Democrats felt they already knew about the Republicans. Beyond that, it is clear that the presidential primary debates were able to generate a large, heterogeneous audience from both parties.

The fall presidential and vice-presidential debates give the public an opportunity for direct, side-by-side comparison of the candidates. The voters are able to examine the candidates, their strengths and weaknesses as individuals, and their ability to handle questions under varying degrees of stress. This experience permits important focused comparisons.

Even when the debates do not contain much substantive information about the issues, they may allow some members of the public a relatively low-effort vehicle to collect information about the candidates in a condensed and structured way. While the candidates may have already

Table 9.4
Presidential Primary Debate Viewing of Television Excerpts, by Political Party

Primary Debate/ Excerpts Viewing	Total	Democrats	Republicans	Independent Other
Yes, News excerpts	12.3%	11.0%	15.2%	9.8%
Yes, Democratic debate live	10.9%	14.1%	6.4%	9.8%
Yes, Republican debate live	1.4%	1.6%	1.6%	0.0%
Yes, Both parties debates live	11.4%	8.9%	12.8%	17.6%
Yes, Democrat live + excerpts	8.3%	12.0%	5.6%	2.0%
Yes, Republican live + excerpts	3.0%	1.0%	6.4%	2.0%
Yes, Both parties lives + excerpts	7.4%	5.8%	7.2%	13.7%
Yes, Saw something but don't don't remember	2.2%	2.1%	1.6%	3.9%
No, Didn't see anything	43.1%	43.5%	43.2%	41.2%
Column N	367	191	125	51
N as % of Total	100.0%	52.0%	34.1%	13.9%

Note: N=367 Registered Voters interviewed during the Spring, 1988 Post-Presidential
   Primary period. Independents, Other party affiliation (N=2, and "Don't Know"
   (N=8) responses were collapsed under an Independent/Other category with the
   Independents.

articulated their individual positions during the campaign, the debates give the public another chance to compare the contenders. This dependence on the debates may depend on education and political interest. This issue will be addressed later in this chapter when we evaluate the opinions of our respondents regarding debates.

The debates put a premium on the showmanship abilities of the presidential candidates. The participants must be able to respond quickly and appropriately within a dynamic environment. They know that their speech, their presentation—their whole image—are under close scrutiny. Chaffee and Dennis (1979) even go as far as to suggest that the televised presidential debates encourage and reinforce a "star system" in which the eyes of the nation focus on just two candidates seeking the presidency, while diminishing the importance of other levels and branches of government. Candidate performance in the debate may or may not have relevance to the ability to govern. While the question of handling issues in the debate may concern many, the candidate's ability to manage the issues in the media may be just as critical in this media age.

The ability to manage is on two levels. First, as Jamieson and Birdsell (1988) suggest, by preparing for the debates, candidates are forced to consider and think through issues ahead of time so that they are prepared for the debate. A second level of managing is the candidate's ability to present himself or herself as competent and in control of a situation or subject area that he or she is being confronted with—in other words, to demonstrate that one is being proactive in thought as well as potentially in action, rather than unaware or ineffectual.

Finally, the debates may serve as entertainment for the audience. The principal feature of debates, according to Dye and Zeigler (1989, 16), may not be simply to enlighten or educate but, rather, "to satisfy the public's thirst for drama and confrontation." While much of the debate is pre-structured, the candidates and those posing the questions are at least trying to create the illusion that the debate is dealing with the important issues of the day.

PUBLIC ASSESSMENT OF THE DEBATES

Respondents to our series of questionnaires provided their evaluations of both the number and utility of the presidential debates. The data from this inquiry were subjected to analysis of variance, Multiple Classification Analysis, and t-tests. Analysis-of-variance tests were performed on all analyses in which there were more than two groups; otherwise, t-tests were undertaken. We were attempting to find out if, for example, a social locator variable such as age made a difference in the evaluation of the debates. The independent variables we examined were age, education, income, political party affiliation, and wave (i.e., time period during campaign). Campaign interest and a measure of cynicism, "mudslinging," were utilized as covariates in many of our analyses.

Specifically, we examined whether respondents thought there were enough televised debates scheduled, whether the debates are a good way to learn about candidates' issue positions, whether the public feels that the candidates avoid questions during the debates, whether the debates are generally a waste of time, and finally whether the debates are the best way to make a final voting decision about the candidates. Each respondent was asked whether he or she strongly agreed, agreed, was neutral, disagreed, or strongly disagreed with the following statements:

Statement 1: "Not enough televised presidential debates have been scheduled."
　(Variable name *Enough*)

Statement 2: "Presidential debates are one of the best ways for me to learn where the candidates stand on the issues." (Variable name *Bestlrn*)

Statement 3: "Presidential candidates always seem to avoid answering the important questions during the debates." (Variable name *Evade*)

Statement 4: "All in all, I think the televised debates have been a waste of time." (Variable name *Wastetime*)

Statement 5: "Televised presidential debates are the best way for people to make their final voting choice." (Variable name *Bestchuz*)

Each of the above ratings was transformed into a 1 to 5 scale, with one being "strongly agree," and five being "strongly disagree." It is important to note that agreement statements for the variables Enough, Bestlrn, and Bestchuz are positive statements for the present situation of debates as a political institution, while they are negative statements for the variables Evade and Wastetime. Only those respondents who expressed an opinion were included in this analysis; those who were neutral were considered as expressing a middle perspective between strongly agree and strongly disagree. The data analyzed here represent the responses of registered voters interviewed during the three fall debate cycles plus November 6. In other words, every registered voter we interviewed during the fall campaign is in this data set, excluding only incompletes and refusals.

Overall, we hypothesized that our social locator variables and the time in which we interviewed respondents during the campaign would make a difference in their evaluations of the debates. Specifically we thought that:

H1. Younger persons would be more likely to evaluate the debates positively than older persons. Voting studies have traditionally shown that generally younger persons, along with the oldest in our society, tend to be the least involved politically. Debates may provide a framework for the young to monitor politics in a limited manner. Thus they may view debates positively. The young may feel that the few debates that are presented are an efficient way to keep up with politics, and thus may even desire more of these condensed information vehicles as an alternative to other information-monitoring mechanisms.

H2. Individuals with more education would be more likely to evaluate the debates positively than those with less education.

H3. People with higher income levels would be more likely to evaluate the debates positively than those with less income.

[For both H2. and H3. the voting literature has consistently shown that those with higher SES tend to be more involved and actively seek out political experiences. Therefore, those with higher educational attainment and income should be more likely to evaluate the debates positively as an institution. One must be aware, though, that they may also be critical of the debates if they do not provide what is expected, because the higher SES groups may recognize this failure more explicitly.]

H4. Democrats would be likely to evaluate the debates more positively than Republicans. For example, in 1988 Dukakis originally led in the polls after the conventions. When he began to trail, the debates were seen as a vehicle to make a comeback.

H5. The further into the campaign period, the lower the public's positive assessment of the debates would be. As voters were able to watch the debates unfold, they may have felt that they had their questions about the candidates answered as fully as they would ever be. Since most had decided early on who would likely win and who they would support, the value of the later debates might diminish.

Four of the five hypotheses were generally confirmed. The overall results of these analyses are presented in Tables 9.5 and 9.6. In our analyses, we first used campaign interest and then mudslinging as covariates. In this way we could control for the effect that each played on the relationships between our series of independent variables and our dependent debate evaluation variables. Our findings, when controlling for both cynicism in the campaign (by using the question item which indicated that there was too much mudslinging going on in the campaign) and for campaign interest revealed similar patterns.

Respondents generally felt that (1) there were enough debates scheduled, (2) the candidates generally avoided answering the important issues that come up in a debate, (3) debates on average were marginally the best way to learn about the candidates and issues, (4) debates were on average marginally a waste of time, and (5) debates were evaluated somewhat marginally negative by the public in their assessment that debates are the best way for people to make their final voting choice. Interestingly, except for the item dealing with candidates avoiding the issues in the debate, the average overall debate evaluations generally hovered in the neutral range.

The covariates, campaign interest and mudslinging, were generally significantly related to our debate evaluation items. Campaign interest was not found to be related to the item that debates are the best way to make a final vote choice, but it was related to all of our other items. The covariate mudslinging was found to be related to Evade, Wastetime, and Bestchuz, but not to Enough and Bestlrn. Tables 9.5 and 9.6 present the Multiple Classification Analysis results and F-values of our covariates for both analytic models.

Age, education, and political party affiliation were the social locator variables which appeared to have the highest degree of discriminating power among the debate evaluation items investigated. Educational at-

News Verdicts, the Debates, and Presidential Campaigns

Table 9.5
Multiple Classification Analysis: Debate Evaluations of Registered Voters* with
Covariate Campaign Interest (1 = strongly disagree; 5 = strongly agree)

Variables	Enough	Evade	BestIrn	Wastetime	Bestchuz
Covariate: Campaign					
Interest F-ratio	14.47[3]	10.56[3]	10.34[3]	138.79[3]	2.02
Independent Variables:					
Age					
18-25	3.06		3.49	2.29	2.71
26-35	3.00		3.36	2.38	2.54
36-45	2.99		3.17	2.60	2.48
46-65	2.74		3.12	2.60	2.42
Over 65	2.58		3.03	2.77	2.59
Beta	.15[3]		.14[3]	.14[2]	.09[1]
School					
0-12 yrs	2.95		3.37		2.86
13-16	2.81		3.24		2.42
Post-grad	3.04		3.41		2.33
Beta	.08[2]		.09[2]		.20[3]
Party					
Republican	2.67	3.61	3.09		2.40
Democratic	3.03	3.77	3.39		2.64
Indep-Other	2.95	3.79	3.16		2.52
Beta	.14[3]	.07[2]	.12[3]		.10[2]
Wave					
Pre 9/25	3.02	3.48			2.85
9/25-10/4	3.10	3.59			2.52
10/5-10/12	2.97	3.86			2.53
10/13-11/6	2.74	3.81			2.48
Beta	.17[3]	.13[3]			.10[3]
Mean	2.90	3.72	3.25	2.51	2.54
Multiple R	.29	.20	.22	.34	.26
N	1327	1324	1338	1338	1331

1	p < .05;
2	p < .01;
3	p < .001
*	Interviews of registered voters during entire fall study period.

Table 9.6
Multiple Classification Analysis: Debate Evaluations of Registered Voters* with Covariate Mudslinging (1 = strongly disagree; 5 = strongly agree)

Variables	Enough	Evade	Bestlrn	Wastetime	Bestchuz
Covariate:					
Mudslinging F-ratio	3.66	41.85[3]	1.58	17.45[3]	4.33[1]
Independent Variables:					
Age					
18-25	3.07		3.49	2.29	
26-35	3.01		3.35	2.42	
36-45	2.95		3.16	2.62	
46-65	2.76		3.13	2.56	
Over 65	2.60		3.05	2.72	
Beta	.143		.133	.133	
School					
0-12 yrs	2.94		3.34	2.61	2.85
13-16	2.81		3.25	2.51	2.43
Post-grad	3.06		3.11	2.36	2.36
Beta	.082		.072	.082	.193
Party					
Republican	2.67		3.09		2.41
Democratic	3.04		3.39		2.65
Indep-Other	2.94		3.16		2.54
Beta	.143		.123		.103
Wave					
Pre 9/25	3.04	3.51			2.85
9/25-10/4	3.11	3.60			2.53
10/5-10/12	2.97	3.86			2.55
10/13-11/6	2.63	3.79			2.49
Beta	.183	.123			.092
Mean	2.90	3.72	3.25	2.51	2.55
Multiple R	.29	.24	.19	.20	.26
N	1325	1320	1332	1332	1326

[1] $p < .05$;
[2] $p < .01$;
[3] $p < .001$
* Interviews of registered voters during entire fall study period.

tainment, which was included in our analytical model using the covariates campaign interest and mudslinging, was not significantly related to any of our debate evaluation items. Thus, while education was included in our statistical analyses, there is no record of it in our tables.

Age was significantly related to the number of debates scheduled, learning from debates, the feeling that debates are the best way to make a voting choice, and whether the debates were, all in all, a waste of time, regardless of the covariate used. The question of whether candidates evade the issues was not differentiated by age. The general pattern established was that younger respondents, while neutral, were more likely to feel that not enough debates were scheduled. They also were more likely to feel that the debates were the best way to learn about the candidates and their issues, that debates were the best way to make final voting choices, and that debates were, all in all, not a waste of time. Younger respondents therefore tend to view the debates in a more positive manner than their elder counterparts.

Depending on whether campaign interest or "too much mudslinging" was used as a control variable, education level did, or did not, predict evaluations of the debates. When controlling for campaign interest, there was no significant difference between educational levels and whether the debaters avoid answering important questions (Evade) or were a waste of time (Wastetime). However, when using mudslinging, our cynicism measure, as a covariate, we found that as educational levels decreased, respondents were more likely to feel that the debates were a waste of time. Similar patterns existed between the various educational levels and our other debate evaluation items. Respondents with the highest educational attainment level were more likely than those at the lowest end to feel that there were not enough debates and that debates are the best way to learn about the candidates and issues. However, the higher educational level group was less likely to feel that debates are the best way to make a final voting decision than those on the lower end. Those with higher educational backgrounds may recognize the value of the debates in presenting information, while at the same time seeking to incorporate a number of other experiences and information sources into their final voting decision.

Political party identification was significantly related to four of the five debate evaluation items when controlling for the covariate campaign interest, and to three of the five items when mudslinging was the covariate. Republicans tended to feel that there were enough debates scheduled, while the Democrats were more neutral in their feelings.

The final variable included in our debate evaluation model was "wave," the period of time in which the interview occurred during the election period. Wave, regardless of which covariate was used, yielded a similar pattern of results; it was significantly related to three of our five debate evaluations, including whether there were enough debates scheduled, whether candidates avoided the issues, and whether debates were the best way to make a final voting choice. Prior to September 25 (the first fall debate) respondents were more likely to express a sense that not enough debates had been scheduled than they were considerably later in the campaign. After the first debate and before the second, the wish for extra debates became even stronger. However, after the October 5 vice-presidential debate, respondents began to express the opinion that perhaps there were enough debates scheduled. This lack of desire for extra debates could be attributed to two points. First, the public may have generally already decided who to vote for. Support for this point was evidenced by the fact that most voters indicated early in the fall campaign (by October) that they knew who they were voting for, as well as often expressing the belief that Bush would likely win the election. Second, having seen at least one of the 1988 debates, respondents were feeling that extra debates would not add enough new information to change their orientations toward the candidates.

As to whether candidates evade the issues, overall the respondents felt that they did. After the vice-presidential debate, they felt so even more. As the election got closer, they were also more likely to feel that the debates were not the best way to make a final voting decision. Perhaps, earlier in the campaign, the public was more receptive to the debates as an institution to promote democratic ideals. But as the campaign progressed, public opinion of debates as an institution to promote democracy generally declined. The good that was to be accomplished through debates had already been done for many of our respondents.

MEDIATED DEBATE COVERAGE AND THE AUDIENCE

As was demonstrated in Table 9.4, even during the primary period most people were monitoring the debates. In the fall, we decided to ask a series of items regarding the importance of watching the actual debate, of watching television coverage, of reading newspaper coverage, of listening to radio coverage, and of engaging in interpersonal communication about the debate in informing the individual about the debate itself. The results of this analysis are presented in Table 9.7.

The data suggest that the public considers watching the actual debate the best source of information about what was presented in the debate. Beyond that, the registered voters interviewed indicated the following order of importance of sources of information about the debate: (1) newspaper articles, (2) conversations with family and friends, (3) television news reports, and (4) radio reports. In our t-test paired comparisons, all of our examined sources were found to be significantly less important than the actual debate as a source of information about the material

Table 9.7
Means and Differences of Importance Self-Assigned by Respondents* to the Actual Televised Presidential and Vice-Presidential Debates vs. Other Sources of Information in Evaluating the Presidential Candidates and the Positions They Present on Issues During the Debate

Source of Information**	Mean	t-value	d.f.	2-tail prob.
Actual Presidential debate	6.20			
Newspaper articles about the debate	5.64	7.80	1603	.000
Talks with family and friends about the debate.	5.60	7.40	1597	.000
TV News reports about the debate	5.56	9.28	1597	.000
Radio reports about the debate	4.70	19.76	1572	.000

*   Interviews collected from September 22, 1988, to November 6, 1988, of registered voters.
**   The question item was: " When you evaluate the presidential candidates and the positions they present on issues during the debates, how important are the following sources of information?   Here, let's use a scale from zero to ten, with zero being not at all important and ten being very important."

presented in the debate. Interestingly, there was little difference in the public's assessments of television news (mean of 5.56 out of 10), newspaper articles (5.64), and conversations with family and friends (5.60). However, radio reports about the debates were scored lower.

At the end of the election period, on November 6, we asked respondents to evaluate a number of sources of information in helping them to decide whether to vote at all. In a period of continually declining participation in presidential elections, we wanted to examine if various information sources were differentially related to the decision to vote at all. Table 9.8 presents the results of this analysis. The data show that the debates themselves were clearly in the middle of the sources in helping potential voters decide whether to vote. Television news coverage about the candidates was clearly on top, followed by newspaper articles. Radio coverage, campaign ads, magazine coverage, and loyalty to one's union or other non-party organization were all less important.

CONCLUSION

Debates provide the public with an opportunity to evaluate candidates and their issue positions in a manifestly politically neutral and artificially

Table 9.8
Means and Differences of Importance Self-Assigned by Respondents* to Televised Presidential and Vice-Presidential Debates vs. Other Sources of Information on the Decision to Vote

Source of Information**	Mean	t-value	d.f.	2-tail prob.
One or more of the debates between either Presidential or Vice Presidential candidates	4.56			
TV news report about what the candidates are saying and doing	5.45	-2.77	85	.007
Newspaper articles about the campaign	5.28	-2.12	84	.037
Interviews with the candidates on television	4.99	-1.39	85	.167
Talks with family and friends	4.84	-.82	85	.417
Loyalty to your political party	4.73	-.44	85	.662
Newspaper editorials	4.44	.28	85	.781
Radio coverage of the Presidential campaign	3.79	2.05	85	.043
Campaign ads for the candidates	3.43	3.37	85	.001
Magazine coverage of the Presidential campaign	3.27	4.07	84	.000
Loyalty to my union or other non-party organization	2.12	5.44	81	.000

*   Interviews of registered voters during entire fall study period.
* *   Respondents were presented with the question "I'd like you to use the same scale (0 lowest to 10 highest) to tell me how important each of the following sources of information was in helping you *to decide whether to vote at all*. How important were . . . ."

structured environment. Overall, the findings of our study indicate that the public wants presidential debates or at least is receptive to having them, even if only initially in the campaign. While they generally felt that there were enough debates scheduled between the 1988 candidates, they also felt that the candidates tend to avoid the issues and that debates are not the best way to make a final voting decision. Respondents were somewhat positive about debates as a vehicle to best learn about the candidates and their issue positions. They also seemed to indicate that debates are not a waste of time. In other words, respondents recognized that perhaps the situation was not ideal, but that debates are a vehicle to gain an insight into the candidates.

We found that the public was generally interested in monitoring the debates, as was evidenced by the large, albeit declining, audience sizes. Furthermore, the voters were interested (although differentially so by party) in viewing the presidential primary debates of the opposition party. During the initial period of the campaign, the debates may play an important role in developing initial impressions of the candidates, particularly with a large and/or somewhat unknown field of candidates.

When asked to evaluate several information channels in terms of their importance in providing debate information, respondents found the debate itself to be the most important source of debate information, with reliance on other sources significantly lower. Perhaps other sources of information, such as daily media coverage, are more important in informing the public about the candidates and their issue positions. But the fact remains that large portions of the American public actively seek out the debates to gather information in a focused manner. Even though the perceived utility of watching the actual debates may be low in many respects, the public's overall sense is that it may be the best game in town. Particularly the more involved members of the electorate may feel that, while little may be gained by viewing the debates, they still should do so. This tendency helps to explain why the audiences for the presidential debates are so large. Perhaps a poorly received channel is perceived as better than the others that might be available—or even worse—none at all.

REFERENCES

Bennett, W. L. 1980. *Public opinion in American politics*. New York: Harcourt.
Chaffee, S. H., and J. Dennis. 1979. Presidential debates: An empirical assessment. In *The past and future of presidential debates*, ed. A. Ranney, 75–101. Washington: American Enterprise Institute for Public Policy Research.
Dye, T., and L. H. Ziegler. 1989. *American politics in the media age*, 3rd ed. Pacific Grove, Calif.: Brooks/Cole Publishing Company.
Edelman, M. 1964. *The symbolic uses of power*. Urbana: University of Illinois Press.
Jamieson, K. H., and D. S. Birdsell. 1988. *Presidential debates: The challenge of creating an informed electorate*. New York: Oxford University Press.
Kraus, S. 1988. *Televised presidential debates and public policy*. Hillsdale, N.J.: Lawrence Erlbaum Associates.
McLeod, J., and L. Becker. 1974. Testing the validity of gratification measures through political effects analysis. In *The uses of mass communication:*

Current perspectives on gratifications research, ed. J. G. Blumler and E. Katz, 137–164. Beverly Hills, Calif.: Sage.

Nielsen Media Research. 1990. Unpublished report. New York.

Paletz, D. L., and R. M. Entman. 1981. *Media power politics*. New York: The Free Press.

Schramm, W., and R. F. Carter. 1959. Effectiveness of a political telethon. *Public Opinion Quarterly* 23:121–126.

Watson, R. A. 1984. *The presidential contest,* 2d ed. New York: Wiley.

10

THE AUDIENCE RESPONDS TO "ATTACK" ADS

Given our restless national media, it may be foolhardy to believe that anything can be engraved indelibly upon media consciousness. But at least one truth about the 1988 campaign has an excellent chance of being passed along in the popular media as "The Lesson of the 1988 Presidential Campaign": Well-produced negative ads that are not vigorously rebutted by the object of the attack will make the victim an unwilling accomplice in his/her own defeat. In other words, Michael Dukakis's unwillingness to get down in the mud with Roger Ailes and George Bush, this media consensus continues, ultimately was the fatal flaw in his campaign. One writer (Barone 1988) even suggested that Dukakis's tactical error was a revealing symptom of his lack of leadership, judgment, and ability to relate to the concerns of the American people. Implicit in "The Lesson" is "The Corollary": The George Bush campaign's attack ads *could* have been rebutted—that is, they had inaccuracies, misrepresentations, overstatements, or other problems with their attacks upon Dukakis. Both of these assumptions were shared in the early academic literature about the 1988 campaign:

In this author's research of ads going back to 1972, negative ads have always been found to be meticulous in their accuracy. No such high standard of accuracy was evident in the 1988 Bush campaign. (Devlin 1989, 396)

[The year] 1988 was the year of the negative ad. George Bush aired 37 ads [in the fall campaign], of which 14 could be labeled negative. Dukakis aired 47 ads, with 23 of those being negative. Dukakis thus had more negative ads, but aside from the "Oval Office" (the ad that raised the possibility of Dan Quayle having to take over if Bush were dead or incapacitated), they just were not very good. The Bush campaign spent over 40% of its budget airing about a half-dozen of its best negative ads. It was these negative ads—"(Boston) Harbor," "(Convicts Through a) Revolving Door," and "(Dukakis in) Tank"—that had an impact. (Devlin 1989, 406).

As we shall see in more detail in the next chapter, the networks may have helped those Bush attack ads to have an impact by largely failing to cover their factual accuracy, while at the same time acting like a giant echo chamber or Greek chorus, repeating the key "attack" portions time after time, just in case we missed seeing them. This brings up a central question no strictly empirical study can answer: If a candidate is unable/unwilling to rebut the inaccuracies in attack ads, is it the responsibility of the news media to do it? Many of us might answer yes, but that response would be based less on empirical grounds than on other considerations.

In any case, the purpose of this chapter is to look for evidence about how the 1988 Bush and Dukakis advertising battle played out in the minds of our respondents. In this chapter, we shall examine such questions as:

• Who did our respondents associate with attack ads: Bush, Dukakis, or both? If Dukakis actually aired 23 attack ads to Bush's 14, did our respondents associate Dukakis more than Bush with attack ads? Perhaps, on the other hand, the Bush campaign's smaller number of repetitively played attack ads made a stronger impression.

• Did the sponsoring candidate have more support when respondents remembered an attack ad or an ad that instead praised its sponsor?

• Did audience recall of attack ads and their sponsors vary with the ebb and flow of positive and negative ads over the length of the campaign?

• Was recall of attack ads related to signs of cynicism and malaise about the campaign?

• How did our respondents feel about political ads as a tool in deciding how they would vote?

THE DATA

During the post-primary interviews in Pennsylvania (March and early April), Illinois (April), and then Oregon (May and early June), we began asking our respondents to report exposure to a presidential campaign ad and whether they felt the ad mostly praised the sponsoring candidate or mostly criticized the opponent. Further questions about presidential campaign ads were asked in the fall interviews, including questions identifying whether the ad was on behalf of Bush or Dukakis. In addition, in the November 6 interview, we asked more direct questions about specific ads, in an effort to see whether respondents remembered and understood them, and we asked respondents to evaluate the usefulness of a number of presidential campaign information sources, including the ads and the debates.

RESULTS

As Table 10.1 suggests, attack ads were recalled far more often later in the campaign than earlier. Generally, our findings for these audience perceptions are consistent with the literature about the actual release of positive and negative presidential spots. For example, Payne, Marlier, and Baukus (1989) concluded that spots during the primaries far less often attacked opponents than they did during the general election campaign. A substantial majority of our respondents during the late winter and spring of 1988 saw the ads they recalled as praising the candidate rather than attacking his opponent. The audience perception shifted dramatically, however, after the first Dukakis-Bush debate, on September 25, when the Bush campaign released a negative spot on crime. As Hoffman and Devroy (1988, 9) put it: "Going into the first debate, the Bush high command had two contingency plans: Go positive on economic prosperity if Bush did well, or go negative on crime issues if he did not.

Table 10.1
Whether Positive or Negative Broadcast Ad Recalled, by Stage of the Campaign

| | Ad Seen As: | |
Interview Done During	Praising Candidate	Criticizing Candidate
Primaries (N=194)	77.3%	22.7%
Sept. 22-24 (N=121)	64.5%	35.5%
Sept. 25-Oct. 4 (N=282)	49.6%	50.4%
Oct. 5-12 (N=261)	28.1%	71.3%
Oct. 13-17, Nov. 6 (N=398)	29.4%	70.6%
Total (N=1256)	44.6%	55.4%

Note: Number of cases refers to those who said they recalled an ad for president and could describe whether it primarily criticized the opponent or praised the sponsoring candidate.
Chi-square = 153.634, df = 4, p < .0001 for entire table.
Chi-square = 72.600, df = 3, p < .001 when primaries excluded.

Television commercials on both topics were sent to all stations. After the debate, the crime ads went up.''

As Table 10.1 suggests, the recall of negative presidential campaign ads continued to climb after the first debate, jumping to more than 70% in the October 5–12 period (after the Quayle-Bentsen debate, but before the final Bush-Dukakis one). Following the Quayle-Bentsen debate, the Dukakis campaign released its "Oval Office" spot, the one pro-Dukakis attack ad that campaign tacticians admired. As mentioned briefly earlier, that ad showed the back of an empty chief executive's chair and raised the question of what would happen if a President Bush were dead or incapacitated vs. what would happen if a President Dukakis were. While we did not break out the results separately for November 6, there was a slight dip downward to 64% in the proportion of negative ads cited, perhaps reflecting a slight upsurge in positive spots near the end of the campaign.

Overall, the Bush ads were recalled more often than were the Dukakis ads–a combined total of roughly 56% Bush ads to 44% Dukakis. More interestingly, perhaps, attack ads were cited more often than positive ads for each candidate, by roughly a 3 to 2 margin in each case. But during the period following the first debate and leading up to the Quayle-Bentsen debate, the Bush campaign decision to "go negative" was reflected in respondents' perceptions; more people cited Bush attack ads than anything else. During this period, Bush ads were far more likely (Chi-square = 8.047, 1 df, p <.01) to be seen as negative than were Dukakis ads.

Many writers have criticized Dukakis's delay in responding in kind to the Bush attack ads, as we have already seen (additional critics include Grove [1988] and Gans [1988]). Interestingly, the belated surge in negative ads by the Dukakis campaign also was quite sensitively reflected by our survey respondents, as Table 10.2 shows. After the October 5 Quayle-Bentsen debate, the Dukakis campaign started running the empty chair ad attacking Quayle's ability to replace an incapacitated President Bush. As we have already seen, this attack ad was intended to take advantage of Quayle's media-defined weak debate performance.

The audience's sensitivity to this shift in the Dukakis ads shows up clearly in the period following the vice-presidential debate (October 5–12), when significantly more people cite negative ads by Dukakis than by Bush (Chi square = 8.698, 1 df, p < .01). In the period following the final debate, marginally more negative ads were attributed to Bush than to Dukakis, but this difference was not large enough to reach statistical significance for the late campaign time period. *In the two periods where ad strategies seemed tied to debate performance,* there were clear discrepancies in whose campaign was seen to have run the more negative ads. Given these rapid perceptual shifts, it is no surprise to find a highly significant overall test, in Table 10.2, of whether attributions of negativity

Table 10.2
Source and Character of Recalled Broadcast Ad, by Stage of Presidential Campaign

Interview Done During	For Bush		For Dukakis	
	Praise	Attack	Praise	Attack
Sept. 22-24 (N=106)	35.8%	22.6%	29.2%	12.3%
Sept. 25-Oct. 4 (N=273)	26.0%	33.7%	24.9%	15.4%
Oct. 5-12 (N=251)	18.3%	29.5%	10.8%	41.4%
Oct. 13-17, Nov. 6 (N=367)	15.5%	42.2%	14.7%	27.5%
Total (N=997)	21.3%	34.6%	18.1%	27.5%

Chi-square = 99.554, df = 9, p < .0001.

to one campaign or the other changed from time period to time period (p < .0001).

One of our study questions for this chapter was whether Bush or Dukakis spots were more often seen as negative. Overall, Bush negative ads were mentioned slightly more often than Dukakis ones, but at least part of that small and insignificant difference probably was due to the more frequent reported recall of Bush ads—both positive and negative.

DID RESPONDENTS FIND THE ADS USEFUL?

Arguably, at least, the interviews done on November 6 allow respondents to look back on the entire presidential campaign and assess the value to them of the debates, the ads, and a variety of other campaign information sources. Based on our November 6 interviews, it seems clear that our respondents did not feel political ads were of much value to them in deciding whether to vote for president. Political ads—not negative ads, just political ads in general—were given ratings significantly below virtually all other potential sources of guidance in voting decisions, as Table 10.3 shows. When the mean rating for political ads was compared against the means for each of 10 other sources, the mean for the ads exceeded only that for the turnout guidance provided by organizational endorsements. The mean for political ads (3.49 on a 0 to 10 scale) was significantly (p < .001) below eight of the nine sources above it. Interestingly, the debates were rated below television news, but well above the ads.

Table 10.3
Political Ads vs. Other Sources of Turnout Guidance, as Rated by November 6
Respondents (N = 100)

Rank[1]	Source	Mean Rating[2]
1	TV News	5.52
2	Newspaper Articles	5.24
3	TV Interviews	5.04
4	People	4.95
5	Political Party	4.70
6	Presidential Debates	4.59
7	Editorials	4.51
8	Magazines	4.10
9	Radio	3.70
10	Political Ads	3.49
11	Organizations	2.14

[1]   Ranking is based on the mean score.
[2]   Means are measured on a 0 to 10 scale. The means for sources 1 through 8 are significantly higher (p < .001) than for Political Ads; mean for Organizations significantly lower (p < .001) than for Political Ads. All tests were t-tests for correlated data.

Attack Ads and Campaign Malaise

Based on the entire series of fall interviews, we can also assess whether recalled exposure to negative campaign ads related to general feelings about the Bush-Dukakis campaign. Throughout the fall, we attempted three general measures of feelings about the campaign. Respondents used a five-point, strongly disagree (1) to strongly agree (5) scale when read each of the three items.

In order to test whether the ads influenced agreement with each item, we constructed a measure of advertising exposure that combined ad sponsorship with whether the ad was seen as mostly praising the sponsor or criticizing his opponent (the same four-way classification reported in Table 10.2). Because recall of the ads might have been selective (it was, to some extent, but only for *positive* ads), and because we wanted to subject the advertising variable to a rigorous test, we always introduced it as the final predictor variable, *after* extracting the influence of other variables in our Multiple Classification Analysis solutions.

In addition, we challenged the advertising variable with a large variety of rival variables, picking out for the solutions to be reported here the rivals which had demonstrated the greatest power to predict attitudes toward the presidential campaign. A second important criterion for selection of each solution was that each optimal solution should be selected independently for each of the campaign attitude measures. Finally, consistent with the other criteria, we chose the solution that incorporated the largest number of cases. (When information was missing on one predictor variable, the entire case was discarded.)

Too Much Mudslinging? The first item asked throughout the fall asserted that there had been too much mudslinging in the presidential campaign. Interestingly, party, gender, race and income were not related to this item. Table 10.4 presents the solution chosen on the basis of the criteria listed above. Agreement with the statement was highest in Eugene-Springfield ("Locale"), highest late in the campaign ("Wave"), and highest with reported exposure to negative Bush *or* negative Dukakis campaign commercials ("Polispot"). Political identification (Republican, Democrat, Independent), introduced as a control variable, did not predict agreement with the "mudslinging" assertion, but it did interact weakly (p = .087) with Locale: Democrats in Eugene-Springfield were *most* likely and Independents in southern Illinois were *least* likely to agree strongly with the mudslinging statement. No matter what other variables were introduced as controls, Polispot withstood the challenge. While agreement about too much mudslinging was strong among all respondents, those recalling attack ads for either Bush or Dukakis were even more likely to agree strongly than those recalling ads that praised either candidate.

Although we did not include in the table the result for exposure to post-debate analysis because the number of respondents would have been reduced to 514, it is worth reporting here that both exposure to post-debate analysis and to attack ads predicted the amount of agreement to the mudslinging statement—but in *opposite* directions. In other words, exposure to attack ads predicted *higher* agreement (p = .005) that too much mud was being slung; exposure to post-debate analysis predicted *lower* agreement (p = .028).

Do I Know Enough? The second item asserted that the respondent did not know enough to make a good choice between the Bush and Dukakis tickets. Unlike the mudslinging statement, agreement was moderately low (mean of 2.26 on a 1–5 scale). Also unlike mudslinging, both gender and another control variable, income, emerged as strong predictors of agreement, while Wave (before debate 1, after debate 1, after debate 2, after debate 3), exposure to analysis and exposure to the ads did not.

Table 10.4
Exposure to Political Ads and Other Predictors of Agreement That There Is Too Much Mudslinging in the Campaign (Range: 1 strongly disagree to 5 strongly agree; Mean = 3.95; N = 908)

Source		df	Sum of Squares	MS	F-Ratio	Prob.
Locale		2	15.009	7.505	7.907	.000
Carbondale	3.92					
Philadelphia	3.81					
Eugene-Springfield	4.07					
Party		2	3.115	1.557	1.641	NS
Wave		3	9.926	3.309	3.486	.015
Sept. 22-24	3.88					
After 1st Debate	3.82					
After VP Debate	3.93					
After Last Debate	4.10					
Polispot		3	18.651	6.217	6.550	.000
Bush, +	3.75					
Bush, -	4.04					
Dukakis, +	3.78					
Dukakis, -	4.12					
Locale x Party		4	7.752	1.938	2.042	.087
Explained Variance		47	76.671			
Error Variance		860	816.293			
Total Variance		907	892.964			

Women, people living in Philadelphia, and low-income respondents were more likely to agree with the statement. In general, the statement seemed to be taken by respondents as referring to their own individual knowledge and competence rather than to the campaign itself, so we have not included this result in a table.

How about "None of the Above"? The final general item tapping attitudes toward the presidential campaign (and asked throughout the fall) asserted that the respondent was not sure whether he/she wanted to vote for either presidential candidate. Mean agreement with this item (2.46) was only slightly above that for the one about knowing enough. Women and independent voters each strongly predicted agreement with this statement of dissatisfaction and uncertainty, as did an interaction of gender with exposure to attack ads (Table 10.5). This interaction can be articulated as follows: While men were more likely to disagree with this statement, men who reported exposure to Dukakis attack ads disagreed even more than did men in general.

Locale and race were unrelated to this item, although income (not tabled) and exposure to post-debate analysis (also not tabled) were. In each case, the inclusion of the variable would have substantially reduced the number of cases available. Once again, lower-income respondents expressed more agreement and those who saw a post-debate analysis more *dis*agreement.

Table 10.5
Exposure to Political Ads and Other Predictors of Agreement That Respondent Not Sure Wants to Vote for Either Man (Range: 1 strongly disagree to 5 strongly agree; Mean = 2.45; N = 894)

Source		df	Sum of Squares	MS	F-Ratio	Prob.
Sex		1	23.487	23.487	16.074	.000
Female	2.61					
Male	2.29					
Party		2	37.985	18.992	12.999	.000
Republican	2.25					
Democrat	2.45					
Independent	2.80					
Wave		3	6.602	2.021	1.383	NS
Polispot		3	1.012	.337	.230	NS
Sex x Polispot		3	12.462	4.154	2.843	.037
Explained Variance		38	104.955			
Error Variance		855	1249.252			
Total Variance		893	1354.207			

Even If Distasteful, Were Ads Influential?

Another piece of conventional wisdom about attack ads—illustrated by, but by no means limited to, the 1988 Bush-Dukakis race—is that voters may not like them, but they are persuaded by them *unless* the ads themselves can be defined as dirty and unfair, in which case voters begin to draw negative conclusions about the campaign that perpetrated them. A recent article about negative ads quoted several campaign consultants to this effect: "Negative ads work because an increasing number of Americans no longer trust their political institutions," [said] George Shipley, a Democratic pollster. On the other hand, the same cynicism that makes negative ads work can also make them backfire—as a number of candidates have discovered this year (Taylor 1990).

In our study, we certainly have evidence that people did not like the ads (Tables 10.3 and 10.4, especially). From the point of view of the attack ad producer, it may be acceptable for people to dislike the attack ads, because that means they notice—and recall—them. Our respondents noticed and recalled them. Regardless of the candidate, attack ads were recalled more often than "positive" ads, even though fewer attack than positive ads were produced. The remaining necessary condition, of course, is that the attack ads have the desired effect on the audience of potential voters. While attack ads represented a smaller proportion of Bush's spots, we have already seen a strong consensus among observers that the Bush attack ads were more likely to achieve their ends than the scattershot, slow-reacting, and thinly replayed Dukakis ones.

But how do we measure the effectiveness of attack ads in the context of the debates, post-debate analyses, partisan predispositions, and the usual collection of rival predictors of voter reactions?

Comprehension. Let us begin with the simple understanding of the point of a given attack ad. If people misunderstand that the ad *is* an attack, we could argue that the ad might even be counterproductive. The only unambiguous measures we have of comprehension occurred on November 6. At each location, we asked the 104 respondents the same question about each of four ads: Was this ad for Bush or was it for Dukakis? Two of the four spots actually were for Bush (one showing Dukakis riding around in a tank, the other was what the question termed "the Willie Horton ad") and two for Dukakis (an "ad about Dan Quayle" and an ad showing Bush campaign planners). Arguably, we could have asked about these ads in several other ways. (For example, there actually were at least three distinct spots about Willie Horton and/or furloughs, with distinctly different visuals). In any case, though, more of our 104 respondents were able to discern who the two Bush ads were for ("Tank," 35; "Willie Horton," 27), compared with the sponsor of the Dukakis spots (the "Quayle ad," 21; "Bush planners," 17). (The numbers cited are raw frequencies. Obviously, a given respondent could correctly identify the sponsor up to four times.) The least successful ad, based on these frequencies, was the Dukakis spot that tried to portray Bush campaign staffers cynically plotting how to divert voters from the fact that Bush had nothing substantive to say.

Candidate Preferences. We have a much stronger data set for attitudes toward the candidates. Since generally the results for such ratings as candidates' leadership or poise closely resemble results for the self-described "odds" of voting for Bush, Dukakis, Bentsen, and Quayle, we will restrict our report to these four generalized "voting-odds" measures. (Of course, we should hasten to add that reported intent to vote a certain way may not be identical to actually voting that way. Nevertheless, our results concerning such demographics as income and race are highly consistent with actual voting patterns in the 1988 election.)

Once again, we used the same criteria to select the optimal solution that were used previously with mudslinging and the two other campaign attitude scales. We deliberately chose as rivals to the campaign advertising variable those demographic and other control variables that had already demonstrated the ability to explain that specific voting-odds scale, while at the same time keeping as many of our respondents as possible in the solution. In other words, we challenged reported exposure to presidential spots to explain voting after we had already explained as much as possible of what was going on.

First, let us consider the chances of voting for George Bush. Income, survey locale, race, party identification, *and* exposure to attack ads each predicted the odds of voting for Bush; gender and when the interview was done ("Wave") did not. The higher the family income of the respondent, the greater the chance of voting for Bush. After controlling for income and all the other predictors in Table 10.6, we find that exposure to attack ads—especially those produced on behalf of Bush—seemed to *reduce*, not enhance, Bush's prospects. Clearly, party identification is the most powerful predictor, as we might expect. But even after it and other predictors are controlled, reported exposure to attack ads makes a big difference. And that difference looks something like a boomerang effect. The variables in Table 10.6 collectively explained almost 51% of the variation in the odds of voting for Bush given by 786 respondents in the fall. That explained variance figure is an unusually high one for the social sciences.

Turning now to Table 10.7, showing the odds of voting for Dukakis, predictably we found a similar result. The only major difference is that race was not a particularly strong predictor of Dukakis voting. Perhaps minorities had stronger feelings about Bush than they did about Dukakis. Overall, our respondents preferred Dukakis over Bush (means of 5.72 and 4.53, respectively), but not by a huge margin. Once again, party

Table 10.6
**Exposure to Political Ads and Other Predictors* of Chances Respondent Would
Vote for George Bush (Range: 0 low to 10 high; Mean = 4.53; N = 786)**

Source		df	Sum of Squares	MS	F-Ratio	Prob.
Income		1	113.834	113.834	13.278	.000
Locale		2	190.967	95.484	11.137	.000
Carbondale	4.52					
Philadelphia	5.38					
Eugene-Springfield	3.98					
Race		3	82.878	27.626	3.222	.022
White	4.68					
Black	3.53					
Asian	4.20					
Other	4.54					
Party		2	4937.416	2468.708	287.949	.000
Republican	8.17					
Democrat	2.03					
Independent	4.54					
Polispot		3	157.532	52.511	6.125	.000
Bush, +	5.40					
Bush, -	4.16					
Dukakis, +	4.47					
Dukakis, -	4.43					
Explained Variance		11	6872.056			
Error Variance		774	6635.829			
Total Variance		785	13507.884			

*   Calculations of all interactions suppressed because of one or more empty cells.

identification was easily the strongest predictor of Dukakis voting, and
the multiple predictors accounted for more than half (53%) of the variance. And once again there was evidence that attack ads hurt rather than
help. For Bush spots, the *lowest* odds for Dukakis came from people who
reported exposure to the broadcast spots praising Bush rather than
attacking Dukakis. For the Dukakis spots, the *highest* odds for Dukakis
came from ads praising Dukakis rather than attacking Bush.

The number of cases for analysis drops when we examine the odds of

Table 10.7
**Exposure to Political Ads and Other Predictors* of Chances Respondent Would
Vote for Michael Dukakis (Range: 0 low to 10 high; Mean = 5.72; N = 785)**

Source		df	Sum of Squares	MS	F-Ratio	Prob.
Income		1	96.343	96.343	11.816	.001
Locale		2	44.378	22.189	2.721	.066
Carbondale	5.68					
Philadelphia	5.34					
Eugene-Springfield	6.01					
Race		3	29.161	9.720	1.192	NS
Party		2	5476.913	2738.457	335.857	.000
Republican	1.91					
Democrat	8.41					
Independent	5.94					
Polispot		3	110.342	36.781	4.511	.004
Bush, +	5.13					
Bush, -	5.90					
Dukakis, +	6.27					
Dukakis, -	5.55					
Explained Variance		11	7088.016			
Error Variance		773	6302.766			
Total Variance		784	13390.782			

*   Calculations of all interactions suppressed because of one or more empty cells.

voting for Bentsen or Quayle. As we mentioned in Chapter 7, we had
actually not planned to ask these questions until it had become evident to
us that we needed to study reactions to the Quayle-Bentsen debate. So
our data set for Tables 10.8 and 10.9 starts with the interviews of October
4. Then, of course, the usual respondent attrition sets in because of
missing data for any single question used in the analysis, and the result is
slightly more than 500 cases for each table.

Even though gender plays a part in only one of the Quayle-Bentsen
tables, we have included it in both Tables 10.8 and 10.9 for what it reveals
about gender-based reaction (and, in one case, *non*reaction) to the two
men. Gender strongly predicts the odds of voting for Bentsen but not the
odds for Quayle: Women were substantially less enthused than men about

Table 10.8
Exposure to Political Ads and Other Predictors of Chances Respondent Would Vote for Dan Quayle (Range: 0 low to 10 high; Mean = 2.84; N = 530)

Source		df	Sum of Squares	MS	F-Ratio	Prob.
Sex		1	13.749	13.749	1.582	NS
Locale		2	3.254	1.627	.187	NS
Party		2	1232.262	616.131	70.895	.000
Republican	5.05					
Democrat	1.49					
Independent	2.48					
Polispot		3	97.561	32.520	3.742	.011
Bush, +	3.74					
Bush, -	2.74					
Dukakis, +	2.22					
Dukakis, -	2.74					
Party x Polispot		6	150.471	25.079	2.886	.009
Explained Variance		31	1719.349			
Error Variance		498	4328.019			
Total Variance		529	6047.368			

Bentsen, even though, like men, women rated their chances of voting for Bentsen, if he were alone on the ballot, far higher (6.67 for women) than their chances of voting for Quayle (2.90). Apparently women sympathized somewhat with Quayle, but interestingly their sympathy showed up in a relative downgrading of Bentsen (for cruelty?) rather than much upgrading of Quayle. The patterns for gender, interesting as they are, are a side issue here. Did attack ads appear to boomerang here, as they did for the two presidential candidates?

As Table 10.8 shows, neither gender nor locale of the survey was related to the odds of a Quayle vote when the other predictors were introduced. (In separate analyses, income and race also were unrelated to the Quayle vote.) Once again, party identification remained the single most powerful predictor of the Quayle vote, as we certainly would expect. In addition, though, we see evidence that attack ads boomeranged on whichever camp produced them. The *worst* odds for Quayle came when

Table 10.9
Exposure to Political Ads and Other Predictors* of Chances Respondent Would Vote for Lloyd Bentsen (Range: 0 low to 10 high; Mean = 7.11; N = 510)

Source		df	Sum of Squares	MS	F-Ratio	Prob.
Sex		1	66.690	66.690	7.313	.007
Female	6.67					
Male	7.52					
Race		3	3.749	1.250	.137	NS
Party		2	1197.423	598.712	65.657	.000
Republican	4.90					
Democrat	8.62					
Independent	6.53					
Polispot		3	59.244	19.748	2.166	.091
Bush, +	7.01					
Bush, -	7.17					
Dukakis, +	7.63					
Dukakis, -	6.60					
Explained Variance		9	1443.612			
Error Variance		500	4559.370			
Total Variance		509	6002.982			

*   Calculations of all interactions suppressed because of one or more empty cells.

people reported exposure to *positive* Dukakis spots, not the attack ads, which of course included the well-regarded "Empty Chair in the Oval Office" spot. Further, Bush spots seemed to pay off with higher Quayle ratings when the spots were positive rather than negative. So positive ads seemed again to have the higher payoff, judging by the candidate ratings made by our respondents.

Party identification interacted with the ad recalled. However, the general pattern we have seen already was not particularly disturbed by the interaction: Whether Quayle fared worst of all with a Dukakis positive ad or a Bush negative ad varied somewhat by party identification. But Quayle did very badly, in all party groups, with both of these two ad-sponsor combinations. Thus, the interaction does not particularly upset the overall finding in Table 10.8 that Quayle's lowest scores occurred for Dukakis positives and Bush negatives.

Table 10.9 provides the optimum solution for the odds of voting for Lloyd Bentsen if he were running without Dukakis. We have already seen that women were less enthused than men about a Bentsen vote. Party identification, as always, was powerfully related to the chances of a Bentsen vote. For the only time in these analyses, the advertising variable did not quite reach the usually accepted $p < .05$ level of statistical significance, although it did reach $p < .10$, and the pattern of means generally was in the now-familiar "boomerang" pattern. For example, Bentsen's chances were *lowest* when a Dukakis attack ad was recalled, *highest* when a positive Dukakis ad was.

Given the importance of exposure to post-debate analysis in the aftermath of the Quayle-Bentsen debate (see Chapter 7), we also introduced exposure to analysis as a control variable in order to see if the advertising remained as a predictor of Quayle and Bentsen voting. However, since measures of Quayle and Bentsen voting took place after the October 13 debate as well as the October 5 one, and since Bush by all odds was defined as the winner October 13, we actually would expect to have an interaction here between interview Wave and exposure to post-debate analysis.

Those exposed to analysis after the October 5 debate, if influenced by the analysis, should give better odds on voting for Bentsen than those who watched that debate but not the analysis. Meanwhile, those interviewed after the October 13 debate should have experienced a post-debate analysis that was strongly favorable to Bush (and, maybe, Quayle). So exposure to post-debate analysis after the final debate should induce better odds for Quayle than would a lack of such exposure: hence, an interaction. The predicted interaction between interview Wave and exposure to post-debate analysis occurred ($p = .059$) for Quayle voting. The advertising variable withstood this additional challenge, remaining a powerful predictor of Quayle voting ($p = .006$).

Since the computer program suppressed any tests of interactions for Bentsen voting, because of an insufficient number of cases, we cannot provide an identical challenge there for the odds of voting for Bentsen. For what it is worth, however, the advertising variable remained significant at $p < .10$ after exposure to post-debate analysis was introduced as a control. (We should also remind the reader here that the best tests of the effects of post-debate analyses are to be found in Chapters 6, 7, and 8, where more cases were available for analysis. Exposure to post-debate analysis was used here merely to pose an additional challenge to the advertising variable.)

CONCLUSION

In contrast to the ads that came to mind during the primaries, following the first debate in the fall, attack ads came to mind more often than ads praising the sponsoring candidate. Our respondents' perceptions of who had "gone negative" seemed to reflect the ebb and flow of the campaign: Bush was more likely to be seen as using attack ads after his first debate with Dukakis, and Dukakis more likely by respondents interviewed in the aftermath of the Quayle-Bensten debate. Meanwhile, these two debate-related changes in the type of ads overlaid a very steep climb in the proportions of people citing negative ads as the general campaign approached election day. As we expected, our respondents rated almost all other sources of presidential voting guidance, including the debates, higher than the ads.

Exposure to attack ads seemed to sour our respondents on the character of the presidential campaign, regardless of party identification, and the later in the campaign, the greater the agreement that there was too much mudslinging. Opponents of attack ads can find grounds for satisfaction in the results reported here. If the reported chances of voting for these candidates were to be translated into actual votes, attack ads seemed consistently to have produced a backlash, regardless of which side produced them.

One obvious alternative explanation of the apparent attack ad backlash is to say that partisans of one candidate are predisposed to remember either their own candidate's positive ads or the bad guy's dirty, rotten attack ads. Interestingly, we found that respondents' party identification did *not* predict whose attack ads would be recalled, although party did predict whose positive ad would be. *If* a positive ad were recalled by Republicans, it was mostly a Bush spot; *if* a positive ad were recalled by Democrats, it tended to be a Dukakis spot. In a sense, though, all this is an interesting side-trip, not central to our argument: *Whatever impact selective recall had on the results had already been extracted by using party identification as a control.*

However, we should consider another possible explanation for the apparent backlash: Perhaps the kind of people most likely to recall attack ads also were the people most likely to be sour on the presidential campaign and to rate *all four* candidates lower. In that case, we would indeed find the patterns we did—an apparent backlash against attack ads from Bush as well as from Dukakis, with that apparent backlash spreading to Quayle as well as Bentsen.

The easiest way to get rid of this rival explanation would be to find that people citing attack ads *did* discriminate among the candidates—that is, they were not downgrading everybody, just the campaign whose negative ads they cited. We therefore split our sample into two groups: the people who recalled an attack ad and the people who recalled an ad praising its candidate. What we wanted to test was whether people citing attack ads discriminated among the four candidates or downgraded them all. If they downgraded all four candidates, correlations among all four of their "odds" ratings would tend to be positive. If that happened—especially in contrast to the pattern of correlations for those recalling positive ads— we would have to conclude that recall of attack ads tells us more about the people recalling them than about their reactions to the ads themselves.

How did the correlations turn out? They were almost identical for both those who cited attack ads and those who cited ads praising their candidate. The patterns of negative and positive correlations are completely identical, and the sizes of the corresponding correlations are often nearly so. For example, correlations between odds of voting for Dukakis and for Bentsen are positive and between .60 and .68 for both attack ad recallers and positive ad recallers. Meanwhile, all correlations between the odds for Dukakis and those for Bush and Quayle are negative for both groups, indicating that attack ad recallers were, indeed, discriminating among the candidates in their ratings, just as positive ad recallers were. Not only was the shift from positive to negative correlations the same for both groups, the respective correlations themselves also were similar. For example, Dukakis odds correlated at − .85 with Bush odds and at − .61 with Quayle odds for those who cited attack ads. The corresponding correlations were − .83 and − .45 for those who cited ads that praised the sponsoring candidate.

All in all, then, our fall survey data suggest that attack ads made a strong impression, but that impression did *not* help either George Bush, the presumed winner of the Battle of the Network Ads, or Michael Dukakis. Are we saying, then, that the Ailes group's negative spots accomplished no aims of the campaign? No. But what they accomplished had more to do with journalists' and other elite reactions rather than directly with how voters responded. If and as journalists defined Dukakis as failing to respond to the "Willie Horton" and furlough ads, for example, the kind of non-elites we were interviewing may have been reacting to the new "attack-ad reality" being defined by journalists and other elites.

REFERENCES

Barone, M. 1988. These Dukakis ads just don't work. *Washington Post*, October 11, A19.
Devlin, L. P. 1989. Contrasts in presidential campaign commercials of 1988. *American Behavioral Scientist* 32:389–414.
Gans, C. B. 1988. No wonder turnout was so low. *Washington Post National Weekly Edition*, November 21–27, 28.
Greenfield, M. 1988. The campaign soap opera. *Washington Post*, October 10, A23.
Grove, L. 1988. Election '88: The negative campaign that came from below. *Washington Post National Weekly Edition*, November 21–27, 12.

Hoffman, D., and A. Devroy. 1988. Bush's road to the White House. *Washington Post National Weekly Edition*, November 21–27, 8–9.

Payne, J. G., J. Marlier, and R. A. Barkus. 1989. Polispots in the 1988 presidential primaries. *American Behavioral Scientist* 32:365–381.

Taylor, P. 1990. The trick is to get vicious carefully: Negative ads work well—if they don't backfire. *Washington Post National Weekly Edition*, July 16–22, 15.

11

DEBATES IN THE CONTEXT OF THE REST OF THE CAMPAIGN

Most of the time, thus far, we have been looking at the 1988 presidential debates in isolation from the rest of the campaign. That perspective, in fact, has been the focus of the project since its inception in 1987: What type of effects did the debates have? How were they covered? How do the public and the media perceive the importance of debates as an institution?

As has been demonstrated, we had an abundance of survey and content data with which to answer those questions. But we also think it is important to provide some analysis of how the 1988 debates fit into the larger context of the entire campaign. How did the candidates and their handlers treat the debates? How important were they in influencing the conduct of the campaign? How important were they in influencing the media coverage of the campaign and how it was conducted? How did the debates compare with the other campaign components with respect to influence?

In this chapter, we attempt to answer these and other questions about the role of debates in the larger campaign context. Previously, we have relied most often on quantitative, social-scientific methods to assess debate impact, but applying those techniques to the entire campaign was beyond the scope of this project. Here, we assess the role of the 1988 debates in a more qualitative, impressionistic fashion than we have in previous chapters, although we will document our impressions with material from network newscasts during the 1988 fall campaign, from the Vanderbilt Television News Index, and from other news media sources.

We assume throughout this analysis that the networks are reflecting with a certain amount of fidelity what is happening in the campaign.

Resource limitations restrict our analytical and interpretative abilities. We cannot, and do not, assess the influence or value of the debates relative to other components of the 1988 campaign, but, instead, evaluate how the debates appear to have fit in with those components. For example, what strategies did the candidates and their campaigns seem to develop for the debates, and how did those debate strategies reflect overall campaign strategies? How important were the debates to the campaigns in comparison with other forms of campaign communications, such as advertisements and free media? When the election was over and the news media could reflect on the campaign, what did they say about the role of the 1988 debates?

STRATEGIES TO DOWNPLAY THE DEBATES

As James Baker put it, "I think the debates . . . have a way of freezing campaigns. . . . Once the debate is over, we'll be free to campaign across the length and breadth of this country."[1] Clearly the intent of those running the Bush campaign was to lessen the impact of the debates—not only on the outcome at the end of the campaign, but also on the campaign itself. The Bush campaign gamesmanship won the day early in the campaign when the two sides agreed to terms: two presidential debates and one vice-presidential; the series of debates completed by mid-October; and the format to include questioning by a panel of journalists. One network news account suggested that Bush aides had celebrated the fact that the agreement had been reached on their terms (Rather 1988). They had succeeded in lessening the potential impact of the debates on the campaign by limiting the number of head-to-head confrontations (the Dukakis people had wanted at least four presidential debates), by having them completed at least three weeks before Election Day (thus allowing time for "damage control," if necessary), and by seeing to it that the format would allow carefully scripted answers to predictable questions from journalists (less opportunity for an infamous Bush verbal gaffe).[2] And what did the Dukakis campaign win in this debate over the debates? Apparently only a concession that the candidates would stand during the debates and that Dukakis could use a riser to offset Bush's six-inch height advantage ("Lectern to Lectern" 1988). And, of course, the opportunity to communicate with 100 million Americans in 35 million households.

Having minimized the possible impact of the institution of presidential debates, the Bush campaign then set out to downplay the importance of the individual debates themselves—but, of course, only for their man. Though James Baker and others within the campaign viewed both presidential debates as mere "hurdles to be crossed" (Hume 1988a), they used every opportunity to increase the importance of the debates for their opponent. In the first debate, the double-barreled effort to lower expectations for Bush and raise them for Dukakis meant emphasizing that the vice president was a veritable debate novice compared with his opponent. "He's not a debater," Baker would tell reporters of Bush, "he's made that point" (Schieffer 1988a). On the other hand, reporters told viewers, Dukakis was a seasoned performer, once the moderator of public broadcasting's debate/discussion program "The Advocates" and the participant in 40 debates during the primary campaign (Hume 1988a). It was in the best interest of the Dukakis campaign to make the debates as important as possible, primarily to attract the largest viewing audience possible. The Dukakis staff members, therefore, made little effort to lower expectations for their candidate. But two examples from network newscasts indicate some attempt to raise expectations for Bush: The Roger Ailes connection to Bush, they said, would make the vice president well-prepared (Morton 1988a), and increased preparation by Dukakis was necessary because "George Bush is a tough debater" (Donaldson 1988a).

The Bush campaign effort to downplay the debates as a whole, and the first debate in particular, did not entirely wash with the news media. The networks, especially, placed a great deal of significance on the debates as the first confrontation approached, despite the Bush efforts to avoid making the debate "the Super Bowl of the campaign" (Hume 1988a). Four nights before the first debate, Peter Jennings led his newscast by calling the debate "that moment in the campaign which could give one or the other a decisive edge" (Jennings 1988a). And two nights later, Jennings started the newscast by suggesting that the debates would be "great" only because the candidates "*both* appear to believe that there's an enormous amount riding on how they impress the voters" [emphasis added] (Jennings 1988b).

Despite the downplay pitch from both sides—mostly by the Bush camp—most network journalists were not buying. Placing the first debate in the context of the entire campaign of "photo opportunities," ABC's Richard Threlkeld called the debate the closest thing to a direct encounter that would occur, ". . . both of them up there answering questions . . . without a safety net" (Threlkeld 1988). Contradicting this view in part was Leslie Stahl of CBS, who asserted that the rigid, controlled debate format the candidates had negotiated would indeed provide a safety net. But, Stahl said, presidential debates historically had helped win elections and lose them. The implication, of course, was that this first debate was a very big deal—for both candidates.

The next debate, on the other hand, was also a big deal—but for neither debater. Throughout the campaign, the Democrats had been on the defensive, for the most part, with the exception of the Dan Quayle "issue." And with the assistance of the national news media, the Dukakis

campaign had succeeded in raising doubts about the abilities and competence of the junior senator from Indiana. Stories ranged from Quayle's
having received special consideration for law school admittance through
a program intended for minorities and underprivileged (Adams 1988a) to
the great extent he was being controlled and handled by Bush media
advisers (Bergantino 1988). Even sympathetic political pundits saw
Quayle as a liability. "I think he will hurt in the end," said conservative
analyst Kevin Phillips. "I think he's going to be a problem" (Bergantino
1988).

It was within this context that the vice-presidential debate took on
great significance. It was important for George Bush that Dan Quayle
perform well, to demonstrate he was not a political lightweight (symbolized by "Doonesbury" cartoonist Garry Trudeau as a feather), to remove
doubts about his competence. It was at least equally important for
Michael Dukakis, for he had not only invested time and money into
making Quayle an issue, he had also invested heavily to make Quayle *the*
issue. The difference between Vice President Bush and himself, Dukakis
would say, is in leadership ability. And one criterion for determining
leadership, Dukakis asserted, was strong decision making. He had been
strong in choosing Lloyd Bentsen; Bush had been weak in choosing
Quayle. The Dukakis people counted on the vice-presidential debate to
provide the incontrovertible evidence.

Just as they had for the first presidential debate, the campaigns played
the appropriate expectation games, but, again, the news media would
have none of it. The Quayle advance story by Jacqueline Adams of CBS
said Senate colleagues thought highly enough of him to wonder why the
Bush campaign advisers were on pins and needles. But Adams also
claimed Quayle had one overriding goal: to convince Americans that he
was smart enough and mature enough to be vice president (Adams 1988b).

Lloyd Bentsen, meanwhile, attempted to raise expectations of Quayle
and simultaneously lower them for himself. But ABC correspondent Ann
Compton insisted that it was important for Bentsen to "set in concrete"
doubts about Quayle (Compton 1988). Peter Jennings, though, best characterized the Quayle-Bentsen debate: "Another one of those important
milestones, crucial . . . to both sides" (Jennings 1988b). Eight days later
the presidential candidates would again confront one another—a meeting
that would become a milestone—and a millstone for Michael Dukakis.

And that final debate was crucial only for Dukakis. By most accounts,
the Bentsen-Quayle debate was a convincing win for the Democrats.
Network correspondents in the days that immediately followed portrayed
it as a clear victory for Bentsen (Donaldson 1988b), as evidence that
Quayle was a liability to the Republicans (Schieffer 1988b), and as the
event that might allow Dukakis to regain momentum in the race (Morton
1988b). But whatever momentum Dukakis might have gained was quickly

offset by successful Bush efforts to distance himself from his running mate and to embrace the crime issue and furlough programs, and state-by-state poll results indicated Bush was gaining a stranglehold on the electoral college.

So even though the Quayle story was still getting play two nights after the debate, it faded behind stories about Willie Horton (see below). And both CBS and ABC showed poll stories three to four days before the final debate that indicated a considerable block of states solidly for Bush. He had a lock in the South, where, as Rebecca Chase pointed out, crime and law-and-order themes appealed to voters (Chase 1988). The evening of the debate, CBS's Bob Schieffer reported 275 electoral votes leaning to Bush, enough to win if he held on to them (Schieffer 1988c). But perhaps the most telling finding in the poll data reported in the days before the debate was the one reported in stories from both ABC and CBS: People liked George Bush more than they liked Michael Dukakis (Scherr 1988; Morton 1988c). And changing that attitude became Michael Dukakis's burden in the last debate.

Throughout the advance stories on the evening newscasts the night of the debate (October 13), correspondents and political pundits hammered away at the likability theme and raised the stakes for Dukakis. "In the first debate, some viewers said they liked Dukakis's impressive grasp of the issues and language," Sam Donaldson reported, "but they didn't particularly like him. Tonight he'll try to project more warmth, more likability" (Donaldson 1988c). Bruce Morton: "Tonight is probably his best single shot at changing the equation" (Morton 1988d).

For Vice President Bush, the reporters said, the strategy was simple and the risks low. Typically, sports metaphors characterized the reporting. For Bush, the debate was "like a ball game in the late innings," Bob Schieffer reported. Bush needed to "hold the lead, protect himself against a surprise" (Schieffer 1988c). "If Michael Dukakis needs to play offensive ball, then George Bush needs to contain the offense and not give any ground," Peter Jennings said (Jennings 1988c). Regardless of which sport provided the metaphor, the message was clear: The election was George Bush's to lose. And in the aftermath of the debate, there was still another sports metaphor: Dukakis had not delivered the "instant knockout" he needed to win the debate and revive his campaign (Donaldson 1988d).

Very little was mentioned about the debates on network television news in the final three weeks of the campaign. About the only reference to them occurred when Dukakis appeared in face-to-face interviews with network anchormen who asked him about his apparent inability to demonstrate emotion on television.[3] And although each debate produced a "moment," none of the three seemed to have changed the course of the election in a way similar to the Gerald Ford Eastern Europe gaffe in 1976 or the Ronald Reagan one-liners in 1980 and 1984. Yet, in our opinion, the debates did play an important role in the 1988 campaign, if mostly in a tactical sense.

Strategically the Bush campaign portrayed the debates as just another day on the campaign trail, despite James Baker's concern to the contrary. Certainly for them the debates provided a rare opportunity to reach millions of voters at one time, but that fact alone did not increase their value for the vice president. To Bush, the debates merely meant that central themes in an overall media strategy would reach more people than if there were no debates.

The Dukakis people, on the other hand, continued to see the debates as discrete events separate from the overall campaign, and as milestones where the stakes became more significant at each point.[4] They had seen their man succeed in a previous "big moment," the Democratic Convention, and to some extent, the strategy was effective for the first debate and the vice-presidential debate. But as ABC's James Wooten put it, the Democrats had faltered when it came to employing a day-to-day operation with a central message (Wooten 1988). That failure, in combination with the Bush campaign success, made potential effects from the first two debates short-lived, at best, and the stakes for Dukakis in the third debate virtually unattainable. It also meant that the lasting effect of the 1988 presidential debates would be a tactical one.

THE NEWS MEDIA AND POLITICAL ADS: A "GREEK CHORUS"?

As we have mentioned earlier, 1988 probably will not be remembered as the year of the great debates, but rather as the year of the negative advertising campaign, or the year of the orchestrated media campaign. In fact, since the election, as we pored through hours of network newscast videotape, we could not help but notice how often stories either made reference to campaign ads or, more importantly, we think, showed excerpts of the actual ads. The amount of attention the networks were paying to the ads made us wonder whether they had done similarly in previous recent campaigns. It also raised the question of how critical the networks actually were as they used the excerpts. In our content analysis of network coverage of the debates, we discovered debate "fact patrol" stories, usually the night after the debate. In these stories, the reporter compared answers the debaters gave with the available record. As often as not, the reporter discovered discrepancies, distortions, or misrepresentations.[5] Did a similar fact patrol exist for the television advertisements? Or did the networks join in the "Greek chorus," repeating and amplifying the political spots uncritically?

One researcher (Devlin 1989) has strongly suggested that the fact patrol was nonexistent for advertising. In fact, Devlin says, journalists abdicated their roles as whistle-blowers during the 1988 election ad campaign. He pointed out that even though some journalists made an attempt to keep the record straight (for example, ABC's Richard Threlkeld critically analyzed the Bush campaign's "Tank" ad[6]), few did enough fact-checking of the ads. In fact, ABC News provided no follow-up coverage, and the ads continued to run.

Devlin's point is well-taken. Network news coverage of the ads did point out misrepresentations only on a hit-or-miss basis, and the coverage was rarely self-initiated. But he overstates the omission of the fact patrol. In fact, most stories on the Massachusetts furlough program and Willie Horton did present certain facts that could have refuted the implications of Republican ads. We believe, however, that even when network correspondents did initiate coverage that included fact-checking of misrepresentations, they contributed to the Greek chorus effect we referred to earlier. That is, their persistence in drawing attention to the campaign claims and their use of stereotypical portrayals gave the furlough and law-and-order issues salience, much in the way that a Greek chorus would compel the audience's attention to important points of a play by repeating story lines and dialogue from the play. While Devlin's argument is valid to a certain extent, it fails to account for the many times when reporters did fact-check advertisements but still gave credence to them by echoing their claims.

For example, Jackie Judd of ABC did a story that was to have presented the facts of the celebrated Horton prison furlough case. The story included excerpts from the Bush campaign's "revolving door" ad and video of the Maryland couple Willie Horton was alleged to have brutalized while on furlough. Judd also pointed out that the Massachusetts furlough legislation had been signed by a Republican governor, that 43 other states and the federal government had similar furlough programs, and that Governor Dukakis had made it tougher for prisoners to earn furloughs. She mixed her message, though, by adding that Dukakis was a "strong advocate" of the furlough program and took "a liberal stand" on crime issues.

Two weeks later ABC ran another story on the furlough program, this one highlighting the appearance of the Maryland couple on the campaign trail for Bush. Again, correspondent John Martin included fact patrol language similar to Judd's, but the story concluded that "Willie Horton has already become a symbol of what can go wrong—and a burden for Michael Dukakis" (Martin 1988). A little more than a week later, excerpts of the "revolving door" ad were included in another ABC story, this time with no refutation (Serafin 1988).

Often the refutation came from the Democrats themselves, although the Dukakis campaign did little to respond directly to attacks on the furlough program and the crime issue until about three weeks before the election, when Dukakis and his surrogates called the Bush tactics "dirty" and "racist." Television production values required, however, that the story place the Dukakis reaction in proper context. That usually meant showing a brief part of the "revolving door" ad or the "Willie Horton" ad that he was complaining about. (The Horton ad was produced by a political action committee for Bush, not by the Bush campaign.[7]) Such references included: "Horton, the black man who raped a white woman while on furlough from a Massachusetts prison" (Donaldson 1988e), and "Horton, who raped a Maryland woman and stabbed her husband, both white, while on prison furlough from Massachusetts" (Hume 1988b). These network stories contained strong reactions from Dukakis, including accusations of racism, but they also included excerpts of the ad itself and the image-laden language about Horton and his victims. And they did *not* contain the fact patrol information available in the previous stories.

We believe that the networks made a greater attempt to fact-check political advertising than Devlin suggests. But, apparently restricted by the routines of "balanced" and "objective" journalism, the journalists used ad excerpts and descriptive language that did little to differentiate the story meaning from the symbolic meaning of the advertising. Furthermore, the constant repetition of brief excerpts of the ads and the issues and players surrounding the ads—in essence, creating an echo chamber—made what they represented salient for potential voters.

Negative television advertising in presidential campaigns has existed since the advent of television (see Diamond and Bates 1984). But what about television news coverage of political advertising in presidential campaigns? We used the Vanderbilt Television News Index to see how many stories the three networks ran about presidential campaign advertising during each of the fall campaigns from 1976 to 1988 (that is, from September 1 through election day). We were especially interested in whether a story included excerpts from the ad the story was discussing. Based on what we saw in 1988, our impression was that showing excerpts of the ads—even if in fact patrol stories—would place the networks in the position of joining the Greek chorus concerning the content discussed in the ad itself. Showing the ad, in essence, would give salience to the issue in the ad. We also noted whether the excerpts shown in the story were from an advertisement for a Republican candidate or a Democratic candidate.

We performed no statistical test on the data, since eyeballing the numbers shows a test unnecessary. In 1976, three stories contained ad excerpts; two of the three had excerpts from both candidates, or the sponsor was unclear. The number of stories containing ad excerpts increased to 21 in 1980, with balance across all categories. The number of stories with ad excerpts in 1984 dropped to eight, five of which contained Reagan ads. But in 1988 the three networks carried 62 stories that included excerpts of political ads, 27 from Bush ads and 17 from Dukakis ads. The other 18 stories included ads from both campaigns, or their source was unclear from the Vanderbilt Index (see Table 11.1).

One way to see how important the debates were in the context of the campaign is to compare the amount of coverage they got with the amount of coverage ads received. We did this for the four most recent presidential election years by taking our data on stories that contained ad excerpts and adding to it data on stories that either showed or mentioned presidential debates, which we also took from the Vanderbilt Television News Index. We also instituted a control for the number of debates in each of the four election years by dividing the total number of stories (both with ad excerpts and debate mentions) by the number of debates that year. Table 11.2 shows that the number of debate stories and stories with ad excerpts parallel each other until 1988. That is, the number of debate stories per debate goes up from 1976 to 1980, but drops in 1984 and 1988. The number of stories with ad excerpts per debate also rises from 1976 to 1980, also drops in 1984, but increases considerably in 1988. We suggest this as evidence that the 1988 debates were no longer as important relative to other forms of campaign communication—namely, televised ads—as they had been in previous campaigns.

Serendipitously, we noticed another interesting fact about the stories with ads in 1988. Before the vice-presidential debate, stories with Dukakis ad excerpts outnumbered stories with Bush ad excerpts, 8 to 4. After the Bentsen-Quayle debate, Bush ads in stories outnumbered Dukakis ads, 23 to 9. This change indicates that the conventional wisdom that the national news media were preoccupied with the media campaign and negative advertising by the Bush side does not hold up, at least when one

Table 11.1
Campaign Stories with Ad Excerpts, by Election Year

Story with excerpt of ad for:	1976	1980	1984	1988
Democratic candidate	--	4	1	17
Republican candidate	1	7	5	27
Other candidate	--	4	--	--
Unclear or more than one candidate	2	6	2	18
Total	3	21	8	62

Table 11.2
Average Number of Stories Mentioning or Showing Debates and Ads, by Year, with Number of Debates Controlled*

Campaign story referring to:	1976	1980	1984	1988
Debates shown or mentioned, per number of debates	42.0	96.5	51.3	43.0
Presidential ads shown or mentioned, per debate	.8	10.5	2.7	20.7

*   Four debates were held in 1976, two in 1980, and three in 1984 and 1988.

looks at the entire fall campaign. Bush may have employed attack methods early in the fall, but they seem to have been in free media-oriented campaign appearances, not in advertising. Either that, or the media had not yet attached much significance to the use of advertising in the campaign. Furthermore, the Democrats also engaged in negative advertising, particularly over the Dan Quayle issue.

DEBATES IN CAMPAIGN REVIEWS

We close this chapter with a look at the campaign retrospectives in various media and how they portrayed the three debates once the campaign had ended. In this portion of the analysis we focus on three print media—the *New York Times*, the *Washington Post*, and *Newsweek* —and public broadcasting's "MacNeil-Lehrer Newshour." These national sources supplied the most thorough, continuous analyses of the campaign within days of election day, both before and after. This section will necessarily be brief because, bluntly, none of these sources—indeed no media source at all—considered the debates turning points in the election. In the overall scheme of the fall campaign, the most important element in the eyes of virtually all analysts was the negativity, especially in the advertising.

Even when these campaign postmortems dealt with debates, it was in the context of the negative campaign. For example, on election night former NBC president Robert Mulholland and former White House aide Michael Deaver appeared on the "MacNeil-Lehrer Newshour" and argued over the best ways to ensure robust exchanges of ideas rather than sound bites and 30-second commercials. Deaver wondered why the television networks had not forced a "true" debate—that is, a debate without a panel of journalists asking questions, only a moderator. But

Mulholland countered that, in fact, one network had offered the candidates a chance to go one on one, but one candidate had refused the offer. In the end, both men agreed that attempting to negotiate a true debate between candidates would be difficult, perhaps even futile ("MacNeil-Lehrer Newshour" 1988).

The frustration about debate format is an indictment of the debates and American media campaigns. Another participant in the same broadcast, *Trenton Times* Managing Editor Ed Baumeister, compared the United States with Canada, where the technologies are the same, but, he suggests, "the culture that surrounds" the media campaign is different. Debates among the three prime-ministerial candidates had no journalist panel and they came, Baumeister said, with a different standard and different expectations for coverage of the campaign ("MacNeil-Lehrer Newshour" 1988).

So retrospective discussion about debates centered primarily on how, in theory, to improve them and, consequently, the campaigns. One exception to this type of discussion came from *Washington Post* columnist Mark Shields on the election night "MacNeil-Lehrer Newshour." Responding to fellow pundit David Gergen's contention that Michael Dukakis had suffered from the emphasis on sound-bite journalism, Shields pointed out that when longer forms such as debates were available to Dukakis, he had not succeeded in using them effectively ("MacNeil-Lehrer Newshour" 1988). It was one of the few November or later television references to the impact of the 1988 debates on the campaign.

The print media we analyzed provided similar emphasis to the negative aspects of the campaign commercials and sound-bite journalism, and little to the impact of the debates. In postmortems the weekend following the election, *New York Times* staffers Robin Toner and Gerald Boyd both referred to specific moments of the two debates, but in neither instance was the moment considered critical to the outcome of the election. Toner's piece on the failure of the Dukakis campaign to develop a coherent strategy (Toner 1988) recounted the two-fisted Bush tactic of defining Dukakis as a liberal and establishing the issue agenda. Dukakis, the story noted, had not counterattacked and missed an opportunity to do so in the second debate. His response to the Bernard Shaw hypothetical about the rape and murder of his wife, Toner wrote, symbolized Dukakis's inability or unwillingness to play hardball. Boyd's reference to the first debate attached even less significance to it than Toner had to the second. Apparently the vice president had been concerned about his debate performance. But, the story related, Bush aides believed he had succeeded in the debate in defining Dukakis as a liberal (Boyd 1988).

In the case of both *New York Times* articles, we see the same emphasis on how the use of television negative advertising and sound-bite journalism influenced the campaign and the electorate. The influence of the debates—the little that did occur—was seen almost entirely as being on the strategy of the campaign, not on the electorate.

A *Washington Post* campaign retrospective provided a similar view of the strategic impact of the debates (Hoffman and Devroy 1988). The story provided a detailed, behind-the-scenes look at how the Bush team planned its campaign, particularly how they planned the use of advertising. According to the story, a critical juncture of the campaign came at the first debate, when the campaign had two plans: If Bush did well in the debate, the campaign would use the theme of economic prosperity to accentuate the positive. But if he did not do well in the debate, the focus would be on crime and accent on the negative. "After the debate," the article concluded, "the crime ads went up."

Finally, *Newsweek's* special issue on the election in mid-November provided more coverage to the debates (seven pages) than any other source ("Lectern to lectern" 1988). But clearly the emphasis of the whole issue was on attack advertising and the negative campaign, from the Bush discovery of how Reagan Democrats in Massachusetts felt toward their governor, to Bush campaign manager Lee Atwater's claim to campaign workers in the summer of 1988 that Willie Horton would be a household word in November.

CONCLUSION

In the eyes of the nation's news media, the 1988 presidential debates had relatively little impact on the campaign, and that is apparently just how the Bush campaign wanted it. The evidence suggests that any impact the debates had on voters came in the second Bush-Dukakis debate, when the bar was raised so high for Michael Dukakis that he was unable to reach it, let alone get over it. Throughout the campaign, though, most media coverage concerned the impact of the debates on campaign strategy and the candidates. This fact appears to be consistent with the findings in our study that deal with how the networks reduced importance of debates to their impact on the campaigns, and with how the news media view presidential debates as an institution.

NOTES

1. Statement from James Baker, Bush campaign manager, on "ABC World News Tonight with Peter Jennings," October 13, 1988.

2. Negotiations over format continued into the week before the first presidential debate, when haggling occurred over the make-up of the panel. The Dukakis campaign wanted the television network anchors to comprise the panel, giving it star quality and, consequently, greater audience appeal. The Bush people, "not

wanting to magnify the event," wanted broadcast and print journalists. Again, the Bush campaign won out (Hume 1988a).

3. The "key" moment the anchors and Dukakis would refer to was the lead-off question from CNN's Bernard Shaw in the final debate. Shaw asked Dukakis if he would still oppose capital punishment if his wife were raped and murdered. Dukakis did not respond with outrage or any other emotion, but rather with scholarly restraint.

4. Before the first debate, Bruce Morton suggested with tongue in cheek that if Dukakis followed the advice from his staff, he would be "an everyday mix of Plato, Shakespeare, Abe Lincoln, and the guy next door."

5. A good example of this type of story is the piece by ABC's James Wooten on September 26, 1988, the night following the first Bush-Dukakis debate. In the story, Wooten questioned several debate statements by both candidates by juxtaposing their answers with previous statements and records. He did the same for the vice-presidential debate and the second presidential debate.

6. The ad was designed to portray Michael Dukakis as weak on defense, but the most memorable part of the ad was the use of news video that had originally been shot as part of coverage of a Dukakis photo opportunity designed to portray the Democratic candidate as strong on defense issues.

7. The Horton ad was produced by a political action committee for Bush, not by the Bush campaign. It contained a mug shot of Horton and the particulars of his furlough and the attack on the Maryland couple.

REFERENCES

Adams, J. 1988a. "CBS Evening News With Dan Rather." September 9.

Adams, J. 1988b. "CBS Evening News With Dan Rather." October 4.

Bergantino, J. 1988. "ABC World News Tonight With Peter Jennings." September 19.

Boyd, G. 1988. How Bush won: picking the right fights and getting the right opponent. *New York Times*, November 12, A8.

Chase, R. 1988. "ABC World News Tonight With Peter Jennings." October 10.

Compton, A. 1988. "ABC World News Tonight With Peter Jennings." October 5.

Devlin, L. P. 1989. Contrasts in presidential campaign commercials of 1988. *American Behavioral Scientist* 32:389–414.

Diamond, E., and S. Bates. 1984. *The spot: The rise of political advertising on TV*. Cambridge: The MIT Press.

Donaldson, S. 1988a. "ABC World News Tonight With Peter Jennings." September 23.

Donaldson, S. 1988b. "ABC World News Tonight With Peter Jennings." October 6.

Donaldson, S. 1988c. "ABC World News Tonight With Peter Jennings." October 13.

Donaldson, S. 1988d. "ABC World News Tonight With Peter Jennings." October 14.

Donaldson, S. 1988e. "ABC World News Tonight With Peter Jennings." October 24.

Hoffman, D., and A. Devroy. 1988. The complex machine behind Bush. *Washington Post*, November 13, A1, A16.

Hume, B. 1988a. "ABC World News Tonight With Peter Jennings." September 21.

Hume, B. 1988b. "ABC World News Tonight With Peter Jennings." October 25.

Jennings, P. 1988a. "ABC World News Tonight With Peter Jennings." September 21.

·Jennings, P. 1988b. "ABC World News Tonight With Peter Jennings." October 5.

Jennings, P. 1988c. "ABC World News Tonight With Peter Jennings." October 13.

Judd, J. 1988. "ABC World News Tonight With Peter Jennings." September 22.

Lectern to lectern. 1988. *Newsweek*, November 21, 120–121.

"MacNeil-Lehrer Newshour." 1988. November 8.

Martin, J. 1988. "ABC World News Tonight With Peter Jennings." October 7.

Morton, B. 1988a. "CBS Evening News With Dan Rather." September 23.

Morton, B. 1988b. "CBS Evening News With Dan Rather." October 6.

Morton, B. 1988c. "CBS Evening News With Dan Rather." October 12.

Morton, B. 1988d. "CBS Evening News With Dan Rather." October 13.

Rather, D. 1988. "CBS Evening News With Dan Rather." September 6.

Scherr, L. 1988. "ABC World News Tonight With Peter Jennings." October 12.

Schieffer, B. 1988a. "CBS Evening News With Dan Rather." September 23.

Schieffer, B. 1988b. "CBS Evening News With Dan Rather." October 7.

Schieffer, B. 1988c. "CBS Evening News With Dan Rather." October 13.

Serafin, B. 1988. "ABC World News Tonight With Peter Jennings." October 16.

Threlkeld, R. 1988. "ABC World News Tonight With Peter Jennings." September 23.

Toner, R. 1988. Dukakis aides acknowledge Bush outmaneuvered them. *New York Times*, November 12, A1, A8.

Wooten, J. 1988. "ABC World News Tonight With Peter Jennings." October 12.

12

CONCLUSIONS

This chapter is divided into two major segments. The first considers what we have found in this multifaceted study. The second looks at the implications of these findings for the political parties, the presidential debates, sponsorship of the debates, the debate format, news media performance, and future research on the debates.

OUR FINDINGS

Candidates, Debates, and Verdicts

Looking across the short time series surrounding each of the three fall debates, our findings fairly consistently suggest that an important verdict effect results from post-debate news specials. How long the effect lasts seems to vary with the particular debate, as does whether the news analysis effect is limited to the beneficiary or also includes the victim of the media verdict about who "won" and who "lost."

Debate Performance. For the two presidential debates, the candidate evaluated most favorably during post-debate news commentary also showed in survey respondents' perceptions as the better performer in the debate. Content analysis showed that of the post-debate news verdicts about Michael Dukakis after the first debate, 70% were positive, compared with only 42% for George Bush. Those figures were almost exactly reversed after the second debate: Bush 76% positive comments, Dukakis only 36%.

Turning now to the surveys, people seeing both the September debate and a post-debate news special gave higher debater-rating scores for Dukakis than those watching the debate only or not watching at all. No parallel influence showed for debater ratings of Bush. As for the second Bush-Dukakis debate, the same "winner-only" pattern existed for Bush (defined as the "winner" this time) but not for Dukakis. On average, debate and post-debate analysis viewers rated Bush as a debater higher than those watching the debate only or not watching at all. Once again, no parallel pattern showed up for the "loser" of this particular debate— in this case, Dukakis.

These results were also supported in our analysis of the responses to the open-ended questions about Bush and Dukakis as debaters. Respondents interviewed immediately after the September debate who had watched both debate and post-debate analysis were more likely to use favorable words in describing Dukakis than those who had watched the debate only. After the October 13 debate, the same pattern of positive descriptions by exposure to post-debate analysis followed for Bush.

What about the Quayle-Bentsen debate? Lloyd Bentsen received 76% favorable verdicts in post-debate news specials, while Dan Quayle received only 36% favorable verdicts about his debate performance. Exposure to post-debate analysis once again strongly predicted favorable ratings of Bentsen's debating skills. Those who saw both the debate and analysis gave Bentsen an adjusted average rating of 7.63 on a 0-to-10-point scale, compared with only 7.11 for those who had watched just the debate. Strictly in terms of his ratings as a debater, the post-debate analysis effect for the loser (i.e., Quayle, as defined by the media) was not as strong ($p < .10$) as for the winner ($p < .02$). Nevertheless, Quayle's ratings as a debater were lower (a mean of 4.51) when people saw both debate and post-debate news special than when they watched only the debate (4.94). Furthermore, people who watched both the debate and analysis were significantly more likely to say that Bentsen won by a lot than those who watched only the debate. So we have a verdict effect for the loser as well as for the media-declared winner in the case of the vice-presidential debate.

We also found evidence for a verdict effect on Quayle in terms of open-ended responses collected between the vice-presidential and second presidential debates. Despite the fact that both his questioners and Quayle himself referred to questions of his competence repeatedly during the debate, it was not until one night later that more than 20% of respondents negatively described Quayle's competence in the debate. This percentage—roughly twice as high as that just after the debate— once it was reached, on October 6, remained remarkably stable through October 12, the end of that time series. Similarly, the idea that Quayle himself might be a campaign issue increased from just 6.6% on debate night to 23.8% the next night. These and the other open-ended responses imply that Quayle's performance looked worse 24 hours after the debate than it did immediately afterward, and this effect held for both Republicans and Democrats.

Over time, Quayle's ratings as a debater remained about the same on debate night (5.14) and the next night (5.20), but kept falling lower and lower on the next three nights we measured (October 9, 11, and 12). Meanwhile, in the case of the two Bush-Dukakis debates, changes around debate night were of relatively short duration (roughly two days). The longer life of the changes for Quayle may reflect the fact that we heard relatively little that was new from or about him, but much that was repeated, in the period after the debate. So if one of the effects of the post-debate coverage was to convert Quayle from debater into campaign issue, and if the reaction of the Bush campaign was to "hide" Quayle, it might not be such a surprise that whatever happened to Quayle's reputation as a debater continued to happen during this time period.

In any case, over the three debates, our evidence strongly suggests that post-debate analysis influences viewers in very predictable ways. The candidate judged most favorably in the media verdicts benefits in the survey responses. In something of a contrast, the least-favored candidate does not necessarily suffer because of exposure to post-debate analysis, although in the case of Dan Quayle, who became a campaign issue to many of our respondents, post-debate analysis as well as media coverage hurt his evaluations as a debater and greatly damaged the chances that people would think he won his debate with Bentsen.

Taken across the three general election debates, then, we report strong evidence of a verdict effect upon debate performance perceptions. This evidence still holds *after* controlling for partisan predispositions and demographic variables.

Image. We used a composite scale to measure the images of the two presidential candidates, and viewer responses on this composite scale were analyzed for the September and October presidential debates. Once again, exposure to post-debate analysis acted the same way on presidential candidate image as it did on debater ratings. The candidate receiving the most favorable post-debate news verdicts immediately after the debate (Dukakis on September 25 and Bush on October 13) also experienced an improvement in his general image as a potential president. For the September debate, viewers watching both the debate and a post-debate analysis rated Dukakis higher (26.33) than debate-only viewers (25.54) or non-viewers (23.03). After the final debate, George Bush had higher image evaluations for debate plus analysis viewers (27.03), followed by debate-only viewers (25.63) and those who watched neither (24.66). No such image measurements were available to us for the two vice-presidential debaters, but it seems clear that debate performance perceptions are used by viewers in evaluating the presidential candidates' overall images as potential presidents. No wonder campaigns worry so much about debate performance verdicts!

For the September 25 debate, simple exposure to the debate itself seemed to influence the image of both presidential candidates. The influence of the debate itself seemed short—one or two days. Once again, many other campaign communications would seem to temper how long the debate itself would influence candidates' general image, unimpeded by other relevant influences.

Voting Preferences. For the candidates, the most important possible impact of the debates obviously concerns whether or not debating adds or subtracts to their vote totals. We have some evidence, at least from the first presidential debate and the vice-presidential one, that it does. The September debate—especially in combination with post-debate analysis—appeared to increase the self-described probability that our respondents were going to vote for Michael Dukakis. In addition, when we moved to a Bush vs. Dukakis forced-choice question, the highest Dukakis percentage (65.7%) was given by people who saw both the September 25 debate and analysis, the next highest by debate viewers only (52.7%), and lowest (48.7%) by non-viewers.

Somewhat to our surprise, the Quayle-Bentsen debate seemed to produce a strong carryover to presidential voting choice. Preferences for Dukakis stood at 58% on October 4, 48% on debate night (October 5), and (consistent with a post-debate analysis effect) increased to 65% on October 6. After that, this 65% preference figure changed hardly at all each night through the night before the final October 13 debate. In the aftermath of the final debate, however, voting preferences seemed to have been established, and no debate (or analysis) effect was visible in our survey data.

Summary. Exposure to post-debate analysis emerges as the strongest debate-related influence on performance impressions, a composite presidential candidate image measure, and voting intentions. For the presidential debates, the post-debate verdict effect seemed more potent for the candidate favored by the verdict, but for the vice-presidential debate the impact seemed to be upon both Quayle, very much the loser in media verdicts, and Bentsen, very much the winner in those verdicts. In general, the verdict effect did not last as long for the presidential debates as it did for the vice-presidential one. In the case of the presidential candidates, many other subsequent campaign events might have shifted attention away from each debate.

Ironically, the effort by the Bush campaign to hide Quayle from further scrutiny might have helped extend the length of time that the Quayle verdict effect lasted. Had this debate been the final debate, or had either of the presidential candidates performed at a Quayle-like level, who knows what the outcome might have been?

The Debates Themselves

Journalists seemed to reduce the importance of the debates to whether they affected the ambitions of the candidates; their importance to voters seemed almost an afterthought. So reduced in importance, the debates were, in effect, being relegated to the same category of concern as those omnipresent attack ads—and suffering, by comparison, in 1988 campaign news. There is little doubt (going back at least to the 1976 campaign, where our records begin) that never was presidential campaign advertising so much a preoccupation of network journalism as in 1988.

Having equated impact upon the campaign with importance, journalists must have thought that *therefore* Roger Ailes and his attack ads were more significant than the debates. But even if those ads succeeded as America's elite journalists imagined they did (we have strong evidence in Chapter 10 that, in fact, the attack ads boomeranged among voters), on what basis did journalists decide that the significance of debates and ads should be measured on that same single effects criterion?

In each presidential campaign year after 1976, favorable institutional verdicts about the debates declined on post-debate newscasts. The decline was so steep that the percentage of favorable verdicts about the debates as an institution fell from 50% in 1976 to barely over 34% in 1988. Altruistic concern about how the debate format and ground rules could be improved in order to foster voters' ability to assess the rival candidates—a concern expressed in 1976 by commentators such as CBS's Eric Sevareid—had virtually disappeared from CBS, NBC, and ABC in 1988. Instead, 1988's correspondents and anchors seemed willing to spend much air time discussing needed changes in format and rules only when they had *personally* confronted the restrictions placed on them as panelists. Perhaps we are too cynical, but it seemed that only when those restraints shackled him or her personally did the network journalist think it worthwhile to share information with viewers about those restraints. When those restrictions happened to Peter Jennings or Andrea Mitchell, for example, Jennings and Mitchell apparently felt the compelling duty to let us all know how constrained they had been.

And ABC gave less air time on October 3 to the League of Women Voters' sudden 1988 withdrawal than it did on another night to panelist Jennings' own post-debate questions to Jim Baker about format and ground rules. With the exception of the *New York Times*, the elite print media also showed little consciousness in 1988 of the debates' potential to assist voters. In common with the networks, such elite newspapers as the *Washington Post* showed little interest in pursuing League complaints about debate format and ground rules.

The withdrawal of the League, which historians may later describe as a landmark event in the possible decline of the presidential debates, was framed by elite television and newspaper journalists in terms of whether the withdrawal would disrupt the staging of the final debate, not as a symptom of what had happened to the debates as a tool for voters. Although few of these 1988 journalists were on the job in 1960, it may be worth reminding the reader that the League supplanted the networks in 1976 as sponsor of the resumed debates. Certainly *Broadcasting*, the industry trade magazine, continually emphasized industry resentment about having been supplanted. In any case, the League received little sympathy from the networks in 1988, although it did get notable editorial support from some newspapers and columnists sprinkled elsewhere throughout the country.

It is in this media context that our survey interviews showed increasing signs of respondents' disappointment with the 1988 debates as those debates unfolded over time. In the early fall, before any Bush-Dukakis debates had been held, respondents agreed very slightly with the statement that not enough debates had been scheduled. Just after the September 25 debate, agreement hovered at about the same spot, but it was downhill after that. With each successive debate, the numbers agreeing fell. By the period after the October 13 debate, mean scores had fallen solidly on the disagree side. Similarly, as interviews moved from September to mid-October to November, more and more people agreed that candidates consistently avoided answering debate panelists' questions. Furthermore, agreement plunged over the fall that the debates were the voters' best way to decide between the candidates.

These three scales, taken together, suggest increasing disappointment with the 1988 debates over time. If only support for holding more debates had declined, that might have reflected the feeling that the debates had already done the job of helping respondents make up their minds. Or— especially for Republicans—it might have reflected only the growing feeling that adding to the number of scheduled debates was a high risk, no win idea for George Bush that could help only Michael Dukakis. However, these explanations cannot account for the growing belief, over time, that the debaters were evading the questions asked them by panelists and that the debates were *not* the best way to decide between the candidates.

As we reported in Chapter 9, people rated the debates themselves as the best first source of information about the debates, significantly above post-debate newspaper articles, discussion with other people, television news reports/analysis, and radio news reports. What this suggests is that people realize the "real thing" (the debate) is still the best way to find out about the debate. But, on the other hand, when we asked November 6 respondents to place the debates in the larger context of helpfulness in deciding whether to vote, the mean ratings of the debates put them squarely in the middle of 11 sources of guidance—five of these other sources above the debates and five below.

On balance, then, disappointment with the 1988 debates grew over time. Nevertheless, the Nielsen ratings for the three 1988 debates showed relatively low falloff during this same time period (see Table 9.1, Chapter 9). In fact, in absolute numbers the 1988 *falloff* after the first debate was smaller than it was in 1960 and 1976. (Unfortunately, of course, the Nielsens for the 1988 debates had already shown a tremendous drop in the ratings for the 1988 debates compared with previous years'. What may be happening is that the presidential debates now will draw a stable core audience, but fewer people will tune in accidentally or casually. Little comfort can be drawn from the fact that just over a third of American households tuned in to each one of the 1988 debates.)

IMPLICATIONS

The Parties and Campaign Organizations

Even in 1988, it appears, attack ads were not working the way campaign insiders thought they were. The lesson that should have been learned during the Bush-Dukakis campaign, based on our interviews throughout the general election campaign, might best be described as follows: *Failure by one side to rebut attacks on it effectively probably has a greater negative influence on the way that side is covered by the news media than it does directly on voters.*

Should the parties and campaign organizations continue to be in control of the debates? We shall take up this issue in sections on debate sponsorship and debate format.

The Debates as a Political Institution

After Michael Dukakis's lead over George Bush evaporated in the late summer of 1988, it became quite clear that the Bush campaign would rather not have debated at all. That they felt they had to debate may be taken as a signal that the fall debates are starting to become institutionalized. That is the good news for people who support the debates; the bad news is that when one candidate debates only because the price paid for refusing is too high, that candidate has many incentives to diminish and restrict the risk posed by the debates.

The surveys showed that, with each debate after the first, voter disappointment with the fall 1988 debates grew. The content analysis of post-debate news specials showed that, compared with previous years, the networks also were less supportive of the debates as an institution. Did these signs of voter and media disenchantment refer only to the 1988 version of the presidential debates, or has long-term damage been done to debates as a political institution?

Debate Sponsorship

Regardless of whether they were interviewed in the spring or on November 6, more of our respondents said they preferred the League of Women Voters if there was to be only a single sponsor of presidential debates. Tellingly, when respondents wanted a single sponsor, a much greater proportion of them (77%) preferred the League over the Commission than did respondents who wanted more than one sponsor (54%). Even most of the minority who favored the party- and campaign-dominated Commission as sponsor *also* wanted somebody else to sponsor an alternative set of debates. This does not strike us as a strong vote of confidence for the Commission—even among the minority who preferred it as sponsor.

There was no change from spring to November 6 in the relatively low preference for the Commission. Apparently, observing the Commission's conduct of the fall Bush-Dukakis debates neither helped nor especially hurt the Commission's standing as debate sponsor. However, when asked on November 6 whether the parties and campaigns had too much control over debate format, those preferring the League as sponsor tended to agree more than those choosing the Commission. Given the obvious ability of the campaigns to control the Commission on Presidential Debates and, through it, to control the ground rules, we wonder what the future of the debates will be if the League or some other currently eligible body, such as the television networks, does not reclaim at least a share of sponsorship of the fall debates.

However, the League or a similar sponsor will fail unless it convinces the campaigns that it is willing to play hard ball with the campaigns, if that is necessary. The only time the League went public with its dissatisfaction about campaign-imposed constraints *while it still was the sponsor*, everyone paid attention, and the League won that battle. Simply withdrawing in protest, as it did in 1988, serves no one except the campaigns. Perhaps the day of the League as sponsor has passed; if so, the next logical alternative to the Commission would be the television networks.

As we saw earlier, many (e.g., Minow and Sloan 1987, and Jamieson and Birdsell 1988) argue that the parties should sponsor the debates, in part because only the parties can require the candidates they nominate to debate. But is the price of institutionalizing the debates too high, if that price involves converting the debates into a kind of extended campaign commercial? Could we really expect that audiences for the debates would remain even as high as they are now if the debates came to be seen that way? John Anderson (1988) has suggested that debate participation ought to be made a condition for receiving Federal campaign funds. Such a proposal, if enacted, would eliminate the principal rationale for involving the parties (or their surrogate, the Commission) as sponsor. Without question it would take intense public pressure to get Congress to enact— and a sitting president to sign—such a law.

Debate Format

While we asked a question about format only on November 6, and while our three-site sample, in any case, would be a precarious base for projecting our exact percentage to the United States as a whole, we did find a strong majority (60 of 96 respondents, or 63%) agreeing that the campaigns had too much control over the debate format and ground rules. No matter who the sponsor is, it is doubtful that candidates and their advisors will not have considerable influence over debate format and ground rules. Furthermore, even if it were possible to prevent the candidates and their advisors from having any influence at all, simple fairness suggests that, as participants in the process and as people who are putting their ambitions at risk, the campaigns *should* have some say about the ground rules. Here again, the question of sponsorship is crucial. It is one thing to have a negotiating position and to play hard ball about the ground rules against an equally formidable rival and an equally formidable sponsor equally willing to play hard ball. It is quite another to control the rules of the game through a surrogate, while avoiding responsibility for imposing those rules; that is what the Commission allows the candidates to do now.

U.S. presidential candidates consistently resist direct confrontation between themselves, invariably opting instead for a panel of journalist-questioners in the belief that the panel is less risky than direct challenging of each other would be. In addition, we are seeing the campaigns increasingly impose restrictions on the possibility of follow-up questions by panelists. Ironically, one result of reducing the threat posed by journalist-panelists is to increase the ambiguity of the debate to viewers and therefore to *increase the risk of media verdict effects*. In other words, if the journalists do not get you with their questions to the debators, they may get you with their verdicts after the debate. This situation suggests that since the First Amendment protects media verdicts and journalists are increasingly wary of campaign-supplied verdicts (an increased wariness evident in our 1988 content analyses), greater candidate control of format has led to a loss of control over the verdict. The question we pose to the campaigns is this: Is not the price you pay for hamstringing the debate format too high, in terms of increasing your vulnerability to verdict effects?

The News Media

As we have seen, ABC, CBS, and NBC—and, possibly, all mainstream news media—concentrated more than ever in 1988 on candidate performance and strategic elements of the debates and less than ever on how the candidates addressed the issues and on whether they showed the necessary competence to lead the country. ABC's James Wooten and CBS's David Martin and Robert Krulvich did try to apply a fact patrol to the statements the candidates made in the debates. We believe this is a useful, important exercise that *all* network news programs should perform in the aftermath of the 1992 debates. Likewise, the print media should use their ability to create and preserve a permanent record to compare debate assertions with the actual records of the candidates.

What are the implications if the news media continue to concentrate on strategy, performance, and debate outcome? What might happen if they fail in their role to interpret the sometimes arcane questions and answers, to monitor candidate statements, and to spotlight inconsistencies and misrepresentations? In short, what if next time we get a repeat media performance of 1988?

We believe that among the strong possibilities are continuing decline in public interest in the election, in voter turnout, and in other forms of political participation. This study is hardly the only evidence of the public's anger at negative campaigning. By election day it seemed as though people were relieved that the end was near, but anxious about the choices they had. The 1988 debates certainly did not escape the public's feelings of disappointment. We acknowledge that the candidates and the campaigns were much of the problem in 1988, but the media seemed far more a part of the problem than ever before and far less part of any solution. Indeed, the 1988 debates seemed almost a perfect microcosm of the whole campaign in the following respects:

- A tightly controlled format that lent itself only to brief, catchy, rehearsed responses.

- Attempts by campaign surrogates to control interpretations of statements during the debates.

- Further attempts by the news media to interpret the interpretations, to discuss what did and did not work, to discern the "sound-biteable" statements, to assess performance (e.g., did Dan Quayle's "steely blue eyes" [Brokaw 1988] offset his debate performance), and so on.

- Little media effort to interpret statements made during the debate (e.g., some of us are *still* wondering about those "thousand points of light"), to discuss ramifications of proposed issue positions, to discern inconsistencies and inaccuracies, and to assess competency.

- Cynicism on the part of the news media themselves about the debates and their usefulness to voters, as the Bush campaign, in particular, tried to downplay and control the debates as a threat/challenge/test of their candidate.

While much criticism of debate format is justified, we believe that diminishing the importance and usefulness of the debates is not in the public interest, especially when the media are part of the reason debates may have lost some of their luster. For example, as we reported earlier, even when the media have recently portrayed the debates as important, they have defined their significance for the candidates, not for the voters.

We believe that the news media, particularly television, may be underestimating the interests and abilities of their audiences by not providing informative, issue-oriented coverage of the debates, rather than concentrating coverage on the "horse race" and whether a candidate's "steely blue eyes" will connect with the television audience. Network underestimation of the audience, however, should come as no surprise. Two decades ago, the networks already had begun to abdicate their role as informer/educator, instead taking on the role of entertainer when covering politics and public affairs. Despite a continuing barrage of generally well-documented criticism of news media trivialization of political campaigns, trends begun two decades ago have, if anything, picked up speed, as our comparisons of debate coverage in 1988 with earlier years suggest.

To the extent that the networks justify the importance of debates solely in terms of their impact on the electoral ambitions of the candidates, it seems a small and easy step for television journalists to focus on their own roles as elite insiders—as brokers and evaluators of how other elites did. That small and easy step seems to have been taken. Journalists' declining concern about how the audience uses the debates leads inevitably to less concern about improving the debates' usefulness to voters by improving their formats. *If journalists don't stick up for their audiences, and if the League has been removed as a surrogate for viewers of the debates, then who will represent their interests?*

Two decades ago, people said they wanted more issue information and less coverage of campaign hoopla (Patterson and McClure, 1976). We think they still feel that way. In reality, people are interested if they receive information they care about. They are well aware that they are not campaign insiders. Paraphrasing an old "Saturday Night Live" gag line, voters do not need to be reminded by network journalists that, in effect, "I'm an insider—and you're not." Feeling shut out of the process cannot help but reduce audience interest and participation.

Continuation of the behind-the-scenes portrayal of the candidate debates, we believe, has important implications for the continued existence and legitimacy of the debates. If the media continue to picture the debates as merely one in an arsenal of alternative political weapons at the disposal of the candidates, an entire generation of Americans will mature without ever considering that debates might serve some other purpose besides furthering the ambitions of Those Politicians. As a result, we probably will see the debate Nielsens—and voter turnout—continue their long decline. If the debates lose their legitimacy as political institutions, ultimately the legitimacy of American elections and the American political system will be threatened. If the debates no longer give Americans the sense that they can be used to make valid assessments of the candidates, it might be better for the legitimacy of the American electoral process to perform a kind of triage—surgically cut off the debates to try to save the legitimacy of the entire process.

News media coverage of negative campaigning and attack advertising has suffered from some of the same shortcomings. In 1988, when news coverage of "polispots" increased dramatically from previous election years, the focus of that coverage was on the strategy of using the ads, how that strategy fit within the campaign as a whole, and whether the ads worked. In the process, television news acted something like a Greek chorus, replaying the "good" parts of those attack ads in sound bites. Occasionally the stories interpreted the meaning of ads, although mostly within the context of overall campaign strategy. Even less often did the stories evaluate the factual accuracy of those ads.

It is true that negative campaigning has been around for a long time, but the amount of network news coverage of attack ads reached an unprecedented level in 1988, probably making the ads' messages more visible and salient than they otherwise would have been. We applaud efforts by the news media *since* 1988—especially in a variety of newspapers—to cover attack ads *as truth claims*, which is certainly what the ads purport to be. As an apparent result of these efforts in 1990, politicians seemed to show greater care in what their ads claimed, and some observers believe that pressure from the news media may even have reduced the number of negative spots (see Lipman 1990, Broder 1990). As encouraging as these developments have been, local television stations seemed less likely than newspapers to apply this kind of coverage to what was happening in their states (KRON-television in San Francisco was a notable exception in 1990).

We encourage the major networks to follow the example of a few affiliates and a growing number of newspapers regarding attack ads. It is the audience that needs help, not the politicians. It is in their own economic interest for the major national news media to encourage voter interest and attention, since greater interest means larger audiences. It is *not* in their economic interest to discourage popular involvement in presidential campaigns—but, based on our evidence, that is what they seemed to have been doing.

Future Research

The first televised general election presidential debate took place in 1960. More than thirty years later, we are still thinking about the need for further research; we are still trying to understand how campaign debates influence those who watch and those who participate. While we think this study has done the most definitive job ever of documenting the impact of post-debate verdicts on the campaign, research questions remain. Although the study has added considerable knowledge about the way journalists construct those verdicts, we need to know more. It has added considerably to our knowledge of how modern journalists treat the debates as political institutions, but more can and needs to be done. And while we think that we have challenged the conventional wisdom about the power of all those 1988 attack ads, the very act of confronting previously unchallenged political wisdom immediately invites vigorous empirical counterattacks. More specifically, here are a few ideas for future researchers:

- We strongly recommend continued reliance on time-series designs, even if existing analytic techniques somewhat restrict interpretation of these designs. Using our design, we were able to locate important changes in the ways our respondents rated the candidates as debaters, judged their images, shifted their voting intentions, and determined the importance of issues. Longer-term time-series studies, perhaps from two weeks before the first of the 1992 debates to the election in November, would allow more sophisticated analysis techniques, since present analytical models are more applicable to a longer series than was possible to use here. More important, a longer time series would allow a more detailed tracking and cross-sectional analysis of other campaign communication events in addition to the debates.

- Now that we are satisfied that the post-debate verdict effect actually occurs, many questions naturally arise about the process at the individual level. For example, could an elaboration likelihood model (Petty and Cacioppo, 1981), perhaps tested in a controlled experiment, illuminate the nature of the process? Another experiment might test the role of format restrictions (such as the agreement not to allow candidates to address each other directly) in so muddying the picture that viewers are made even more dependent on the news media for clarification of who did better. A third experiment might test the impact of verdicts given by studio audience members vs. those given by "experts." And so on.

- What are the factors that seem to limit the impact of the debates and post-debate analysis over time? Why, generally, do these influences most often last only a day or two? Under what conditions would they last longer? Why did a

1988 verdict effect seem more often to occur for the candidate whose verdict was favorable than for the one whose verdict was unfavorable?

- A common tendency in research books such as this is to call for replication in other years, with other candidates, other debates, other campaign ads, and so on. Such a call may seem a cliché, but that does not mean it is not valid. Perhaps the longer life span of the verdicts after Quayle-Bentsen and the carryover of impact to the loser as well as the winner for only one debate was a characteristic of only this particular set of debates and candidates.

- The impact of post-debate analysis particularly requires that we better understand how commentary is organized and conducted. What are the agendas, hidden or otherwise, of the commentators? Interviews with network producers and other gatekeepers, plus observation of the mounting of the production itself, are clearly called for here, as are further content studies in subsequent years. What determines whether network personnel decide to interview campaign spin doctors or ignore them? What evidence do network personnel think they have that the audience *wants* to hear from or about spin doctors? Or verdicts exclusively from network personnel, for that matter? Would audiences prefer to hear how others like them—such as members of a studio audience— are reacting, or would they rather hear from "experts"? Would a combined content analysis and behind-the-scenes study of production reveal that, left to their own devices, studio audience members would rather talk about things that do not fit into the networks' win-lose, zero-sum-game model of the debates?

REFERENCES

Anderson, J. B. 1988. *A proper institution: Guaranteeing televised presidential debates. A Twentieth Century Fund Paper.* New York: Priority Press Publications.

Broder, D. S. 1990. Negative campaigning revisited. *Washington Post National Weekly Edition*, September 10–16: 4.

Brokaw, T. 1988. "NBC News post-debate analysis with Andrea Mitchell and John Chancellor." October 5.

Jamieson, K. H., and D. J. Birdsell. 1988. *Presidential debates: The challenge of creating an informed electorate.* New York: Oxford University Press.

Lipman, J. 1990. Newspapers dissect negative political ads. *Wall Street Journal*, July 27, B3.

Minow, N. N., and C. M. Sloan. 1987. *For great debates: A new plan for future presidential TV debates.* New York: Priority Press Publications.

Patterson, T., and R. D. McClure. 1976. *The unseeing eye.* New York: G. P. Putnam's Sons.

Petty, R. E., and J. T. Cacioppo. 1981. *Attitudes and persuasion: Classic and contemporary approaches.* Dubuque, Iowa: Wm. C. Brown.

Appendix

POST-FIRST PRESIDENTIAL DEBATE QUESTIONNAIRE

Post-Debate 1 Questionnaire

1988 Debates Study

Location: **1. C'dale**   2. Phil   3. Eug

Questionnaire No. at this location
(0001 to 9999)   _ _ _ _

Attempts (Allow **8** Rings)

Telephone _ _ _-_ _ _ _

	Date	Time
(Record date	1. _____	_____
and time of	2. _____	_____
attempt)	3. _____	_____
	4. _____	_____

Interviewer

Hello, my name is _____, and I'm calling from the Mass Communication Research Center at Southern Illinois University.

We are doing a survey about the 1988 presidential election campaign and, because this is a scientific sample, I need to speak to someone who is at least 18 years old, who is in your house right now, and who has the next birthday coming up. **(IF NECESSARY, REPEAT ABOVE INTRODUCTION OF YOURSELF TO PERSON WHO COMES TO PHONE NEXT.)**

NEXT SAY THIS IF A NEW PERSON: This interview is part of a national study, dealing with the presidential campaign. **(IF THEY SAY THIS ISN'T A GOOD TIME, MAKE AN APPOINTMENT AND GET THEIR FIRST NAME.)**

Call back at: Day _____ Time of Day_____ First name_____

We'd like to ask you some questions about your media use during this campaign.

1. First, some questions about television.

   1a. Over the past **week**, how many nights did you watch **local** television news programs?

   ____ (0 to 7 nights)
   (8) Don't know
   (9) Refused

   1b. During this week, how many nights did you watch **national** television news programs?

   ____ (0 to 7 nights) **(If they watched national news, go to Q 1c)**
                        (If they did not watch national news, go to Q 1d)
   (8) Don't know **(Go to Q 1d)**
   (9) Refused **(Go to Q 1d)**

   1c. Which national television news program or programs do you usually watch? **(Place an "X" by the correct choices.) (Probe: Any other?)**

   __ ABC (with Peter Jennings, Channel 3)   __ CNN
   __ CBS (with Dan Rather, Channel 12)   __ Nightline
   __ NBC (with Tom Brokow, Channel 6)   __ Other
   __ PBS (with McNeil-Lehrer, Channel 8)

   1d. Of all the television news stories you have seen, do you remember any that were about tonight's presidential debate?

   (1) Yes **(Go to Q 1e)**   (8) Don't remember **(Go to Q 1g)**
   (2) No **(Go to Q 1g)**   (9) Refusal **(Go to Q 1g)**

   1e. **(Ask of respondents who recalled seeing debate stories)** Which story about tonight's debate do you remember best? **(Probe: Ask for specifics.)**

   Description of story (candidate, theme, issue, etc.): _____

   _____

   _____

   _____

   1f. When did you see this story? Did you see it before the debate or just after the debate was held?

   (1) Before the debate   (8) Don't remember
   (2) After the debate   (9) Refusal

   1g. Again, **besides stories about tonight's debate**, do you remember seeing any television **news** stories about the presidential campaign?

   (1) Yes **(Go to Q 1h)**   (8) Don't know **(Go to Q 2)**
   (2) No **(Go to Q 2)**   (9) No response **(Go to Q 2)**

   1h. **(Ask of respondents who recalled seeing stories about the presidential campaign)** Which of these stories about the campaign do you remember best? **(Probe: Ask for specifics.)**

Description of story (candidate, theme, issue, etc.): _____

_____

_____

2. Do you recall seeing any paid political advertisements for any of the presidential candidates on television?

(1) Yes **(Go to Q 2a)** (8) Don't know **(Go to Q 3)**
(2) No **(Go to Q 3)** (9) Refused **(Go to Q 3)**

2a. Think of the ad you remember best. Was it a pro-Bush or pro-Dukakis ad?

(1) Pro-Bush **(Go to Q 2b)** (8) Don't know **(Go to Q 3)**
(2) Pro-Dukakis **(Go to Q 2b)** (9) Refusal **(Go to Q 3)**

2b. Would you say this ad praised the virtues of the candidate it was for or did it mainly criticize that candidate's opponent?

(1) Praised virtues (8) Don't know
(2) Criticized opponent (9) Refusal
(3) Both praised and criticized

3. Now I would like to ask you about **newspaper reading**. Think back carefully over the **past week**? How many of the seven days of the week did you read at least part of the main news section of the newspaper?

____ (0 to 7 days) **(If subject did not read a newspaper, go to Q 5)**
(8) Don't know **(Go to Q 5)**
(9) Refused **(Go to Q 5)**

3a. **(Ask only if respondent read a newspaper or newspapers)** Which newspaper do you rely on most? **(Record Name)**

_____

3b. Thinking back over the past several days, do you remember reading any stories in the newspaper about tonight's presidential debate?

(1) Yes **(Go to Q 3c)** (8) Don't know **(Go to Q 3d)**
(2) No **(Go to Q 3d)** (9) Refusal **(Go to Q 3d)**

3c. **(If they remembered a story about the debate)** Which story about tonight's debate do you remember best? **(Probe: ask for specifics.)**

Description of story (candidate, theme, issue, etc.): _____

_____

_____

3d. Excluding stories about tonight's presidential debate, do you remember reading any other newspaper stories over the past several days that were about the presidential **campaign**?

(1) Yes **(Go to Q 3e)** (8) Don't know **(Go to Q 4)**
(2) No **(Go to 4)** (9) Refusal **(Go to Q 4)**

3e. **(Ask of respondents who recalled reading stories about the presidential campaign)** Which of these stories about the campaign do you remember best? **(Probe: Ask for specifics.)**

Description of story (candidate, theme, issue, etc.): _____

_____

_____

4. Over the past several days, do you recall reading any paid political advertisements for any of the presidential candidates in the newspapers?

    (1) Yes **(Go to Q 4a)**   (8) Don't know **(Go to Q 5)**
    (2) No **(Go to Q 5)**   (9) Refused **(Go to Q 5)**

    4a. Think of the ad you remember beest. Was it a pro-Bush or pro-Dukakis ad?

        (1) Pro-Bush **(Go to Q 4b)**   (8) Don't know **(Go to Q 5)**
        (2) Pro-Dukakis **(Go to Q 4b)** (9) Refusal **(Go to Q 5)**

    4b. Would you say this ad praised the virtues of the candidate it was for or did it mainly criticize that candidate's opponent?

        (1) Praised virtues   (8) Don't know
        (2) Criticized opponent   (9) Refusal
        (3) Both praised and criticized

Now some questions about this political campaign.

5. First, do you consider yourself a Republican, Democrat, Independent, or what?

    (1) Republican   (4) Other
    (2) Democrat   (8) Don't Know
    (3) Independent   (9) Refusal

6. Are you currently registered to vote?

    (1) Yes **(Go to Q 7)**   (8) Don't know **(Go to Q 8)**
    (2) No **(Go to Q 8)**   (9) Refusal **(Go to Q 8)**

7. Did you vote in the presidential primary earlier this year?

    (1) Yes **(Go to Q 7a)**   (8) Don't Know **(Go to Q 8)**
    (2) No **(Go to Q 8)**   (9) Refused **(Go to Q 8)**

    7a. **(Ask only if respondent voted in presidential primary.)** For whom did you vote in the presidential primary?

        (1) Dukakis   (5) Another Democrat
        (2) Jackson   (6) Another Republican
        (3) Bush   (8) Don't know
        (4) Dole   (9) Refused

8. At this time we'd like to ask you some questions about some of the things that people are doing or have done during this fall's presidential campaign.

Have you done any of the following things during this fall's campaign?

8a. Have you donated any money to the campaign of one of the presidential candidates?
    (1) Yes   (8) DK
    (2) No   (9) NR

8b. Did you watch at least part of George Bush's acceptance speech **live** on television during the Republican convention?
    (1) Yes   (8) DK
    (2) No   (9) NR

8c. Have you worn a campaign button, displayed a bumper sticker, or put up a lawn sign for one of the presidential candidates?
    (1) Yes   (8) DK
    (2) No   (9) NR

8d. Have you worked in the presidential campaign as a volunteer (any office/issue)?
    (1) Yes   (8) DK
    (2) No   (9) NR

8e. Did you watch at least part of Michael Dukakis's acceptance speech on **live** television during the Democratic convention?
    (1) Yes   (8) DK
    (2) No   (9) NR
8f. Have you discussed the presidential campaign with friends?
    (1) Yes   (8) DK
    (2) No   (9) NR

9. As far as you are **personally** concerned, what are the one or two **most important** issues in this presidential campaign? Begin with the issue you think is **most** important. **(Probe after the first issue: Is there anything else?)**

    9a. Most Important Issue: _____

    _____

    _____

    9b. Second Mentioned Issue: _____

    _____

    _____

Now I'm going to ask you some questions about presidential debates.

10. First, I'm going to read you several statements about presidential debates and ask you whether you **strongly agree, agree, are neutral, disagree,** or **strongly disagree** with each statement.

	SA	A	Neu	D	SD
10a. Not enough televised presidential debates have been scheduled.	(5)	(4)	(3)	(2)	(1)

10b.	Presidential debates are one of the best ways for me to learn where thecandidates stand on the issues.	(5)	(4)	(3)	(2)	(1)
10c.	Presidential candidates always seem to avoid answering the important questions during the. debates.	(5)	(4)	(3)	(2)	(1)
10d.	All in all, I think the televised presidential debates have been a waste of time.	(5)	(4)	(3)	(2)	(1)
10e.	Watching the actual debate is not necessary because people can get the highlights on television news programs.	(5)	(4)	(3)	(2)	(1)
10f.	Televised presidential debates are the best way for people to make their final voting choice.	(5)	(4)	(3)	(2)	(1)

11. **Before** Sunday's presidential debate was held, who did you think was going to win?

   (1) George Bush (8) Didn't know
   (2) Michael Dukakis (9) Refusal

12. Did you watch or listen to Sunday's presidential debate between Michael Dukakis George Bush?

   (1) Yes **(Go to Q 13)** (2) No **(Go to Q 12a)**

   12a. **(Ask of respondents who did not watch or listen to the debate)** Even though you didn't watch the debate, have you seen or heard anything about the debate?

   (1) Yes **(Go to Q 12b)** (2) No **(Go to Q 14)**

   12b. Would you say that what you have learned about Sunday's debate came primarily from television news, from family or friends, from radio, from newspapers, from the TV analysis after the debate, or from some other source?

   (1) Television news (5) Newspapers
   (2) Family and friends (6) Other source
   (3) Radio (8) Don't know
   (4) TV analysis (9) Refusal

   12c. Based on what you have heard or seen about Sunday's debate, who do you think won?

   Bush **(Go to Q 12d)** (8) Don't know **(Go to Q 14)**
   (3) Neither **(Go to Q 14)** (9) Refusal **(Go to Q 14)**
   Dukakis **(Go to Q 12e)**

12d. Would you say that George Bush won by a lot or by a little?

    (1) A lot   (2) A little

12e. Would you say that Michael Dukakis won by a lot or by a little?

    (4) A little   (5) A lot

12f. If you had to choose a word or two to describe the performance of George Bush during the debate, what would those one or two words be? (**Write in "88" for "Don't know," 99 for "Refusal."**)

_____

12g. If you had to choose a word or two to describe the performance of Michael Dukakis during the debate, what would those one or two words be? (**Write in "88" for "Don't know," 99 for "Refusal."**)

_____

12h. Was there any **one** issue or topic that came up during the debate that think will influence which candidate people will vote for in November?

    (1)   Yes **(Go to Q 12i)**   (8) Don't know **(Go to Q 14)**
    (2)   No **(Go to Q 14)**   (9) Refusal **(Go to Q 14)**

12i. Can you describe what that was? (**Probe: Ask for specifics.**)

_____

_____

_____

12j. Which of the two candidates do you think came out best on that issue? (**Go to Q 14**)

    (1) Bush   (8) Don't know
    (2) Neither (even)   (9) Refusal
    (3) Dukakis

13. **(Ask Q 13a-13m only if respondent watched or listened to the debate)** We'd like to ask you some questions about Sunday's presidential debate.

  13a. Did you watch the Sunday's debate on television or listen to it on radio?

    (1)   Television **(Go to Q 13b)** (8) Don't Remember **(Go to Q 13c)**
    (2)   Radio **(Go to Q 13c)**   (9) Refusal **(Go to Q 13c)**

  13b.(**If they watched on TV**) Which channel were you watching?

    (1) ABC (Channel 3)   (5) CNN
    (2) CBS (Channel 12)   (6) Other
    (3) NBC (Channel 6)   (8) Don't Remember
    (4) PBS   (9) Refusal

13c. How much of the debate itself would you say you watched or listened to?
All of it, **most** of it, **some** or it, or a **little** of it?

(1) All of it   (4) A Little
(2) Most of it   (8) Don't know
(3) Some of it   (9) Refused

13d. What about right after the debate, did you watch or listen to any analysis of
the debate?

(1) Yes   (8) Don't remember
(2) No   (9) Refusal

13e. Who do you think won Sunday's presidential debate?

       Bush (Go to Q 13f)   (8) **Don't know (Go to Q 13h)**
(3)   **Neither (Go to Q 13h)**   (9) **Refusal (Go to Q 13h)**
       Dukakis (Go to Q 13g)

13f. Would you say that George Bush won by a lot or by a little?

(1) A lot **(Go to Q 13h)**   (2) A little **(Go to Q 13h)**

13g. Would you say that Michael Dukakis won by a lot or by a little?

(4) A little **(Go to Q 13h)**   (5) A lot **(Go to Q 13h)**

13h. If you had to choose a word or two to describe the performance of George
Bush during the debate, what would those one or two words be? **(Write
"88" for "Don't know," "99" for "Refusal.")**

_____

13i. If you had to choose a word or two to describe the performance of Michael
Dukakis during the debate, what would those one or two words be? **(Write
"88" for "Don't know," "99" for "Refusal.")**

_____

13j. Was there any **one** issue or topic that came up during the debate that
you think will influence which candidate people will vote for in November?

(1) Yes **(Go to Q 13k)**   (8) **Don't know (Go to Q 13m)**
(2) No **(Go to Q 13m)**   (9) **Refusal (Go to Q 13m)**

13k. Can you describe what that was? **(Probe: Ask for specifics.)**

_____

_____

13m. Which of the two candidates do you think came out best on
that issue?

(1) Bush   (8) Don't know
(2) Neither (even)   (9) Refusal
(3) Dukakis

14. Again, relying on what you know and what you have read, seen, and heard about candidates, how would you rate each of them in terms of the following characteristics? Use a scale running from zero to ten, where zero means that the candidate is **very weak** and ten that the candidate is **very strong. (Enter 00 for zero, 01 for one, . . ., 09 for nine, 10 for 10, 88 for Don't remember, and 99 for a Refusal)**

    14a. Michael Dukakis's knowledge of domestic issues. . . . .   _____

    14b. George Bush's knowledge of domestic issues. . . . .   _____

    14c. George Bush's ability to lead the country. . . . .   _____

    14d. Michael Dukakis's ability to lead the country. . . . .   _____

    14e. George Bush's poise and self–confidence under pressure. . . .   _____

    14f. Michael Dukakis's poise and self-confidence under pressure. .   _____

    14g. Michael Dukakis's knowledge of foreign and defense policy. . .   _____

    14h. George Bush's knowledge of foreign and defense policy.. . . . .   _____

15. Based on what you know about each candidate so far, how would you rate the candidates as debaters? Use a scale running from zero to ten where zero means that they are **very weak** debaters and ten that they are **very strong** debaters. **(Enter 00 for zero, 01 for one, . . ., 09 for nine, 10 for 10, 88 for Don't remember, and 99 for refusal)**

    15a. First, George Bush. As a debater, how would you rate George Bush on a scale from 0 **(very weak)** to 10 **(very strong)**?

    _____

    15b. Now, Michael Dukakis. As a debater, how would you rate Michael Dukakis on a scale from 0 **(very weak)** to 10 **(very strong)**?

    _____

16. Based on what you have heard or seen written by reporters on television, in the newspapers, on radio, or in news magazines, which of the candidates do you think press thought was the winner of Sunday night's debate?

    (1)   Bush   (8)' Don't know

    (2)   Neither   (9)   Refusal

    (3)   Dukakis

17. Who do you think will win the next presidential debate?

          Bush **(Go to Q 17a)**   (8) Don't know **(Go to Q 18)**

    (3)   Neither **(Go to Q 18)**   (9) Refusal **(Go to Q 18)**

          Dukakis **(Go to Q 17b)**

    17a. Would you say that George Bush will win by a lot or by a little?

        (1)   A lot   (2)   A little

    17b. Would you say that Michael Dukakis will win by a lot or by a little?

        (4)   A little   (5)   A lot

18. When you evaluate the presidential candidates and the positions they present on issues during the debates, how important are the following sources of information? Here, let's use a scale from zero to ten, with zero being **not at all important** and ten being **very important. (Enter 00 for zero, 01 for one, . . ., 09 for nine, 10 for 10, 88 for Don't remember, and 99 for refusal)**

   18a. How important is the actual presidential debate? . . . . _____

   18b. How important are the TV news reports about the debate? . . . . . _____

   18c. How important are the newspaper articles about the debate? . . . . . . _____

   18d. How important are radio reports about the debate? . . . . _____

   18e. How important are talks with family and friends about the debate? . . _____

19. Can you tell me where Sunday night's debate was held?

   (1) Winston-Salem **or** Wake Forrest **or** North Carolina)
   (2) Someplace else
   (8) Don't Know
   (9) Refusal

20. At this stage of the 1988 campaign, how would you describe your interest in the presidential campaign? Would you say that you are **un**interested or interested in the campaign?

   Uninterested **(Go to Q 20a)**　　　　(8) Don't know **(Go to Q 21)**
   (3) Neither **(Go to Q 21)**　　　　　(9) Refusal **(Go to Q 21)**
   Interested **(Go to Q 20b)**

   20a. Would you say you are very uninterested or somewhat uninterested?

   　　(1) Very uninterested　　　　　　(2) Somewhat uninterested

   20b. Would you say you are very interested or somewhat interested?

   　　(4) Somewhat interested　　　　　(5) Very interested

21. What would you say the odds are that you might or might not vote in this presidential election? Would you say that you **definitely will** vote, **probably** vote, that there is about a **50-50 chance** that you will vote, that you **probably will not** vote, or that you **definitely** will **not** vote?

   (1) Definitely will vote **(Go to Q 22)**　　(8) Don't know **(Go to Q 22)**
   (2) Probably will vote **(Go to Q 22)**　　　(9) Refusal **(Go to Q 22)**
   (3) 50-50 chance **(Go to Q 22)**
   (4) Probably will not vote **(Go to Q 22)**
   (5) Definitely will not vote **(Go to Q 23)**

22. Based on a scale from zero to ten, where zero means that you **definitely** would **not** vote for the candidate and ten that you **definitely would** vote for that candidate, what would you say, from zero to ten, describes your likelihood of voting **(Enter 00 for zero, 01 for one, . . ., 09 for nine, 10 for ten, 88 for Don't remember, and 99 for refusal)**

   22a. for Michael Dukakis? . . . . _____

22b. for George Bush? . . . . _____

23. If you **had** to vote **today** for one of the candidates, who would you vote for?

(1) Bush
(2) Dukakis
(3) Other

(4) Wouldn't vote
(8) Don't know
(9) Refusal

24. Who did you vote for for president in November of 1984?

(1) Reagan
(2) Mondale
(3) Other candidate
(4) Not eligible

(5) Not registered
(6) Didn't vote
(8) Don't remember
(9) Refusal

25. Now I'm going to read you several statements about this presidential campaign. Tell me if you **strongly agree, agree,** are **neutral, disagree,** or **strongly disagree** with each statement.

		SA	A	Neu	D	SD
25a.	This campaign has relied too much on mudslinging and name calling.	(5)	(4)	(3)	(2)	(1)
25b.	I don't think I know enough about any of the candidates to make an intelligent voting choice.	(5)	(4)	(3)	(2)	(1)
25c.	From what I've learned so far about the candidates, I'm not sure I want to vote for anybody.	(5)	(4)	(3)	(2)	(1)

We're just about through. Let me ask a few of questions about your background.

26. How old are you ? _____ (Write in present age)

27. What was the last year in school that you completed?

0 1 2 3 4 5 6 7 8 9 10 11 12 13 14 15 16 17 18 19, 19+

28. Which of the following **best** describes you current occupational status? **(Read the list below)**

(1) Full-time employed
(2) Part-time employed
(3) Full-time student
(4) Retired

(5) Homemaker
(6) Unemployed at the moment

(8) Don't know **(Don't read)**
(9) Refusal **(Don't read)**

29. What is your total yearly household income range? Under $10,000? $10,000 to $20,000? Over $20,000 but less than $30,000? $30,000 to $50,000? or more than $50,000?

(1) < $10,000
(2) $10,000 to $20,000
(3) > $20,000 but < $30,000
(4) $ 30,000 to $50,000

(5) > $50,000

(8) Don't know
(9) Refusal

30. What is your race? White, Black, Asian, Hispanic, American Indian, or other?

(1) White	(5) American Indian
(2) Black	(6) Other
(3) Asian	(8) Don't Know
(4) Hispanic	(9) Refusal

Thank you very much for your help. It's very important to us.

INTERVIEWER CIRCLES SEX OF RESPONDENT.

(1) Female   (2) Male

BIBLIOGRAPHY

Adams, B. 1988. Bush probably gained more than Dukakis from match. St. Louis *Post-Dispatch,* October 14, A8.

Adams, J. 1988a. "CBS Evening News With Dan Rather." September 9.

Adams, J. 1988b. "CBS Evening News With Dan Rather." October 4.

And then there were two. 1980. *Newsweek,* September 22, 25.

Anderson, J. B. 1988. *A proper institution: Guaranteeing televised presidential debates. A Twentieth Century Fund Paper.* New York: Priority Press Publications.

Barone, M. 1988. These Dukakis ads just don't work. *Washington Post,* October 11, A19.

Becker, L. B., D. H. Weaver, D. A. Graber, and M. E. McCombs. 1979. Influence on public agendas. In *The great debates: Carter vs. Ford, 1976,* ed. S. Kraus, 418–428. Bloomington: Indiana University Press.

Bennett, W. L. 1980. *Public opinion in American politics.* New York: Harcourt.

Bergantino, J. 1988. "ABC World News Tonight With Peter Jennings." September 19.

Berquist, G. F., and J. L. Golden. 1981. Media rhetoric, criticism and the public perception of the 1980 presidential debates. *Quarterly Journal of Speech* 67:125–137.

Bishop, G. F., R. W. Oldendick, and A. J. Tuchfarber. 1978. The presidential debates as a device for increasing the "rationality" of electoral behavior. In *The presidential debates: Media, electoral and policy perspectives,* ed. G. F. Bishop, R. G. Meadow, and M. Jackson-Beeck, 179–196. New York: Praeger Publishers.

Bode, K. 1988. "NBC Nightly News With Tom Brokaw," October 14.

Boisvert, L. B. 1988. No wonder the League withdrew. Letter to the editor, *Washington Post*, October 12, A18.

A boost for the stay-at-home. 1980. *Newsweek*, October 6, 40–42.

Bothwell, R. K., and J. C. Brigham. 1983. Selective evaluation and recall during the 1980 Carter-Reagan debate. *Journal of Applied Social Psychology* 13:427–442.

Boyd, G. 1988. How Bush won: picking the right fights and getting the right opponent. *New York Times*, November 12, A8.

Broder, D. S. 1990. Negative campaigning revisited. *Washington Post National Weekly Edition*, September 10–16: 4.

Brokaw, T. 1988a. "NBC Nightly News With Tom Brokaw," October 14.

Brokaw, T. 1988b. "NBC Nightly News With Tom Brokaw," October 17.

Brokaw, T. 1988c. "NBC News post-debate analysis with Andrea Mitchell and John Chancellor." October 5.

Campbell, D. T., and J. C. Stanley. 1963. *Experimental and quasi-experimental designs for research*. Chicago: Rand McNally.

Carmines, E. G., and R. A. Zeller. 1979. *Reliability and validity assessment*. Beverly Hills, California: Sage.

Chaffee, S. H., and J. Dennis. 1979. Presidential debates: An empirical assessment. In *The past and future of presidential debates*, ed. A. Ranney, 75–101. Washington: American Enterprise Institute for Public Policy Research.

Chase, R. 1988. "ABC World News Tonight With Peter Jennings." October 10.

Cheney, R. B. 1979. The 1976 presidential debates: A Republican perspective. In *The past and future of presidential debates*, ed. A. Ranney, 107–136. Washington: American Enterprise Institute for Public Policy Research.

Compton, A. 1988. "ABC World News Tonight With Peter Jennings." October 5.

Comstock, G., S. Chaffee, N. Katzman, M. McCombs, and D. Roberts. 1978. *Television and human behavior*. New York: Columbia University Press.

Cook, T. D., and D. T. Campbell. 1979. *Quasi-experimentation: Design & analysis issues for field settings*. Chicago: Rand McNally.

Davis, D. K., and J. Lee. 1980. Time-series analysis models for communication research. In *Multivariate techniques in human communication research*, ed. P. R. Monge and J. N. Capella, 429–454. New York: Academic Press.

Davis, M. H. 1982. Voting intentions and the 1980 Carter-Reagan debate. *Journal of Applied Social Psychology* 12:481–492.

Deaver, M. 1988. Sound-bite campaigning: TV made us do it. *Washington Post*, October 30, C7.

The debate and the spin doctors. 1984. *New York Times*, October 21, E22.

Debates, domesticated. 1988. *New York Times*, September 27, A34.

Dennis, J., and S. H. Chaffee. 1978. Legitimation in the 1976 U.S. election campaign. *Communication Research* 5:371–393.

Dennis, J., S. H. Chaffee, and S. Y. Choe. 1979. Impact on partisan, image, and issue voting. In *The great debates: Carter vs. Ford, 1976*, ed. S. Kraus, 314–330. Bloomington: Indiana University Press.

Devlin, L. P. 1989. Contrasts in presidential campaign commercials of 1988. *American Behavioral Scientist* 32:389–414.

Diamond, E., and S. Bates. 1984. *The spot: The rise of political advertising on TV*. Cambridge: The MIT Press.

Diamond, E., and K. Friery. 1987. Media coverage of presidential debates. In *The presidential debates: 1988 and beyond*, ed. J. L. Swerdlow, 45–53. Washington, D.C.: Congressional Quarterly, Inc.

Donaldson, S. 1988a. "ABC World News Tonight With Peter Jennings." September 23.

Donaldson, S. 1988b. "ABC World News Tonight With Peter Jennings." October 6.

Donaldson, S. 1988c. "ABC World News Tonight With Peter Jennings." October 13.

Donaldson, S. 1988d. "ABC World News Tonight With Peter Jennings." October 14.

Donaldson, S. 1988e. "ABC World News Tonight With Peter Jennings." October 24.

Donaldson, S. 1988f. On the Dukakis campaign trail. *Gannett Center Journal* 2 (4):87–118.

Dye, T., and L. H. Ziegler. 1989. *American politics in the media age*, 3rd ed. Pacific Grove, Calif.: Brooks/Cole Publishing Company.

Edelman, M. 1964. *The symbolic uses of power*. Urbana: University of Illinois Press.

An empty chair. 1980. *New York Times*, September 11, A18.

Engstrom, E., J. Gentry, and G. Melwani. 1989. *Evidence for differential effects on males and females in the wake of post-debate analyses*. Paper presented to the annual meeting of the Committee on the Status of Women, Association for Education in Journalism and Mass Communication, August, Washington, D.C.

Excess baggage. 1980. *Broadcasting*, November 3, 106.

Extra baggage. 1984. *Broadcasting*, October 15, 98.

Fazio, R. H., and C. J. Williams. 1986. Attitude accessibility as a moderator of the attitude-perception and attitude-behavior relations: An investigation of the 1984 presidential election. *Journal of Personality and Social Psychology* 51:505–514.

Ferguson, M. A., B. A. Hollander, and G. Melwani. 1989. *The "dampening effect" of post-debate commentary: The Bentsen-Quayle debate*. Paper presented at annual meeting of the Political Communication Division of the International Communication Association, May, San Francisco.

Finn, S. 1987. Electoral information flow and students' information processing: A computerized panel study. In *Communication yearbook 10*, ed. M. L. McLaughlin, 517–532. Newbury Park: Sage.

For the people. 1988. *Broadcasting*, September 12, 114.

Gadziala, S., and L. B. Becker. 1983. A new look at agenda-setting in the 1976 election debates. *Journalism Quarterly* 60:122–125.

Gans, C. B. 1988. No wonder turnout was so low. *Washington Post National Weekly Edition*, November 21–27, 28.

Garramone, G., C. K. Atkin, B. E. Pinkleton, and R. T. Cole. 1990. Effects of negative political advertising on the political process. *Journal of Broadcasting & Electronic Media* 34: 299–311.

Geer, J. G. 1988. The effects of presidential debates on the electorate's preferences for candidates. *American Politics Quarterly* 16:486–501.

Germond, J. W., and J. Witcover. 1989. *Whose broad stripes and bright stars? The trivial pursuit of the presidency 1988.* New York: Warner.

Graber, D. A. 1988. *Processing the news: How people tame the information tide,* 2d ed. New York: Longman.

The great debate. 1984. *Newsweek,* October 15, 30–34.

Greenfield, J. 1980. *Playing to win: An insider's guide to politics.* New York: Simon & Schuster.

Greenfield, M. 1988. The campaign soap opera. *Washington Post,* October 10, A23.

Grove, L. 1988. Election '88: The negative campaign that came from below. *Washington Post National Weekly Edition,* November 21–27, 12.

Hagner, P. R., and L. N. Rieselbach. 1978. The impact of the 1976 presidential debates: Conversion or reinforcement? In *The presidential debates: Media, electoral, and policy perspectives,* ed. G. F. Bishop, R. G. Meadow, and M. Jackson-Beeck, 157–178. New York: Praeger Publishers.

Hershey, M. R. 1989. The campaign and the media. In *The election of 1988: Reports and interpretations,* ed. G. M. Pomper, R. K. Baker, W. D. Burnham, B. G. Farah, M. R. Hershey, E. Klein, and W. C. McWilliams, 73–102. Chatham, N.J.: Chatham House.

Hoffman, D., and A. Devroy. 1988. Bush's road to the White House. *Washington Post National Weekly Edition,* November 21–27, 8–9.

Hoffman, D., and A. Devroy. 1988. The complex machine behind Bush. *Washington Post,* November 13, A1, A16.

Horvath-Niemeyer, P. S., and M. A. Ferguson. 1989. *Effects of post-debate analyses on biased processing: The Bentsen/Quayle debate.* Paper presented at annual meeting of the Theory and Methodology Division, Association for Education in Journalism, August, Washington, D.C.

Hume, B. 1988a. "ABC World News Tonight With Peter Jennings." September 21.

Hume, B. 1988b. "ABC World News Tonight With Peter Jennings," October 13.

Hume, B. 1988c. "ABC World News Tonight With Peter Jennings." October 25.

In the way again. 1980. *Broadcasting,* September 29, 90.

Jackson-Beeck, M., and R. Meadow. 1979. The triple agenda of presidential debates: Media, electoral, policy perspectives. *Public Opinion Quarterly* 43:173–180.

Jamieson, K. H. 1988. For televised mendacity, this year is the worst ever. *Washington Post,* October 30, C1, C2.

Jamieson, K. H., and D. S. Birdsell. 1988. *Presidential debates: The challenge of creating an informed electorate.* New York: Oxford University Press.

Jennings, P. 1988a. "ABC World News Tonight With Peter Jennings." September 21.

Jennings, P. 1988b. "ABC World News Tonight With Peter Jennings." October 5.

Jennings, P. 1988c. "ABC World News Tonight With Peter Jennings." October 13.

Judd, J. 1988. "ABC World News Tonight With Peter Jennings." September 22.

Just, M., A. Crigler, and L. Wallach. 1990. Thirty seconds or thirty minutes: What viewers learn from spot advertisements and candidate debates. *Journal of Communication* 40 (Summer):120–133.

Katz, E., and J. J. Feldman. 1977. The debates in the light of research: A survey of surveys. In *The great debates*, 1st paperback ed., ed. S. Kraus, 173–223. Bloomington: Indiana University Press.

Kelly, J. R., and J. E. McGrath. 1988. *On time and method*. Newbury Park: Sage.

Kerlinger, F. N. 1973. *Foundations of behavioral research*, 2d ed. New York: Holt, Rinehart and Winston.

Kraus, S. 1988. *Televised presidential debates and public policy*. Hillsdale, N.J.: Lawrence Erlbaum Associates.

Krippendorff, K. 1980. *Content analysis: An introduction to its methodology*. Beverly Hills: Sage.

Lang, G. E., and K. Lang. 1978. The formation of public opinion: Direct and mediated effects of the first debate. In *The presidential debates: Media, electoral and policy perspectives*, ed. G. F. Bishop, R. G. Meadow, and M. Jackson-Beeck, 61–80. New York: Praeger Publishers.

Lazarsfeld, P. F., B. Berelson, and H. Gaudet. 1948. *The people's choice: How the voter makes up his mind in a presidential campaign*, 2d ed. New York: Columbia University Press.

Lectern to lectern. 1988. *Newsweek*, November 21, 139.

Lemert, J. B. 1981a. *Simple reductionism in the study of media effects: How we got there, and are we stuck with it?* Invited paper presented to the Spring Conference, Mass Communication and Society Division, Association for Education in Journalism, Kent, Ohio, March 21.

Lemert, J. B. 1981b. *Does mass communication change public opinion after all? A new approach to effects analysis*. Chicago: Nelson-Hall.

Lemert, J. B., W. R. Elliott, K. J. Nestvold, and G. R. Rarick. 1983. Effects of viewing a presidential primary debate. *Communication Research* 10:155–173.

Lemert, J. B., W. L. Rosenberg, W. R. Elliott, J. M. Bernstein, and K. J. Nestvold. 1989. *Impact of the Bentsen-Quayle debate and of news "verdicts" about the debate—a time-series analysis*. A paper presented to the annual meeting of the American Association for Public Opinion Research, St. Petersburg, Fla.

Lewis-Beck, M. S. 1986. Interrupted time series. In *New tools for social scientists: Advances and applications in research methods*, ed. W. D. Berry and M. S. Lewis-Beck, 209–240. Beverly Hills: Sage.

Lights-camera-candidates! 1976. *New York Times*, September 24, A24.

Lipman, J. 1990. Newspapers dissect negative political ads. *Wall Street Journal*, July 27, B3.

Long shot. 1976. *Broadcasting*, August 30, 66.

Lowry, D. T., J. A. Bridges, and P. A. Barefield. In press. The effects of network TV "instant analysis and querulous criticism" following the first Bush-Dukakis debate. *Journalism Quarterly*.

Major, A. M., and L. E. Atwood. 1990. *The U.S. press covers two presidential elections*. Paper presented at the International Communication Association, Dublin, Ireland, June.

Martin, J. 1988. "ABC World News Tonight With Peter Jennings." October 7.

"MacNeil-Lehrer Newshour." 1988. November 8.

McCleary, R. M., and R. A. Hay, Jr. 1980. *Applied time series analysis for the social sciences*. Beverly Hills: Sage.

McDowall, D., R. McCleary, E. E. Meidinger, and R. A. Hay, Jr. 1980. *Interrupted time series analysis*. Beverly Hills: Sage.

McGrory, M. 1988. The League puts its foot down. *Washington Post*, October 6, A-2.

McLeod, J., and L. Becker. 1974. Testing the validity of gratification measures through political effects analysis. In *The uses of mass communication: Current perspectives on gratification research*, ed. J. G. Blumler and E. Katz, 137–164. Beverly Hills, Calif.: Sage.

McLeod, J. M., J. A. Durall, D. A. Ziemke, and C. R. Bybee. 1979. Reactions of young and older voters: Expanding the context of effects. In *The great debates: Carter vs. Ford, 1976*, ed. S. Kraus, 348–367. Bloomington: Indiana University Press.

McLeod, J. M., Z. Pan, S. W. Sun, and K. Hein. 1989. *To know them is to what? Media influences on knowing and feeling in the 1988 election campaign*. Paper presented at annual meeting of Theory and Methodology Division of the Association for Education in Journalism and Mass Communication, August, Washington, D.C.

Meadow, R. G. 1983. Televised campaign debates as whistle-stop speeches. In *Television coverage of the 1980 presidential campaign*, ed. W. C. Adams, 89–102. Norwood, N.J.: Ablex.

Meadow, R. G. 1987. A speech by any other name. *Critical Studies in Mass Communication* 4:207–210.

Miller, A. H., and M. MacKuen. 1979. Informing the electorate: A national study. In *The great debates: Carter vs. Ford, 1976*, ed. S. Kraus, 269–297. Bloomington: Indiana University Press.

Minnow, N. N., and C. M. Sloan. 1987. *For great debates: A new plan for future presidential TV debates*. New York: Priority Press Publications.

Morton, B. 1988a. "CBS Evening News With Dan Rather." September 23.

Morton, B. 1988b. "CBS Evening News With Dan Rather." October 6.

Morton, B. 1988c. "CBS Evening News With Dan Rather." October 10.

Morton, B. 1988d. "CBS Evening News With Dan Rather." October 12.

Morton, B. 1988e. "CBS Evening News With Dan Rather." October 13.

Morton, B. 1988f. "CBS Evening News With Dan Rather." October 17.

A naked look at the debate. 1980. *New York Times*, October 17, A30.

Neuman, N. 1990. Telephone interview with Lemert, March 8.

Nielsen Media Research. 1989. Nielsen measures presidential debates. November 1988.

Nielsen Media Research. 1990. Unpublished report. New York.

Nimmo, D. 1989. Episodes, incidents, and eruptions: Nightly network TV coverage of candidates '88. *American Behavioral Scientist* 32:464–478.

North, R. C., O. R. Holsti, M. G. Zaninovich, and D. A. Zinnes. 1963. *Content analysis: A handbook with applications for the study of international crisis*. Evanston: Northwestern University Press.

Ostrom, C. W., Jr., and D. M. Simon. 1989. The man in the teflon suit? The environmental connection, political drama, and popular support in the Reagan presidency. *Public Opinion Quarterly* 53:353–387.

Out of their League? 1980. *Newsweek*, September 8, 21.

Paletz, D. L., and R. M. Entman. 1981. *Media power politics*. New York: The Free Press.

Patterson, T. A. 1980. *The mass media election: How Americans choose their president*. New York: Praeger Publishers.

Patterson, T., and R. D. McClure. 1976. *The unseeing eye*. New York: G. P. Putnam's Sons.

Payne, J. G., J. L. Golden, J. Marlier, and S. C. Ratzan. 1989. Perceptions of the 1988 presidential and vice-presidential debates. *American Behavioral Scientist* 32:425–435.

Payne, J. G., J. Marlier and R. A. Barkus. 1989. Polispots in the 1988 presidential primaries. *American Behavioral Scientist* 32:365–381.

Petty, R. E., and J. T. Cacioppo. 1981. *Attitudes and persuasion: Classic and contemporary approaches*. Dubuque, Iowa: Wm. C. Brown.

Playing hardball. 1988. *Newsweek*, October 3, 22–26.

Political device. 1976. *Broadcasting*, September 27, 106.

Rabbits and reality in Louisville. 1984. *New York Times*, October 7, E20.

Rather, D. 1988a. "CBS Evening News With Dan Rather." September 6.

Rather, D. 1988b. "CBS Evening News With Dan Rather." October 12.

Rerun. 1980. *Broadcasting*, September 1, 74.

The rise and fall of the age issue. 1984. *Newsweek* special issue, November/December, 103–109.

Rosenberg, W. L., and W. R. Elliott. 1987. Effect of debate exposure on evaluation of 1984 vice-presidential candidates. *Journalism Quarterly* 64:55–64.

Rouner, D., and R. M. Perloff. 1988. Selective perceptions of outcome of first 1984 presidential debate. *Journalism Quarterly* 65:141–147, 240.

Running against the television party. 1980. *New York Times*, September 14, E20.

Scherr, L. 1988. "ABC World News Tonight With Peter Jennings." October 12.

Schieffer, B. 1988a. "CBS Evening News With Dan Rather." September 23.

Schieffer, B. 1988b. "CBS Evening News With Dan Rather." October 7.

Schieffer, B. 1988c. "CBS Evening News With Dan Rather." October 13.

Schramm, W., and R. F. Carter. 1959. Effectiveness of a political telethon. *Public Opinion Quarterly* 23:121–126.

Sears, D. O., and Chaffee, S. H. 1979. Uses and effects of the 1976 debates: An overview of empirical studies. In *The great debates: Carter vs. Ford, 1976*, ed. S. Kraus, 223–261. Bloomington: Indiana University Press.

Serafin, B. 1988. "ABC World News Tonight With Peter Jennings." October 16.

Shapiro, W. 1988. The phantom race: Call it politics Lite, with lots of froth and little annoying substance. *Time*, September 19, 18–19.

Shields, M. 1988. The teflon campaign manager. *Washington Post National Weekly Edition*, November 21–27, 29.

Sigelman, L., and C. K. Sigelman. 1984. Judgments of the Carter-Reagan debate: The eye of the beholders. *Public Opinion Quarterly* 48:624–628.

Simonton, D. K. 1977. Cross-sectional time-series experiments: Some suggested statistical analyses. *Psychological Bulletin* 84:489–502.

Smith, W. E. 1989. *The shrinking sound bite: Two decades of stylistic evolution in television news.* Paper presented to the Association for Education in Journalism and Mass Communication, August, Washington, D.C.

Stahl, L. 1988a. "CBS Evening News With Dan Rather." October 14.

Stahl, L. 1988b. CBS poll report. "CBS Evening News With Dan Rather." October 6.

Stanford, S. W. 1989. Statistical designs in survey research. In *Research methods in mass communication*, 2d ed., ed. G. H. Stempel, III, and B. H. Westley, 173–199. Englewood Cliffs: Prentice Hall.

Steeper, F. T. 1978. Public response to Gerald Ford's statements on Eastern Europe in the second debate. In *The presidential debates: Media, electoral, and policy perspectives,* ed. G. F. Bishop, R. G. Meadow, and M. Jackson-Beeck, 81–101. New York: Praeger Publishers.

Stein, M. L. 1988. Discouraging negative political ads: *Washington Post* columnist says press should do a better job of it. *Editor & Publisher*, December 3, 15.

Stempel, G. H., III, 1989. Content analysis. In *Research methods in mass communication*, 2d ed., ed. G. H. Stempel, III, and B. H. Westley, 124–136. Englewood Cliffs: Prentice Hall.

Stempel, G. H., III, 1989. Statistical designs for content analysis. In *Research methods in mass communication*, 2d ed., ed. G. H. Stempel, III, and B. H. Westley, 137–149. Englewood Cliffs: Prentice Hall.

Stovall, J. G., and J. H. Solomon. 1984. The poll as a news event in the 1980 presidential campaign. *Public Opinion Quarterly* 48:615–623.

Sure loser in the debate: The format. 1988. *New York Times*, October 15, 30.

Sussman, B. 1988. *What Americans really think: And why our politicians pay no attention.* New York: Pantheon Books.

Taylor, P. 1990. The trick is to get vicious carefully: Negative ads work well—if they don't backfire. *Washington Post National Weekly Edition*, July 16–22, 15.

Threlkeld, R. 1988. "ABC World News Tonight With Peter Jennings." September 23.

Toner, R. 1988. Dukakis aides acknowledge Bush outmaneuvered them. *New York Times*, November 12, A1, A8.

Too much of a bad thing. 1988. *Broadcasting*, October 17, 98.

The veep showdown. 1988. *Newsweek*, October 10, 40–41.

Walker, C. E. 1979. Discussion following R. B. Cheney paper. In *The past and future of presidential debates*, ed. A. Ranney, 134. Washington, D.C.: American Enterprise Institute for Public Policy Research.

Wall, V., J. L. Golden, and H. James. 1988. Perceptions of the 1984 presidential debates and a select 1988 presidential primary debate. *Presidential Studies Quarterly* 18:541–563.

Watson, R. A. 1984. *The presidential contest,* 2d ed. New York: John Wiley and Sons Inc.

Weber, R. P. 1985. *Basic content analysis.* Beverly Hills: Sage.

Why not debate now? 1984. *New York Times*, October 8, A26.

Wimmer, R. D., and J. R. Dominick. 1987. *Mass media research: An introduction,* 2d ed. Belmont, Calif.: Wadsworth.

Wooten, J. 1988. "ABC World News Tonight With Peter Jennings." October 12.

INDEX

ABOUT THE AUTHORS

JAMES B. LEMERT, Professor and Journalism Graduate Studies Director in the School of Journalism at the University of Oregon, is the author of two previous books and dozens of research articles. His previous books are: *Does Mass Communication Change Public Opinion After All?* (1981) and *Criticizing the Media: Empirical Approaches* (1989). Dr. Lemert teaches courses in public opinion, journalists' craft attitudes, and mass communication theory.

WILLIAM R. ELLIOTT, Associate Professor and Head of Graduate Studies in Journalism at Southern Illinois University at Carbondale, is the author of numerous journal articles and papers on media influences on the political process. At Southern Illinois University at Carbondale, Dr. Elliott teaches courses in mass communication theory, research methods, and theory construction.

JAMES M. BERNSTEIN, Assistant Professor in the School of Journalism at Indiana University, teaches courses in broadcast journalism, public opinion, and the media as social institutions. Dr. Bernstein's research interests include public opinion, political communication, and television and politics.

WILLIAM L. ROSENBERG, Associate Professor and Director of the Drexel University Survey Research Center, has presented many papers and has authored numerous articles on politics and communication. In addition to serving as a media analyst during election campaigns, as well as a research consultant for local, state and national agencies, Dr. Rosenberg teaches courses in political communication, public opinion and propaganda, and research methods in the History and Politics Department of Drexel University in Philadelphia, Pennsylvania.

KARL J. NESTVOLD, Professor and Associate Dean, is Head of the Broadcast News Sequence, School of Journalism, University of Oregon. Dr. Nestvold's research interests include the FCC theory of diversity, television news and public affairs, broadcasting in Great Britain, and the Soviet Union's external information programs.